Self-Leadership and Personal Resilience in Health and Social Care

SAGE was founded in 1965 by Sara Miller McCune to support the dissemination of usable knowledge by publishing innovative and high-quality research and teaching content. Today, we publish more than 750 journals, including those of more than 300 learned societies, more than 800 new books per year, and a growing range of library products including archives, data, case studies, reports, conference highlights, and video. SAGE remains majority-owned by our founder, and after Sara's lifetime will become owned by a charitable trust that secures our continued independence.

Los Angeles | London | Washington DC | New Delhi | Singapore

Self-Leadership and Personal Resilience in Health and Social Care

JANE HOLROYD

WITH CONTRIBUTIONS FROM KEITH BROWN AND AARON TURNER

Los Angeles | London | New Delhi
Singapore | Washington DC | Boston

Learning Matters
An imprint of SAGE Publications Ltd
1 Oliver's Yard
55 City Road
London EC1Y 1SP

SAGE Publications Inc.
2455 Teller Road
Thousand Oaks, California 91320

SAGE Publications India Pvt Ltd
B 1/I 1 Mohan Cooperative Industrial Area
Mathura Road
New Delhi 110 044

SAGE Publications Asia-Pacific Pte Ltd
3 Church Street
#10–04 Samsung Hub
Singapore 049483

Library of Congress Control Number: 2014957419

British Library Cataloguing in Publication Data

A catalogue record for this book is available from
the British Library

Editor: Kate Wharton
Production controller: Chris Marke
Project management: Swales & Willis Ltd,
Exeter, Devon
Marketing manager: Tamara Navaratnam
Cover design: Wendy Scott
Typeset by: C&M Digitals (P) Ltd, Chennai, India
Printed in Great Britain by Henry Ling Limited at
The Dorset Press, Dorchester, DT1 1HD

MIX
Paper from
responsible sources
FSC
www.fsc.org   FSC™ C013985

ISBN 978-1-4739-1623-4
ISBN 978-1-4739-1624-1 (pbk)

At SAGE we take sustainability seriously. Most of our products are printed in the UK using FSC papers and boards.
When we print overseas we ensure sustainable papers are used as measured by the Egmont grading system.
We undertake an annual audit to monitor our sustainability.

Contents

List of illustrations   vii

About the author   ix

Foreword and invitation   xi

Introduction   xiii

1   Leadership theories   1

2   What is self-leadership?   23

3   The foundations of self-leadership   43

4   What determines state of mind?   63

5   Self-leadership: neuroscience implications   79

6   Self-leadership and resilience: a key to
    appropriate professional judgement
    under pressure   105

Appendix: a new framework for easy, effective
and sustainable leadership development   137

References   155

Index   177

Illustrations

Figures

1.1	McGregor's theory X and Y	7
1.2	Identified important leadership behaviours	7
1.3	Functional and accompanying attributes of servant leaders	12
2.1	An example of self-regulation in an individual	26
2.2	Common themes from reports	35
3.1	The foundations of self-leadership	43
3.2	Evidence of a poor state of mind	46
3.3	Evidence of an improved state of mind	47
3.4	Distributed, dispersed and shared leadership	58
3.5	The foundations of self-leadership	62
4.1	Thought	76
5.1	The SCARF model	100
6.1	Resilience factors	106
6.2	Some key components of the professional judgement process	109
6.3	What professional practice involves	110
6.4	Continuum of reflection	111
6.5	Kolb's experiential learning cycle	112
6.6	The top five national key areas of change within the workplace	116
6.7	Signs and symptoms of work stress	117
6.8	Factors that cause stress in organisations	117
6.9	Three questions to test self-awareness	119
6.10	The foundations of great leadership	119
6.11	Balanced leaders should focus on three areas	124
6.12	Cyclical thinking feedback loop	127
6.13	Siegel's triangle of well-being	128
6.14	Five facets of mindfulness	129
A.1	State of mind as an underlying driver of performance	139

Tables

1.1	Historical leadership theories	2
1.2	Transformational Leadership Questionnaire	14
1.3	A comparison of charismatic, ideological and pragmatic leadership	18
2.1	Leading self and leading others	30

2.2	Reviews that point to ineffective leadership	34
3.1	Evaluation outcome levels example	61
5.1	System 1 and System 2	86
5.2	Potential biases, System 1	87
6.1	Model I and Model II behaviours	115
6.2	Research evidence in relation to the effectiveness of mindfulness	133

About the author

Jane Holroyd MBE has over 25 years' experience in the development and delivery of services within the NHS. She was awarded an MBE for her achievements and services to nursing and critical care. Seconded to the Leadership Centre, where she was responsible for Medical and Nurse Director Leadership programmes and associated links with Europe, she was the author of *Improving Personal and Organisational Performance in Social Work* and the co-author of *Performance Coaching Skills for Social Work*. She specialises in leadership and organisational development and is a public sector coach.

Foreword and invitation

At the Centre for Leadership, Impact and Management in Bournemouth (CLiMB), we are committed to challenging and supporting individuals to develop the skills and knowledge they need to be effective, both now and in the future. Constantly scanning the environment within which leadership and management is likely to be practised and identifying evolving theory helps us to contribute to shaping this complex aspect of Health and Social Care.

While much leadership theory evolves slowly over time, occasionally a new and novel set of ideas comes to light more rapidly, often as the result of one or two enthusiastic advocates. Often there can be few if any texts or articles to support a new theory, so three main lines of action are available to CLiMB.

- Wait for the theory to become respected or refuted and then adopt or reject it accordingly.

- Adopt the theory without evidence, accepting that it could be discredited at some point.

- Undertake an initial assessment of the ideas and, where appropriate, stimulate debate about the new theory, thus placing the university at the forefront of new thinking about leadership.

At CLiMB we are committed to exploring 'next practice', prompting shifts in thinking, behaviour and organisational design at pace. Given this position, the option of waiting for theory or concepts to be validated or at least adopted by others is a timid and inadequate response. Fully adopting a theory or concept without some testing and exploration, however, is little short of reckless. We believe we have a duty to contribute to the thoughtful generation, testing and dissemination of leadership and management theory that has had some validation and testing but requires further development.

Self-leadership

We believe that self-leadership is an example of a concept that offers fresh insights and possibilities for leaders and that needs further testing and thought. As part of this process of testing we have designed and are piloting a Master's-level unit that addresses self-leadership and is the outcome of four years of research and development based on our Improving Personal and Organisational Performance (IPOP) work. This new text takes our thinking further forward and is offered to stimulate further consideration of self-leadership in the context of Health and Social Care.

The invitation

As you are an early reader of this text we would like to hear your thoughts about self-leadership and seek feedback, observations and questions. This feedback will help us widely with our development of this theory.

We ask that you approach the contents of this text with a spirit of enquiry and an open mind, yet at the same time being critical. The content, tone and approach of this text reflect an extensive literature review, but we accept this is not the only way that 'self-leadership' can be defined or explained. We would like to test our thinking and value your input at this point.

Clearly there have been many reported cases of poor, inadequate or simply unacceptable levels of care in recent months within the Health and Social Care sectors, often with an emphasis on poor or inadequate leadership. Our view is that leadership is not for the few but for all, in that all professionals have some leadership responsibility even if it's only for the clients they are directly responsible for. Supporting professionals to make better decisions under pressure, as they learn to manage their own stress and build personal resilience, is our key focus and emphasis. To this end, we trust that this new text makes a major contribution to this debate and also to the delivery of professional practice of the highest order.

Please join in the discussion about self-leadership by emailing or posting comments to Professor Keith Brown, the Series Editor, by visiting **www.buclimb.com**.

Professor Keith Brown

Director of the National Centre for Post-Qualifying Social Work and the Centre for Leadership, Impact and Management in Bournemouth (CLiMB), at Bournemouth University

Introduction

Self-Leadership and Personal Resilience in Health and Social Care is a textbook for professionals making significant judgements under pressure. It presents self-leadership, which is a pivotal concept for all practitioners within the sector, to appreciate and leverage capability in its fullest potential, and to sustain effective interventions when it counts, in the moment of interaction whatever the conditions. The focus is on the quality of the leader's thinking, self- and social awareness, self-regulation and self-management and the fundamentals of sustained resilience.

Self-leadership is about preparing individuals not only to survive but also to thrive within environments that are constantly changing – it's getting them to think in different ways to be mindful of their state of mind and how this impacts everything they do, from every interaction, action and reaction. A central tenet is creating relationships and communication based on consistent, compassionate exchanges. It is about establishing clarity in thinking, freeing individuals to be more creative and innovative, and to use their professional judgements appropriately, blending intuition in the right state of mind, to be able to fully perceive and read situations appropriately without being distracted or overwhelmed and, therefore, to be able to make the right, fully informed decisions. It is enlightened by developments and discoveries from the world of neuroscience, from behavioural economics and from psychology.

Chapter 1

The book takes a journey in first examining some of the most popular leadership theories in history to deconstruct the differing emphasis and influences within the field. It demonstrates that the leadership approaches matched the perceived needs of the time, for example the heroic, Great Man Theory – the premise that leaders are born, which gave way to the concept that leaders could be developed through learning a set of behavioural competencies. Each of the advantages of the identified theory is countered by criticisms and disadvantages as the focus shifted across the decades. Concentrating on the leader, for example, precludes the importance of leadership and collective leadership as a process. Fixing on a select few leaders with the title not only conceivably precludes human potential; today, in the current climate of leaner, fast-paced environments of constant change, it is no longer viable. Beginning to build the case for self-leadership leads naturally to the next chapter.

Chapter 2

Self-leadership as a concept is explored and defined. The key facets are identified and discussed under the two central themes of 'Leading self' and 'Leading others', for self-leadership is about the importance of leadership based on relationships. Some of the brutal truths are examined as the current landscape in Health and Social Care is reviewed. Common themes are identified with self-leadership proposed as providing the solutions. The concern for quality services, while also an international feature, has resulted in significant investment in the public sector in leadership development, but with a perceived lack of compassion or compassion fatigue and disengagement, the evidence of such investment is arguably difficult to discern. With the need for integrated care spelt out within the policy directives, a leadership model and approach that fits is required – self-leadership is proposed as the way forward.

Chapter 3

The foundations of self-leadership are presented within this chapter and are identified as: the fundamental role state of mind plays in terms of performance; the concept of everyone needing to count; and the important role devolved structures play in creating the right conditions to support rapidly changing organisational environments moving towards integration and networks of care. The final and somewhat controversial concept is the importance of evaluating impact. For, despite the significant amounts of investment in leadership development, there is very little evaluation and therefore accountability in terms of the 'so what?' Evaluating impact focuses on what really makes a difference, on continuously adapting and matching operational service needs, and on transformation of services rather than merely the acquisition of knowledge.

Chapter 4

The focus of this chapter is one of the key four foundations of self-leadership – state of mind. The premise is that state of mind is so integral to improving all individuals' abilities, implicitly maximising the quality of every interaction, for state of mind so fundamentally impacts the outward discernible results of leadership. It is therefore proposed that a leader's state of mind has a direct correlation with his or her potential to lead well. This is about what happens under pressure and the ability through a clear state of mind to manage and direct ourselves effectively. It notably explores what determines state of mind and some misconceptions.

Chapter 5

This chapter examines some of the significant neuroscientific research findings and their implications for self-leadership. The magnitude of detecting mirror neurones in the brain, for example, was equated with the discovery of DNA. The important ability to understand our emotions and, therefore, to appreciate how these can impact our thinking and reasoning has been explored. Two systems of thinking are presented in terms of unconscious biases and the brain's incredible neuroplasticity. The disastrous implications of multitasking, the role of emotional intelligence and the impact of the resonant leader are discussed.

The staggering effect on the brain of change is explored in terms of how to reduce these potential detrimental implications for performance.

Chapter 6

Being able to 'do the right thing' in terms of exercising appropriate professional judgement under pressure is examined in the context of resilience. Resilience is, therefore, put under the microscope together with identifying some of the key components of professional judgement and practice. Reflection as an integral aspect is explored. It presents some of the key findings in relation to neuroscience and the influence of mindfulness as an approach and practice that has received considerable attention in terms of research and evidence base. Benefits in relation to mental resilience, learning powers of attention, concentration, courage, kindness and patience have been identified. The role of compassion and mindfulness, together with research in the field, is presented. The surprising fact that increases in compassion also improve an individual's resilience is discussed.

Chapter 1
Leadership theories

Introduction

This chapter examines some of the most popular leadership theories in history, presenting the advantages, disadvantages and criticisms of each and the reported research. It starts to build the case for why self-leadership works in the current context of the public sector and, in particular, Health and Social Care.

Some authors conceptualise leadership as a set of traits, the personality of the leader and their behaviours, whereas others see it as an ability to manage the situation, or from a relationship standpoint, transforming or serving others. Northouse (2013) defines leadership as a 'process whereby an individual influences a group of individuals to achieve a common goal'. This focus away from a distinctive preoccupation with the importance of traits and characteristics to an 'event . . . between the leader and the followers', is an interactive process consisting of observable behaviours that Northouse (2013) argues can be learnt.

This is one explanation; throughout history there have been many different leadership theories, with each losing its initial popularity as the latest approach fails to meet expectations, or exceptions to the theory became more apparent. Examining these influences and perspectives on leadership before discussing self-leadership provides not only the historical background, but a case to support self-leadership as a fundamental approach. Before examining these theories it is important to address two linked concepts: management and leadership.

Management versus leadership

Key distinctions between management and leadership were reinforced by Bennis and Nanus's (1985, p221) statement that managers 'do things right', and 'leaders do the right thing'. This distinction artificially intimated that leadership was more important, and in some way better, although there is a considerable amount of interplay between the two concepts of management and leadership. Making arbitrary distinctions between the two can therefore oversimplify the concepts, for unquestionably leaders both manage and lead, and managers likewise.

Interestingly, Brookes and Grint (2010) describe New Public Management (NPM) as 'dead in the water', for it is about dealing with complicated but essentially 'tame problems', compared to leadership, which they stress is about 'coping with wicked problems involving complexity and change', which, currently arguably, is a feature of everyday public sector services.

They suggest that management is more mechanical, and that New Public Leadership (NPL) works better in a 'networked governance environment where the overall aim is the delivery of public value'. With this specific focus, managing a steady state is no longer compatible with the significant changes required within Health and Social Care. Indeed, change has been an ongoing feature of all public sector organisations for some time, and therefore leadership rather than management has dominated discussions; because of this emphasis, leadership will be the main feature throughout this text.

A historical overview of leadership theories

This section examines historical leadership theories, with Table 1.1 capturing some of the most well known. Historically there was a concentration on the individual as the leader who was perceived as genetically born to lead, and the importance of leader traits and behaviours continued this fascination with the individual leader. The situation or context became an important emphasis, followed by the notion of transforming others into leaders, and finally all this has come full circle, returning to individual leaders, but more specifically to the way they think.

Table 1.1 Historical leadership theories

Period	Theory	Description	Key writers
A focus on the individual as leader			
1840s	Great Man Theory	Leaders are exceptional and are born.	James (1880); Carlyle (1888).
1940s	Trait Theory	List of personal qualities or characteristics a leader should have.	Bowden (1926); Gibb (1947); Weber (1947); Stogdill (1948) – an important critique.
1940s	Behaviourist theories	Concentrate on what leaders do – behaviours can also be categorised as 'styles of leadership'.	Katz et al. (1951); Fleishmann (1953); Halpin and Winer (1957); Likert (1967).
A focus on the situation or context			
1960s	Contingency theories	Identifying the contingent variables that best predict the most effective leadership style required.	Tannenbaum and Schmidt (1958); Fiedler (1967); House (1971); Vroom and Yvetton (1973); Adair (1973).
1970s	Situational theories	Leadership approach and style specific to the situation.	Hersey and Blanchard (1969–93).
A focus on the followers			
Late 1970s	Servant Leadership Theory	Supports the notion that the main purpose of leaders is to provide service to others.	Greenleaf (1970).
	Transformational Leadership Theory	Central concept is change and the role of leadership is envisioning and transforming organisational performance. Leaders inspire and transform followers.	Burns (1978, 2003); Bennis and Nanus (1985); Tichy and Devanna (1986); Bass (1998); Kouzes and Posner (2002).

		Is in contrast to Transactional Leadership Theory – where an emphasis is on the leader, follower, rewards or recognition in return for commitment.	
1990s	Relational Leadership (psychodynamic) theories	Concentrates on the quality of the relationship of leader and direct report, or group members. Described as the leader–member exchange (LMX).	Graen and Uhl-Bien (1995).

A focus back on the individual as leader			
1990s	Authentic Leadership Theory	A form of transparent and ethical leader behaviour that fosters openness and acting in accordance with the true authentic self. The importance of self-awareness, and follower involvement, is recognised.	Terry (1993); George (2003); Avolio and Gardner (2005).
2000s	Cognitive theories	Focus on how leaders think, decide and make 'sense' of the situation for followers.	Connelly et al. (2000); Mumford et al. (2007a).

A focus on the individual as leader

Great Man Theory

The Great Man Theory of the 1840s proposed that leaders are born with a set of innate qualities and characteristics, or 'traits', which only 'great' people inherited (Northouse, 2013). The emphasis therefore was on the belief that leaders were born and not shaped or made, were implicitly destined to lead and were primarily male, hence the 'Great Man' (Glynn and DeJordy, 2010). Some lists of traits would also include a person's height (Yukl, 1998). They were often distinctly Western and from the military (Bolden et al., 2003, p6).

There was a perceived connection with being brave and heroic, mythical interactions made popular by the writings of Thomas Carlyle (1888) in his book, *On Heroes, Hero Worship and the Heroic in History*. This fantasy with the 'hero' and associated conviction of courage and bravery is a feature that played into the sense of being saved by a 'super' human being; inferences are clearly discernible today with the fascination for studying great leaders, and reading their autobiographies with a fixation on a 'heroic concept of leadership' (Vroom and Jago, 2007, p18). This emphasis focused attention on the individual's so-called unique personal qualities, with an inference that the many were led by a few gifted and talented individuals.

Advantages

The romantic idea of the leader as a 'hero' arguably satisfied the so-called follower's concept, need and ideology of a 'great leader' at that time. This perpetuated the belief that individuals, or a situation, could be protected or rescued by the right person – that a great leader would take control and save the day.

Criticisms – disadvantages

There was a real focus on the leader, and his innate character, as the shaper of history, and not the followers, or the situation that prevailed. This great leader was not only perceived to be male but also of a certain social class. In contrast, contributions of the 'Great Women' leaders in history, for example Joan of Arc, Catherine II (the Great), Empress of Russia, and Florence Nightingale, were largely ignored. The concept of one brave super hero to some extent has remained elusive and attractive; although in the National Health Service (NHS), The King's Fund (2011) has recognised this as conceptually flawed.

Depending on a 'Great' leader links to Wilfred Bion's work, described by Stokes (1994, p19) as 'the unconscious at work in groups and teams'. Group members, Stokes suggests, can 'become pathologically dependent, easily swayed one way or another, by their idealisation of the leader', and with it there is a loss of challenge, or criticism of the leader, an important feature of a 'healthy group life' (1994, p19). Today, Johnson (2005, p3) reminds us that there is more discussion about 'fallen heroes' and that the image of the leader as a hero, 'has been shattered by one ethical scandal after another'.

Importantly, there was no scientific validity to support this theory. In contrast self-leadership focuses on all individuals counting, not a privileged few. The Great Man Theory is clearly linked to the next category, Trait Theory.

Trait Theory

Early trait theories

Trait Theory continued the focus on the individual leader and, while popular in the 1930s, Stogdill's (1948) critique of the ever growing list of traits ensured it lost some of its credibility and therefore its appeal, to see a resurgence in terms of interest from the 1990s onwards.

This theory proposes that leaders have distinct traits (either inherited or acquired), which are part of their personality and which enable them to influence others to achieve (Northouse, 2013). An emergent or effective leader, it was believed, possessed a certain set of particular traits that were relatively stable over time, and were distinct from a person's mood (Roberts and DelVecchio, 2000). According to Beeler (2010), 'traits' describe thinking preferences, personality, motivation and how leaders interact with others. Bass and Bass (2008, p103) suggest that, 'when traits are requirements for doing something they are called competencies'.

Individuals who were *more dominant*, *more intelligent* and *more confident* about their own performance were more likely to be identified as leaders by other members of their task group, and these three traits could be used to identify emergent leaders (Smith and Foti, 1998). Kirkpatrick and Locke (1991, p59) supported the notion that individuals could be born, or learn the six key traits they identified: *drive, motivation, integrity, confidence, cognitive ability* and *task knowledge*. Others included *social intelligence* (Zaccaro et al., 2004). Social intelligence is described by Marlowe (1986) as the ability to recognise one's own and others' feelings, behaviours and thoughts, and to respond accordingly.

Northouse (2013) advocated similar key traits: *intelligence, self-confidence, determination, integrity* and *sociability.* Kouzes and Posner (2002, p25) interviewed 75,000 individuals to establish the top perceived characteristics needed in a leader (the data were extrapolated from six different continents: Africa, North and South America, Asia, Europe and Australia); the following are the top ten traits identified:

- Honest
- Forward looking
- Broad minded
- Dependable

- Competent
- Intelligent
- Supportive
- Inspiring

- Fair minded
- Straightforward

Others, such as Judge et al. (2002), suggested that *extraversion* was the most significant factor, followed by *conscientiousness, openness* and *low neuroticism.*

Advantages
This theory supports the notion that there is a set of individuals, with special gifts, who can achieve great things. It fulfils the need for individuals to see their leaders as 'gifted people' (Northouse, 2013).

In addition, it provides lists of reported traits that individuals can be assessed and measured against to determine suitability for the role of leader, and while individual traits present little clue, or indicative significance, in combination they can produce predictive patterns. Invariably, whole industries of psychometric testing have emerged to attempt to identify leadership potential, measured against a set of predetermined traits (thinking preferences, personality and predisposition in terms of motivation). Zaccaro (2007) advocated another look at the leadership traits, suggesting that the move away from this area had been premature.

Criticisms – disadvantages
The trait approach was challenged in terms of its universal application by Northouse (2013), for this emphasis concentrates on the leader and her or his personality, and not the context, or the individuals being led. Focusing on the individual traits distracted attention from the fundamental importance of the relationship between individuals.

The lists of traits that emerged over time have become almost limitless and, without an agreed definitive grouping of tried and tested traits, this has produced long subjective lists. Matthews et al. (2003, p3), for example, refer to Allport and Odbert's (1936) inventory of almost 18,000 personality-relevant terms. The studies supporting the Trait Theory have been described by Northouse (2013) as, 'ambiguous and uncertain at times', not robust and consistent. Bolden et al. (2003, p6) concur that, although some traits were identified across studies, there were 'no consistent' and conclusive groupings that could be isolated with any degree of universal accuracy; implicitly isolated traits do not define a leader.

Earlier researchers also found no significant differences between the traits of followers and leaders, and also on leadership effectiveness in relation to identified traits (Fleenor, 2007). Implicitly they did not provide 'sufficient predictors of leadership effectiveness' (Hernandez et al., 2011).

Concentrating solely on individuals' traits also fails to take into consideration the impact of the situation (Friedrich, 2010). A person who possesses certain traits can make a leader in one situation, but not in another. Churchill is a classic example of a leader who may not have been recognised for his greatness and specific abilities, had it not been for the Second World War. Traits are also a poor predictor of behaviour. Others may have traits that help them to emerge as leaders but that are not sustained over time. Identifying a prescriptive and definitive list of traits is therefore not only reductionist, and excludes potential, but is also subjective and therefore somewhat flawed. Indeed, according to Bass and Bass (2008, p49) the 'pure trait theory eventually fell into disfavour'.

Being a leader is far more than simply being intelligent, self-confident and sociable (Caughron, 2010). Indeed, Stogdill and Bass (1990) concluded, after extensive research, that there was no one set of traits that could be linked to successful leadership in all situations.

This reductionist approach arguably leaves no room for potential growth and development, an important and contrasting feature of self-leadership. Despite this the interest and reliance on 'trait'-type assessments continue in terms of popularity.

A legacy still evident is within the so-called associated 'leadership fads'. One example is the popularity of using instruments such as the Myers-Briggs Type Indicator (MBTI), which can contribute significantly to the development of self-awareness and understanding of others. However, these instruments have limitations. Zaccaro and Horn (2003, p779) remind us that 'some fundamental questions remain about the validity of the MBTI to predict leadership outcomes'. They also suggest that there can be an overemphasis by the consumer on identifying particular MBTI types as better leaders (Zaccaro and Horn, 2003, p780).

With MBTI, individuals receive four letters as part of an assessment report which are often consigned to the drawer or worn as a label to live by; for example, I am an ENTJ. Step Two with its facet analysis can lead to a much richer understanding of type and is potentially powerful – less likely to be used as a label but more likely to be consigned to a drawer due to the complexity and level of investment taken to understand it.

Behaviourist theories

Behaviourist theories of the 1940s–1950s moved away from personal characteristics or traits to actions, or things leaders do – behaviours that bring about a change (Gosling et al., 2012). Skinner (1974) suggested that leadership is a learned behaviour and therefore, if the specific behaviours were identified, they could also be learnt. Indeed, behavioural theorists would probably argue, in contrast to some of the earlier trait theorists, that leaders can be made (Caughron, 2010). The different patterns of behaviours can be classified as 'styles of leadership' (Bolden et al., 2003, p6).

McGregor's (1960) theory X and Y stance would explain a leader's underlying style (Bolden, 2004). For example, theory X leaders would view individuals as having an inherent dislike of work, and avoidance would be the primary motivation, requiring a controlling and coercive, or dominating, style. In contrast, theory Y leaders would believe individuals inherently want to work and be responsible, and would therefore adopt a much more supportive, developmental and encouraging style (see Figure 1.1).

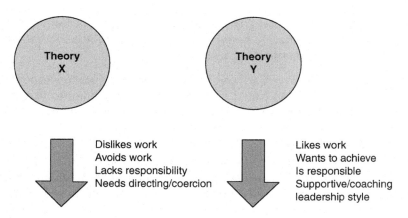

Figure 1.1 McGregor's theory X and Y

Behaviours related to *initiating structure, consideration, task orientation* and *relationship focus* (see Figure 1.2) were identified in early studies as important activities (Katz et al., 1951; Fleishmann, 1953; Likert, 1967). *Initiating structure* could include planning and organising a work group, monitoring standards, meeting deadlines and providing rules for communication, and *relationship-focused* behaviour and participation relates to involving others (Beeler, 2010). *Consideration* is described by Beeler (2010) as showing concern for staff well-being. Staying on *task* is also an important feature of any leadership behaviours. Yukl (2006) would add change-oriented behaviours to capture the specific role some leaders play in bringing about and facilitating change.

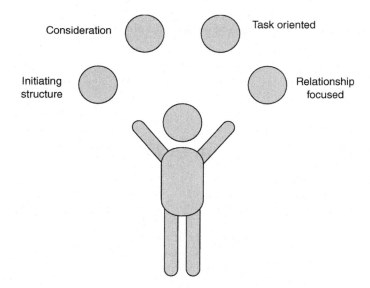

Figure 1.2 Identified important leadership behaviours

Advantages

Behaviourist theories supported the notion that, unlike the Great Man Theory, leaders could be developed, from any cultural or social background, male or female. In contrast to the Trait Theory, it was proposed that a set of behaviours could be learned. The concept of being able to copy, or imitate, a certain person's set of behaviours to become a great leader is potentially both appealing and simplistic.

Role modelling can play an important part in terms of learning positive leadership behaviours. Indeed, Macaulay (2010) would suggest that 'research indicates that the biggest influence on employee engagement is an individual's direct line manager'.

Criticisms – disadvantages

Negative behaviours, however, can equally be learnt through role modelling (Cruess et al., 2008). Furthermore, behavioural theories tended to focus on an abstract concept of behavioural types that were often difficult to identify (Yukl, 1989, cited by Glynn and DeJordy, 2010). In addition, like traits, no universal style was established as effective across different settings and, like Trait Theory, there were far too many categories of leader behaviours (Friedrich, 2010). The research in the field was also found to be unacceptable (Howell and Costley, 2006).

Individuals who were successful leaders in one environment, often failed in another organisation. Research also relied upon follower observations, their accuracy for capturing everything potentially influenced by subjective perceptions. There is an implied and simplistic inference that the outward behaviour of an individual could be imitated, or copied, to be an effective leader. In copying there is not only a potential loss of 'self', but also with it a loss of authenticity and diversity, which it will be argued self-leadership integrally preserves.

Bolden and Gosling (2006), however, talked of the attractiveness of competencies or styles, still prevalent today, which offer a structured and consistent framework. However, they describe this simplistic, narrow and reductionist emphasis as negating:

> [the] more subtle qualities, interactions, situational factors and the collective [focus of] building on individual strengths and differences with a focus on outcomes rather than behaviours.
>
> (Bolden and Gosling, 2006, p150)

A focus on the situation or context

Contingency theories

Contingency theories of the 1960s proposed that different situations may require differing leadership approaches. Then contingent variables included the nature of the task, the followers, the leader's style and the complexity of the organisation (Vroom and Jago, 2007). Others would add that the 'certainty of the task' impacts the approach the leader takes (Lorsch, 2010). Contingency theorists Tannenbaum and Schmidt (1958) focused on the behaviour of the leader in terms of a continuum of appropriate leadership styles, including *autocratic, persuasive, consultative* and *democratic*, which were contingent on, and therefore matched to, what was perceived to be required.

Other early contingency research focused on the leader's motivation and the particulars of a situation, to assist in predicting group performance (Fiedler, 1967). Avolio (2007, p26) describes Fiedler's theory as a 'trait contingency model'. This theory suggests that in certain given situations particular leaders would be effective and in different situations ineffective, or less well equipped (Caughron, 2010). Matching more closely therefore the leader's style to the situation, or fitting the role to the individual leader, in Fiedler's model would arguably improve the outcomes (Vroom and Jago, 2007).

House (1971) developed a path–goal theory by combining behavioural and motivational approaches. Path–goal theory assumes that the leader's purpose is to provide subordinates with anything that is missing in the situation and to help them overcome limitations in their abilities (Northouse, 2013). This approach emphasised the leader's remit in managing the so-called 'path' of the subordinates, for example, by providing rewards, if these are absent, to improve job satisfaction (House and Mitchell, 1974).

Adair's (1973) action-centred leadership model, although categorised as a leadership style by Gill (2011), arguably fits within the contingency parameters in that it relates to the leader keeping in balance three important elements or contingents: the *task*, the *team* and the *individual*. Implicitly, it focuses on achieving the task, building and managing the team, and succeeding in the development of the individual. The effective leader is the individual who focuses equally on all three, keeping them in balance.

Advantages
The value of contingency theories is that they recognised the systemic impact upon leadership, introducing important elements, or contingents, other than the individual leader. They therefore stressed the need for the leader to 'react', rather than simply 'act' (Stone and Patterson, 2005).

They considered both the task and the social and emotional needs of the individual and team. They also supported the notion that individuals with a preference for tasks over relationships, and vice versa, could be better matched to the required situation to improve the potential outcomes (Gosling et al., 2012).

Criticisms – disadvantages
Fielder's theory produced a significant degree of controversy (Vroom and Jago, 2007). Lorsch (2010) criticised the earlier models for being too simplistic, while others described the later models as 'highly complex and often difficult to apply', according to Glynn and DeJordy (2010, p124), as there are endless contingencies (Gill, 2011). Indeed, including the wider context such as cultural aspect and political influences, together with demographic differences, to name just a few, ensured that the concept potentially was unspecified and unwieldy. Hackman (2010) suggested that paradoxically the more complete and complex a contingency model is, the more it requires the individual leader to be almost superhuman in being able to translate the leadership style required, in order to match the changing contextual elements.

Friedrich (2010) also suggested that the contingency theory failed to satisfy the 'how and the why' questions; for example, a relationship between certain leader traits and group performance was found, but the process was unknown. Much of the research related to the path–goal leadership theory proposed by House (1971), which is described as flawed by Wofford and Liska (1993).

Stogdill (1974) would argue that the situational stance attributed differences in outcomes distinctly to the environment. Indeed, much of the research related to contingency models produced inconclusive evidence with criticism about methodology and analysis (Gill, 2011). Self-leadership, however, it will be argued, starts with every individual and is an 'inside-out' model that is more immune to changes and fluxes in the environment – an approach that instead fosters resilience and adaptability whatever the environmental, team or individual contingencies.

Related to contingency is the impact of the situation, and adapting leadership styles to better match differing situations.

Situational theories

While the contingency theorist would suggest that a leader has a certain style, and should not to stray from this, the situational theorist would argue that leaders should adapt their style to fit (Caughron, 2010). Situational theories, therefore, proposed that different situations required different combinations of behaviours, and that the leader should be able to appreciate when to change his or her leadership style. In crisis situations, leaders who articulated a vision that shared their followers' values and goals were more likely to be accepted by the followers (Hunt et al., 1999).

According to Barrett (2010), the most commonly discussed situations are the environment, organisation, culture, crisis and change. Situational variables significantly influence leadership behaviours (Vroom and Jago, 2007).

The most well-known theory is the Hersey and Blanchard (1969) Situational Leadership Theory (Graeff, 1997). The earlier writings described an important situational relationship between the task behaviour, relationship behaviour and maturity (Graeff, 1997). The developmental levels of the subordinates, or followers' maturity (readiness), were proposed as playing the most significant role in determining the leadership style (Bolden et al., 2003; Gill 2011).

This involved moving through different stages or phases: of *telling, selling, participating* and *delegating*. A subordinate who lacks understanding, experience or capability (as examples) would require the leader to adapt her or his style to be more directive or 'telling'. Maturity in this case alluded to the experience, motivation and readiness of followers to take responsibility (Caughron, 2010). The more proficient and confident the subordinate becomes, the more the reciprocal leadership style is adapted to be more 'delegating' and empowering.

This model requires the leader to be able to recognise the situational ability of the individual, or subordinate, and the behavioural flexibility to adapt the leader's own style (Gill, 2011). In 1993, Hersey and Blanchard focused on two leadership behaviours in different situations: *supportive* and *directive*. *Delegating* and *coaching* were added to make four proposed leadership styles, adapted to match the developmental/maturity level of the followers (Friedrich, 2010).

Advantages
Similar to contingency theories' advantages or strengths, Hersey and Blanchard's theory recognised that situational factors can impact the effectiveness of leaders so that one style therefore might not work in all situations (Gill 2011). Bass and Bass (2008) describe it as an intuitively popular model despite its lack of reliability and validity. They suggest that this is

linked to its simplicity and ease of use in terms of the information that can be made available on a 'single small card' (Bass and Bass, 2008, p521).

Criticisms – disadvantages

Barrett (2010) and Mumford (2010) warn that, despite this theory being applied in management, very few studies have identified whether or not it 'actually works'. Graeff (1997, p164) also suggested an absence of supportive research for the original of, and subsequent adaptations to, the Situational Leadership Theory and concludes that the adaptations made to the original model were confusing.

Gill (2011, p81) adds that the model fails to explain how leadership styles vary in relation to the different levels of leaders, and provides the example of executive leaders. And, like contingency theories, there was a lack of specificity in terms of 'how' leaders can change their styles (Gill, 2011, p81).

Applying exactly the right style to match complex and different situations is hard (Johnson, 2005). For no two leadership situations or dilemmas are identical. Anyone who has been on-call, or managed a department, can encounter similar issues, but in reality, when all the facts are established, each situation becomes a unique experience. Indeed, prejudging a situation to be similar, or the same, can have disastrous consequences, resulting in missing information and misdiagnosing the leadership intervention.

Nicholls (1985) suggested that the model could perpetuate paternalistic and very prescriptive approaches. The potential overprescriptive approach to leadership is stressed by Northouse (2013). Bass and Bass (2008) allude to the problem of constantly switching leadership styles in terms of a lack of consistency, and potential confusion in terms of subordinate expectations. Northouse (2013) also criticises the model for not providing guidance in terms of how leaders use this approach in groups, or with teams. Self-leadership, it will be argued, instead starts with the individual, the authentic self, and avoids simply copying a style. It is more about judging each moment in the now and as integrally unique, responding with a state of mind that produces wisdom and flexibility to adapt to the situation. It moves away from a prescription of how to act.

Both contingency and situational theories and models move away from the leader as the main feature and begin to hint at the importance of the follower. The next grouping of leadership approaches concentrates more on the follower(s). A 'follower' in this context is 'anyone who works with a leader towards a common goal' (Barrett, 2010).

A focus on followers

Servant Leadership Theory

The Servant Leadership concept was introduced by Robert Greenleaf in the 1970s. The emphasis was on the notion of the leader wanting to serve instead of lead; of putting the needs and interests of others above his or her own (Johnson, 2005). Arguably, with the emphasis on service to others, this is well placed within the public sector (Gill, 2011). Robert Greenleaf's (1977) *Servant Leadership* text was described by Van Wart (2003, p217) as 'the first major text devoted to ethical issues' in leadership; however, it did not receive 'mainstream attention', with which Bolden et al. (2003) concur.

The need to serve a cause is common to this model of leadership, as Greenleaf (1970, cited by Bolden et al., 2003, p12) states: 'The servant-leader is servant first'. The following are the key central tenets:

- service to others;

- holistic approach to work;

- promoting a sense of community;

- sharing power in decision making.

Whetstone (2002) connected moral concerns for others with Servant Leadership, and Russell and Stone (2002) identified the functional and accompanying attributes of servant leaders shown in Figure 1.3. They also included the role of teacher, encouraging others, good communication, delegation, listening, competence and credibility.

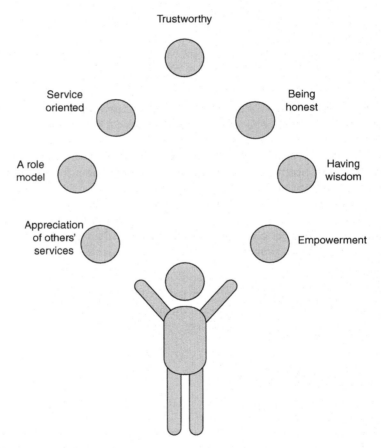

Figure 1.3 Functional and accompanying attributes of servant leaders

Advantages
Russell (2001) suggests that the value systems held by servant leaders are different, and contrast with other types of leaders and leadership theories. The Servant Leadership

model respects the followers' abilities, shares power and empowers followers to perform (Spears, 1995; Russell, 2001). As Manz (1998, p99) would suggest, 'Wise Leaders lead others to lead themselves.'

An important priority for the servant leader is the well-being and development of, and collaboration with, the followers (Gosling et al., 2012). This focus of the importance of 'follow-ship' is identified by Gosling et al. (2012) as a significant feature of this theory. 'Partners, not subordinates' is also the emphasis (Johnson, 2005, p174).

Criticisms – disadvantages

Servant Leadership as an approach has been criticised for a lack of empirical evidence and, therefore, remained more of a philosophical model (Stone et al., 2004). Eicher-Catt (2005, p17) suggests that the values attributed to Servant Leadership promote a 'patriarchal' inference and a theological stance. McCrimmon (2010) and Smith et al. (2004) both concur, suggesting it is paternalistic and that, 'some writers have alluded to servant leadership in moral terms' (Smith et al., 2004, p82). McCrimmon (2010) believes that, as an approach, it would reduce the individual worker's initiative, sense of responsibility and accountability. It will be argued that self-leadership, as an approach, is about human potential and about the capacity to respond with ability.

The importance of the followers is captured in the more contemporary leadership theories, particularly in relation to Transformational Leadership Theory, outlined below.

Transformational Leadership Theory

According to Bass and Bass (2008, p50), Transformational Leadership was first proposed as a theory by Burns, in 1978, and relates to leadership as a transformational progression that ensures followers achieve through a process of change, with the leader as the 'primary catalyst' (Glynn and DeJordy, 2010, p125). This theory concentrated on how a leader is able to influence and motivate followers through strong relationships, to change how they see themselves and the challenges they face (Mumford, 2010). Transformational leaders are able to elicit achievements in others that are above and beyond what individuals believed they could attain. This again is a style of leadership.

Burns' (1978) original discussions about Transformational Leadership, importantly, focused on the concept of working towards a greater collective good, and the importance of self-development as a feature. The main difference between Transformational Leadership and Servant Leadership is the leader's focus. The principal emphasis of Servant Leadership is on service to the followers, while in Transformational Leadership the individual is important, and the organisational transformation is also a key feature (Stone et al., 2004).

Bass (1985) would add that charismatic leadership was 'the largest factor' in Transformational Leadership, but only one feature. Tichy and Devanna (1986) emphasised that Transformational Leadership could be learned and focused on the process of deliberately analysing systems to bring about changes, which would positively impact on productivity. Gill (2011, p85) advises that 'transformational leaders tend to use consultative, participative and delegative styles as well as the directive style'.

This remained in stark contrast to a leader who, in a structured environment, directs and increases performance by rewards, or punishment, but does not create the change in the individuals; this was described as a *transactional* style of leadership (Stogdill and Bass, 1990). Sponsors of Transformational Leadership Theory would suggest that transformational approaches are more effective than transactional ones, most of the time (Caughron, 2010). However, Bass (1985) advised that both transactional and transformational approaches formed an important combination for effective leadership. Gill (2011, p85) critically reported that Transformational Leadership is prevalent at higher, rather than the lower levels of organisations, although the effectiveness of this approach is 'the same at all levels'.

Laissez-faire leadership, in contrast with both transactional and transformational approaches, allows things to simply happen, representing either an absence, or avoidance, of leadership with management by exception (Bass and Riggio, 2006). Operationally, this is an approach that can potentially be disastrous.

In the NHS and local government, Alimo-Metcalfe and Alban-Metcalfe (2001) developed a Transformational Leadership Questionnaire (TLQ) to identify Transformational Leadership behaviours. It was originally based on 9 scales, increased to include the 14 that are outlined in Table 1.2. They reported that an engaging style of leadership, a shared process, positively impacted employee productivity.

Table 1.2 Transformational Leadership Questionnaire (Alimo-Metcalfe and Alban-Metcalfe, 2011)

Leading and developing	Leading and developing the organisation
• Showing genuine concern	• Supporting a development culture
• Being accessible	• Inspiring others
• Enabling	• Focusing the team effort
• Encouraging change	• Being decisive
Leading the way forward	**Personal qualities and values**
• Building a shared vision	• Being honest and consistent
• Networking	• Acting with integrity
• Resolving complex problems	
• Facilitating change sensitively	

Advantages

A sustainable focus is achieved through developing and transforming the followers (Bass and Riggio, 2006). A role model is also provided with whom individuals can identify (Stone and Patterson, 2005). More satisfaction and follower commitment are produced by Transformational Leadership approaches (Dumdum et al., 2003). In addition, increased creativity can be achieved through transformational rather than transactional methods (Jung, 2001).

Criticisms – disadvantages

Creating a significant bond, Caughron (2010) would propose, is only one way, and results can be achieved without the need for this type of attachment. Often a crisis is required for this form of leader to emerge, or be parachuted in (Mumford, 2006). Tourish (2013, p21) suggests that if a leader achieves enough 'power to adjust the psyche of his, or her followers, in transforming [them] . . . such power could just as likely be used for the sectional good of the designated leader . . . the Hitler problem'. He would also stress that there is the connotation that 'powerful leaders' act upon 'powerless others' (Tourish, 2013, p20).

Similarly, Bass and Avolio (1997) describe the rise of pseudo-transformational leadership interventions where an unhealthy competitive, us and them, self-interest can prevail and where authoritarian approaches are used inappropriately. Self-leadership as a concept, in contrast, negates all of these pseudo-transformational leadership characteristics.

Currie and Lockett (2011) also advise that this model overemphasises the role of the leader in the change process, and Avolio et al. (2009, p430) inform us that Transformational Leadership lags 'behind all other areas of leadership research'. Another more contemporary theory of leadership that fits within the follower category is the leader–member exchange (LMX).

Relational Leadership theories – leader–member exchange

Gill (2011, p76) describes LMX as a 'psychodynamic theory', where there is a focus on the 'characteristics of the leader, their followers and their relationship'. It is different from other leadership theories in that it centres on the relationship development over time between a leader and each individual follower. Graen and Uhl-Bien (1995) describe three stages an exchange relationship may go through, from a more formal relationship, to an acquaintance phase, to a more mature relationship of equal commitment to each other.

Importantly, the theory concentrates on the fact that leaders, instead of treating all individuals in the same way, might handle each follower differently depending on their specific relationship. Within this model is the concept of the 'in-group', identified as those individuals who are given 'extra roles or responsibilities', and the 'out-group', where the relationship is simply based on the more formal employment contract, or defined roles (Northouse, 2013). Each relationship is therefore described as unique and thus different; if the leader gets on well with an individual the latter becomes part of the in-group, receiving more 'information, influence, confidence and concern' from the leader. A reciprocal relationship develops where in-group members do additional things for the leader, and the leader does the same for them (Northouse, 2013).

Advantages
Research confirmed that the 'in-group' scenario created greater employee retention, better performance and greater organisational commitment with more promotions (Graen and Uhl-Bien, 1995). There was therefore a clear gain for organisations in which good relationships are developed.

Criticisms – disadvantages
According to Mumford (2010), it is 'difficult to discern what constitutes whether a relationship between a leader and follower is high or low' or, indeed, how high-quality exchanges are developed or accurately measured. Gill (2011, p77) suggests that it seems to support the notion of 'privileged groups' in organisations. The obvious downside is the impact on the out-group of the in-group privileges. Treating all direct reports the

same, rather than one group differently from another, surely should be a priority. When we examine David Rock's (2010) SCARF model in Chapter 5, creating an 'in-group' and an 'out-group' produces a sense of threat that adversely impacts performance. Gill (2011, p78) also complains that the LMX theory does not define how 'specific leadership behaviours create high-quality relationships', but rather generalisations relating to trust, respect, openness, autonomy and discretion. In contrast, self-leadership is about relationships, but not at the expense of 'in- or out-groups', which Rock (2010) would describe as potentially damaging.

The next leadership area focuses back on the individual as the leader.

A focus back on the individual as leader

Outstanding Leadership approaches are referred to by Mumford (2006) and involve examining exceptional or outstanding leadership, being distinct from the Great Man Theory, which supported the notion that all leadership was 'good'. This grouping denotes the 'breadth of a leader's impact', good or bad (Friedrich, 2010).

Mumford (2006) suggested three categories of Outstanding Leadership: *charismatic*, *ideological* and *pragmatic*. Charismatic leaders were oriented to idealised future visions; ideological leaders focused on an idealised past; and the pragmatics focused on problem solving rather than visions, the reality of the now (see summary comparison in Table 1.3). Mumford (2006, p49) stresses the unique 'sense-making' role of all three outstanding leaders relating it to an ability to interpret the current leadership challenges.

Charismatic leadership

Vessey (2010) describes charismatic leaders as basing their vision on 'forecasting', or predicting what the world would be like, perhaps with a perceived problem resolved. To gain support the charismatic leader has to identify a problem and its resolution, which followers can relate to, and will also sign up to the collective greater good (Avolio et al., 2003). These leaders also empower others by increasing followers' self-efficacy, and emerge as leaders in a crisis, or through an opportunity to change.

Bass and Bass (2008, p50) suggest that charismatic leaders are 'highly expressive, articulate and emotionally appealing . . . their followers want to identify with them, have complete faith and confidence in them, and hold them in awe'.

Advantages
Charisma has been described as motivating individuals to follow a vision or strategy (Mumford, 2006). This can be an important element, especially when change is required. Choi (2006) would also support the notion that charismatic leaders are individuals who are capable of great empathy, in addition to envisioning and empowering individuals.

Criticisms – disadvantages
Collins' (2001, p27) identification of level-five leadership qualities found that the most effective leaders of 'great companies' were 'self-effacing', 'humble' and not the so-called charismatic leaders, often parachuted into organisations. An important message here is that if individuals below the charismatic leader perceived the gap between themselves and

the leader to be too great, implicitly they could never see themselves being like the leader, and their performance would be adversely impacted (Collins, 2001). Indeed, Mumford (2006, p7) supports this finding, suggesting that charisma has been found to 'not necessarily result in better performance in business organizations'. In addition, Shipman (2010) reminds us that charismatic leaders may also be destructive, using their persuasive skills in manipulating and convincing followers to collude to meet a negative goal.

Ideological leadership

Emerging as a consequence of a crisis and with a past-oriented vision are the key characteristics of this style of leadership (Strange and Mumford, 2002). Harking back to a past, idealising tradition, culture, a set of rules or behaviour exemplifies this stance (Vessey, 2010). Addressing current issues with traditional, tried and tested methods can be a feature of this approach. The appeal for 'follow-ship' is that these leaders represent the same traditional values that should be promoted and maintained (Post et al., 2002). Vessey (2010) suggests that ideological leaders principally believe that external focuses are the key issue, not individuals.

Advantages
This nostalgic stance can create powerful motivation and influence over others. Learning from the past is an important feature of not repeating mistakes, or reinventing the wheel – an approach that can also fit better with individuals who are averse to change.

Criticisms – disadvantages
This approach can perpetuate on an unconscious level the group dynamic of hope, distracting away from the primary task, the main business or service, in terms of an ideological wish, to return in the future to something more reminiscent of the past (Stokes, 1994). This arguably prevents individuals from acting in the now and being responsive to obvious future changes in direction, something akin to burying your head in the sand, or wearing rose-tinted glasses.

Pragmatic leadership

Described as outstanding problem solvers, pragmatic leaders are therefore talented at identifying and analysing problems (Mumford and Van Doorn, 2001). The key features of their approach are described by Vessey (2010) as knowledge management, expertise, problem solving and consensus building.

Pragmatic leaders are focused on the here and now, not the past, or future, and are not preoccupied with change unless this solves the issue being addressed. They are more inclined to examine the positive and negative consequences, and also to implement unpopular decisions.

The followers of pragmatic leaders are influenced by previous performances; this builds trust and commitment over time. The followers are also more likely to offer their own creative solutions to problems (Mumford and Licuanan, 2004).

Advantages
The emphasis is on knowledge management, expertise and problem solving, rather than building and relying on a 'loyal following' (Mumford, 2010). Often this type of leader has

an ability to think through complex problems and is therefore more flexible (Mumford et al., 2006).

Criticisms – disadvantages

Acting in the now, while laudable, can create reactive responses not thought through, or not allowing the grace of time to reveal a clearer path. While the followers of pragmatic leaders may be listened to and provide ideas for the solution, this ideology, however, relies on one great individual.

Table 1.3 A comparison of charismatic, ideological and pragmatic leadership (adapted from Mumford, 2006, p33)

	Charismatic	Ideological	Pragmatic
Time frame	Future	Past	Present
Experience focus	Positive	Negative	Both
Nature of outcomes	Positive	Transcendent	Malleable
Number of outcomes	Many	Few	Variable
Model adapted from	External	Internal	External
Overall focus	People	Situations	Interactive
Degree of control	High	Low	Selective

The charismatic, ideological and pragmatic leader concepts relate to individuals, as distinct from self-leadership, which is about everyone counting and being at their best in all interactions.

Another type of focus on the individual leader, which emerged to satisfy a need of the time, is the Authentic Leadership Theory, which with recent leadership scandals and failings remains popular and relevant.

Authentic Leadership Theory

The Authentic Leadership paradigm is one type of recent Outstanding Leadership approaches that relates to the alignment of a leader's personal values and beliefs (Avolio et al., 2004). The authentic leader gains the trust of the followers by demonstrating that their values and actions are congruent, and that they believe in what they are doing; the principle method is through role modelling, setting an example (Gardner et al., 2005).

Two authors, Terry (1993) and George (2003), who advance this model, present two different emphases. Terry (1993) focuses on identifying the problem and the truth of the situation, and George (2003) concentrates on the qualities, or characteristics, of authentic leaders. Because the focus is on the leader this links to the style of leadership.

Discussions about the lack of 'authenticity' within corporate leadership seems to have resulted in needing to specify, and propose, an approach based upon being 'true to self' (Kouzes and Posner, 2002), and of finding one's values of being 'genuine and real' (Northouse, 2013). The model has been described by a number of authors; Sparrow (2005), for example, alludes to 'consistency', which he believes results from 'self-awareness' and 'self-regulation'. 'Self-regulation' is further related to setting internal standards and addressing any inconsistencies through self-adjustment (Gardner et al., 2005).

Avolio et al. (2009) describe four features of Authentic Leadership, which include the crucial 'self-awareness' (in terms of values, identity, emotions and motives) and the following three other dimensions:

- 'balanced processing' – for example objectively analysing before deciding;
- 'internalised moral perspective' – being guided by internal ethical standards;
- 'relational transparency' – being open and sharing.

Humility and vulnerability are also two key characteristics of authenticity. Others have mentioned self-sacrifice, spirituality, ethical leadership and authentic behaviours (Gardner et al., 2005; Klenke, 2005). Luthans and Avolio (2003) stressed the importance of a positive outlook, which was made up of the leader's confidence, hope, resilience and optimism. Vessey (2010) proposes that a confident leader has faith in his or her own ability, which in turn creates trust and confidence in followers. He also suggests that they create hope, specifically, that a goal can be achieved, resilience in managing setbacks or obstacles and optimism, which is related to an expectation that things will work out positively. One important feature is the leader's morality/ethics – an individual's personal beliefs about right and wrong.

Advantages

Underlying this model of leadership is the concept that the leader should do what is right, and in order to do the right thing she or he must know what is 'true' to self, the organisation and the wider stakeholders (Northouse, 2013). According to Northouse (2013), it satisfies society's need for honourable and trustworthy leaders. In addition, Avolio (2010) advocates that authenticity as a characteristic can be learnt.

Criticisms – disadvantages

Sparrow (2005), however, would stress that authenticity as a process is not advanced, independent of any interaction, but requires continued interpretation that can only be provided by others. Northouse (2013) would also warn that this concept is relatively new and likely to undergo more changes as the research in this area develops. In addition, he suggests that there is no single recognised definition of Authentic Leadership, and stresses the important influence of life experiences. Authenticity is not a fixed trait, according to Northouse (2013), who believes it can be developed usually through life experiences and triggered by a significant event.

Walumbwa et al. (2008) propose that Authentic Leadership has a behavioural basis that is forged from a leader's positive inner characteristics and strong ethics. The ethical, moral facet, however, seems to presuppose that if you are not 'authentic', you are therefore 'inauthentic'. Alimo-Metcalfe and Alban-Metcalfe (2011, p8) also point out that, although authenticity provides a concept of an individual's characteristics, it does not 'directly address the question as to how to engage employees in the work of the organisation'.

Gill (2011) reminds us that authenticity, while described as a positive leadership characteristic, may have negative consequences when a leader says exactly what he or she is thinking in the heat of the moment.

Cognitive theories

These theories refer to understanding how leaders think and make decisions; their thought processes, for example the impact when stressed; and how other individuals think of their leader (Friedrich, 2010). This included research on intelligence, problem-solving skills and the cognitive processes involved in planning, evaluating and monitoring interactions.

The two aspects of *intelligence* and *experience* were described as 'resources' and formed the Cognitive Resources Leadership Theory (Fiedler and Garcia, 1987). In this theory it is thought that performance of the leader, and subsequently the followers, is shaped by the leader's cognitive resource, his or her behaviour and the particular facets of a situation (Byrne, 2010).

Intelligence and experience are two specific variables in the theory, with intelligence measured by IQ tests, and experience incorporating skills and behaviours learned over time. These two variables, it is proposed, can impact a team's performance.

The theory suggests that leaders with more intelligence would make better decisions; however, this proved not always to be the case, especially in stressful situations, where experience improved decision making (Caughron, 2010). Intelligence, therefore, is the main factor in low-stress situations, so long as the leader provides direction.

Mumford et al. (2003) confirmed these results by examining the cognitive process that leaders undergo to solve problems, and later how they react to crisis (Mumford et al., 2007b). A distinction was made between intelligence and problem solving, implicitly that the two are not one and the same. Byrne (2010) proposed that there is a substantial body of evidence advocating that good leaders have key creative problem-solving skills. Cognitive Resources Leadership Theory supporters would suggest, therefore, that leaders need intelligence, experience and good problem-solving skills to be effective (Byrne, 2010). Most of the work, however, in this sphere covers two areas: crisis or innovation.

This cognitive group of theories also included the impact of both the follower's and leader's perceptions about how effective the leader is (Byrne, 2010), for each individual has her or his own perception of what makes a good leader; and furthermore these are beliefs, or presuppositions, about how a successful leader should act, rather than being based on the leader's actual performance (Mumford, 2010).

Advantages

Understanding the important influence of stress, especially on thinking, is useful information for all leaders. The theory therefore helps predict whether a certain type of person will be able to lead in a given stressful situation.

Criticisms – disadvantages

The research in this area, however, is limited as it is a relatively new theory, and has been focused within the military arena (Byrne, 2010). In addition, the definition and measurement of experience is not accurate enough, and other cognitive abilities should be included.

Stress tolerance and the relationship between intelligence and experience are insufficiently explained, for someone with both intelligence and experience may feel the impact differently. There are many different forms of stress, which arguably is a subjective concept.

Other cultures may also have features that are more important than intelligence and/or experience. In addition there are different forms of intelligence, for example social and emotional, which may impact differently and have not been considered.

Self-leadership as an approach stands in contrast to this, perhaps oversimplistic, model which focuses on two aspects. Self-leadership is instead about embracing the diversity and complexity of each individual, implicitly human potential in its fullness.

Summary

This chapter has comprehensively examined the many different historical leadership theories presented, each essentially with some merits but mainly with key flaws. The different influences are clearly discernible in terms of historical flavours from the Great Man, to a focus on the individual, the situation or context, the followers and back full circle to the individual, each with the advantages identified and countered with the criticisms and disadvantages.

Focusing on the leader, for example, precludes the importance of leadership as a process and its systemic impact. Both will be demonstrated to be essential, as part of self-leadership and its foundations. Trying to find one leader with all the right traits and behaviours not only arguably creates clones and misses the fundamental importance of diversity, but also excludes the significance of the potential of others; this human potential of all is at the heart of self-leadership.

In addition, expecting individuals to change their style of leadership to better match the changing situation is simplistic, and loses the operational reality of organisational complexity, particularly within the public sector. The foundations of self-leadership provide the particular bedrock to be flexible whatever the situation.

A preoccupation with differentiating between management and leadership, when each does both, provides an important focus on leadership as the approach required to deal with change and 'wicked problems' (Brookes and Grint, 2010), the unprecedented nature of which would suggest a focus on leadership is ever more significant. However, in the next chapter, in building the case for self-leadership and its foundations, it will be proposed that there is an exaggerated emphasis on traditional leadership as the 'panacea to cure all organisational ills' (Holroyd and Brown, 2011, p11). A less well explored area is the importance of professional leadership to be distinct from public leadership.

This chapter therefore draws to a close with no one theory of leadership being better or having sufficient research to set it apart from the rest. Leadership as a concept therefore remains elusive despite everyone knowing when they have encountered a great leader or great leadership. The following chapters will identify what self-leadership is, its foundations and why these are crucial for better leadership from the bottom to the top of organisations.

Chapter 2
What is self-leadership?

Introduction

Self-leadership within this text is **the ability to bring out the best in individuals in any circumstances for the ultimate aim of realising better outcomes**. It is about achieving full potential, crucially when needed, to accomplish whatever the tasks and challenges might be. It relates to an individual changing his or her behaviour as a result of a better state or presence of mind. For as school children we are not taught about the powerful impact the mind and our thinking have on everything we do, even though 'what we achieve at work is driven by what we think' (Rock, 2007, p288).

This chapter will therefore discuss what self-leadership comprises. The facets of 'leading self' are *self-observation*, *self-regulation*, *self-management*, *self-awareness* and, crucially, *self-compassion*. The facets of 'leading others' for self-leadership are not about simply self. The importance, therefore, of *social awareness*, *relationship management* and *effective communication* will be discussed and explored. It will be argued that leadership development thus far has followed an 'outside-in' model, rather than the 'inside-out' dimension that self-leadership focuses upon.

The significant and compelling context within the Health and Social Care sectors will also be discussed to demonstrate the case for self-leadership. It has been established in Chapter 1, for example, that many historical leadership theories emerged to attempt to meet and match the outstanding needs of those time periods. A preoccupation with the romantic idea of the single hero leader model has dominated the historical landscape, and is still prevalent to date with concepts of parachuting individuals into failing organisations, not uncommon in the Health and Social Care sectors. This has somewhat distracted attention away from the central and powerful process of leadership towards individual leader models.

The process of leadership is therefore an important foundation for self-leadership and will be explored further in Chapter 3. However, examining and defining key terms is an important starting point for this chapter.

Self-leadership as a concept

The first and best of all victories, the victory of oneself over oneself.

(Plato's Laws, 626e, Pangle, 1980, p5)

'Leadership starts with self' is proposed by Braye (2002, p300), so we need to go there first, knowing and understanding as much about self in order to better appreciate others, and how this can impact interactions. It is extraordinarily difficult to change people; you only have to think about partners, children and colleagues to realise this. Managing and regulating 'self' better, to maximise the full potential of each individual, is what this is about, rather than focusing on manipulating others, which leadership can become, particularly when someone is trying too hard to be the right leader.

Leadership is the ability to influence others; this influence is the theme of many definitions of leadership (Johnson, 2005; Mumford, 2010; Northouse, 2013). Self-leadership is the ability to influence self, and bring out the very best of who we are, and who we can be. This relies on a working appreciation of what allows individuals to function at their best, and what inhibits them. An appreciation that individuals can influence this human potential is key.

Self-leadership, however, points to something more fundamental than traits, behaviours, skills (competencies) and knowledge. The focus, instead, is on the moment-to-moment human capability to use these resources effectively, in order to achieve the best outcome in all actions, reactions and interactions.

Self-leadership as a concept is not new, for Charles Manz in 1983, and later with Christopher Neck, used the term to describe 'the process of influencing self' (Neck and Manz, 2010, p4). They focused, however, more on the social impact of others on an individual, an 'outside-in' model, rather than the purely 'inside-out', natural capability individuals have. State of mind, therefore, is more integral to this concept of self-leadership, which will be discussed further in Chapters 3 and 4.

In their text, Neck and Manz (2010, p1) also suggest that 'self-leadership' is not about the 'leadership of others'. However, within this book the author stresses that all leadership involves others, in that interactions in human systems are about connection, communication and interfacing with, implicitly, relationships. Invariably leadership cannot happen without such exchanges with others, otherwise leadership does not exist. Leadership is therefore more akin to Kouzes and Posner's (2002, p20) concept of 'leadership as a relationship': a relationship with 'self and others'. Indeed, as Hersey et al. (2013, p189) state, 'effective leaders focus on others'.

Self-leadership defined

Self-leadership therefore has a personal and a social consequence, and within the Health and Social Care sectors is:

> *the ability to bring out the best in individuals in any circumstances for the ultimate aim of realising better outcomes.*

This definition importantly captures the concept of leadership as a process. Self-leadership is therefore about the leader who asks the right questions, listens deeply to others to ensure they feel listened to, and creates a culture based on learning, sharing, challenging, tackling conflict and instigating difficult conversations. Co-creating strategy from the bottom and integrating it within services, being mindful of sustainability and supporting independence in others to be comfortable with innovation and change are all features of self-leadership.

Self-leadership includes *self-observation*, the ability to *self-regulate* and *self-manage*, being *self-aware* and exercising *self-compassion*. There is an important process of learning about self and 'learning as a change in behaviour' is crucial (Hersey et al., 2013, p10). Self-observation is the first of these facets.

Self-observation

De Mello (1990, p35) suggests that self-observation is the 'most important thing of all' and is about looking at everything as though unconnected, as 'a passive, detached observer'. Self-observation is being aware, or conscious in the moment, of our reactions, which are interpreted as thoughts and feelings, and to realise the impact of thinking and feeling, for as human beings our thoughts influence our feelings with biochemical reactions as markers (Borghi and Cimatti, 2010). We have a thought that produces a chemical response, a feeling (emotional response) that produces a reaction and a potential action. A scary thought, for example, prepares the body for flight or fight, the same response whether simply imagined or real, as the brain is not so discerning. Emotional responses such as self-criticism trigger the same flight or fight response. Cortisol is one of the resultant hormones released, which, over prolonged periods of time, plays havoc with the ability to feel pleasure, potentially resulting in depression (Neff, 2011).

Becoming more observant allows an individual to better predict the impact different situations, conversations and individuals can have, together with their current level of tension (stress) and subsequent clarity of thought. It is noticing when our thinking is less clear, for example standing in the middle of a room trying to remember what it is you were doing there – potential clue to being preoccupied. Being quick to anger or easily distracted, judging self or others harshly, or becoming easily irritated might also provide evidence of a potential poor state of mind and a lack of presence in the moment.

Self-observation can be an important precursor to change, described by Neck and Manz (2010, p18) as providing, 'the foundations for managing our behaviour'. Significantly, however, this involves a commitment to being present in the moment, how to act, rather than react, and to simply observe without overanalysing and 'evaluating everything', to see what is really there (De Mello, 1990, p37). Importantly, this is about everyone being capable of self-observation, of tuning into the now. It is not returning over and over to thoughts, thinking of the past or future, for both do not exist in strict real terms – only the 'now' exists. For churning over past thoughts and future worries creates an in the moment distraction, coloured potentially with flavours of sadness, preoccupation, worry, tension or something else, other than being fully present and in the best state of mind to interact.

Thinking we are always fully present, fully concentrating is common; however, the concentrating brain uses a significant amount of energy in the form of glucose and oxygen, not stored by the brain, so it often shortcuts through unconscious pattern formation (Kahneman, 2011). Think of the last time, while listening to someone, your thoughts wandered off, thinking about a family member or row with a colleague, a shopping list must-have item, a to-do list crucial task, or '*I wonder what they are doing or how they are getting along . . .*'.

Whybrow and Wildflower (2011, p7) suggest that self-observation produces 'greater awareness' by helping individuals to 'notice any disconnect between what [they are] saying, and the behaviour [they are] exhibiting'. This is an awareness 'in action' – an ability to understand our emotional responses, our mood and importantly the realisation that these are transient. De Mello (1990, p47) describes self-observation as 'stripping down to the I'; the 'I' observing the 'me' and that it is indeed one of the 'most important things'. He crucially stresses that it is not about a method or a technique; it is about watching and observing without judgement, 'as if it were happening to someone else' (De Mello, 1990, p36). This is therefore about being aware of momentary, fleeting feelings and significantly their impact on our thinking. Linked to this important concept is self-regulation.

Self-regulation

Ringleb and Rock (2012, p373) describe self-regulation as being better able to handle 'stressors', to 'call upon cognitive resources regardless of one's emotions, and/or mental state in order to enhance performance'. Goleman et al. (2013, p158) refer to it as 'emotional self-control'. Koole et al. (2011, p34) would concur that self-regulation is closely related to 'emotion regulation'. Having insights into one's own emotions has also been linked with resilience, and 'the resilient personality' (Skodol, 2010, p114). Resilience has been defined as 'an outcome of successful adaptation to adversity' (Zautra et al., 2010, p4). Being resilient is a key feature of self-leadership and therefore something that will be discussed further.

Caver and Scheier (2011, p3) suggest that self-regulation is a 'purposive process, the sense that self-corrective adjustments are taking place as needed to stay on track, for the purpose of being served . . . and the sense that the corrective adjustments originate within the person.

Koole et al. (2011, p28) refer specifically to the 'regulation of emotions', with emotions defined as 'people's . . . positive or negative reactions to events that they perceive as relevant to their ongoing concerns'. They discuss this in terms of 'virtually any stimulus' that results in changes in the emotions, in which they include 'specific emotions such as anger or fear, along with global mood states, stress and all kinds of affective responses' (Koole et al., 2011, p23). Koole et al. (2011, p25) suggest that regulation of negative emotions can occur at any of the four stages shown in Figure 2.1.

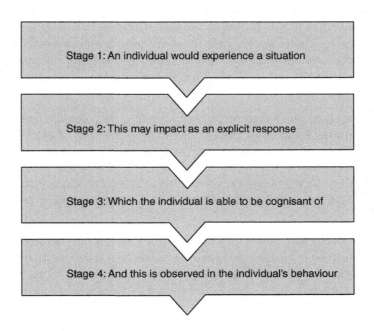

Figure 2.1 An example of self-regulation in an individual (adapted from Koole et al., 2011, p25)

Two approaches advocated, for example, were distraction and reappraisal – distraction was found to be effective at any stage, with early acknowledgement more effective than reappraisal in the latter stages (Koole et al., 2011). Other methods, such as controlled breathing and muscle relaxation, were described as effective in successfully reducing emotional stress.

This concept of regulation is described as a process to control and is more effortful; Chapter 4 describes managing state of mind through an intuitive, instinctive automatic ability, which is more effortless, and is more about being aware in the moment and the impact of an individual's thinking; and with this realisation comes the ability to choose how to react, or simply not react and do nothing. Simply quieting, slowing down will allow individuals the space within to listen to their internal wisdom, their intuition. Another linked concept and the third facet is self-management.

Self-management

Goleman et al. (2013, p45) suggest that a 'leader's primal challenge' is 'self-management' and they discuss this in terms of the principal context of controlling emotions. The impact emotions can have on the brain has been shown by functional magnetic resonance imaging (fMRI) scans (Gyurak et al., 2009). Implicitly, being stressed can impact adversely the individual's ability to think clearly. This is referred to as an 'amygdala hijack' (Goleman et al., 2013, p45), for the amygdala plays an important part in processing emotions (Blakemore and Frith, 2005).

Negative thinking has also been shown to adversely impact the ability to react and respond (Dispenza, 2007). Indeed, Goleman et al. (2013) talk about the important contagion effect of emotions (good or bad) and the implications for leaders. They discuss, for example, the explicit impact on team members who take their 'emotional cues from each other, for better or for worse' (Goleman et al., 2013, p178).

Tang and Posner (2009), however, propose that the ability to regulate our emotions can be learnt and enhanced. This will be discussed further in Chapter 5. Leaders' flexibility and adaptability are significant correlates with emotional self-management.

Senge (2006, p27) asks if we are 'prisoners of our own thinking', for he proposed that many problems within organisations are related to 'basic ways of thinking and interacting' rather than any other explanation. These are often habitual ways of thinking.

Developing a consistent sense of self is an important concept, not changing on a daily basis – one day autocratic, another democratic – and being authentic across all aspects of life (George et al., 2011); for we do not arrive at work without the influence of home sometimes bleeding into our daily lives, as much as people attempt to build artificial boundaries between the two. It is about managing this through self-observation, being aware it is happening in the moment and the potential impact on state or presence of mind, decision making and all interactions. Better management of self is therefore a crucial concept when it comes to emotions.

'Managing yourself' is part of both the *Leadership Qualities Framework for Adult Social Care* (National Skills Academy for Social Care, 2013, p14) and the *NHS Clinical Leadership Framework* (Leadership Academy, 2011, p15). The NHS document suggests, for example, that competent leaders 'Manage the impact of their emotions on their behaviour with consideration of the impact on others' (Leadership Academy, 2011, p114). This, the author would propose, is the 'ripple effect' of self-leadership, for the individual who is experiencing a better state or presence of mind will impact positively everyone he or she interacts with.

The next concept, 'self-awareness', is very much connected to the management of emotions and is also part of both the *NHS Clinical Leadership Framework* and the *Leadership Qualities Framework for Adult Social Care*.

Self-awareness

'Clinicians show leadership through developing self-awareness' (Leadership Academy, 2011, p12); and 'in order to develop self-awareness leaders must be willing to examine their own values, principles and assumptions, while also learning from their experiences' (National Skills Academy for Social Care, 2013, p14).

Self-awareness is defined by Goleman et al. (2013, p40) as 'having a deep understanding of one's emotions, as well as one's strengths and limitations and one's values and motives'. It helps individuals 'to understand the effect that behaviour has on followers and to find congruence between observable behaviour, and the deeply held beliefs, drives, motivators and other elements of their inner theatre' (Kets de Vries and Korotov, 2012, p266).

As Goleman et al. (2013, p40) suggest, it allows leaders 'to act with conviction and authenticity'. Indeed, self-awareness is a key feature of self-leadership, and encompasses the ability to observe behaviours and their potential triggers. Goleman (2000, p4) would add 'as well as recognise their impact on work performance, relationships, and the like'. Awareness, is not overanalysis, or explicit knowledge, it is more tacit. It is not self-judgement or self-criticism, but instead informs the sense of self. Invariably, 'individuals with more differentiated knowledge of self and emotion show greater efficiency in emotion regulation' (Koole et al., 2011, p31).

Hersey et al. (2013, p189) describe self-awareness as the 'cornerstone of developing yourself as a leader'. Starkey and Hall (2012, p89) suggest that it allows individuals to 'reframe experience and abandon old negative or habitual modes of thinking and experiencing'. De Mello (1990, p37), however, would emphasise that it is 'awareness without evaluating everything' with 'no judgement'.

It is an 'inside-out' approach, for individuals can be so preoccupied with what is happening in the external world (outside-in) that they miss what is really impacting the internal environment. Individuals become lost within busy systems buffered by reactive knee-jerk responses with little ability to process, self-reflect and understand the inner impact and outward resultant behaviour.

Health clinicians and social workers alike are encouraged to recognise their own values, appreciating how these may be different from those of others. Social workers and health clinicians, with self-awareness, are able to express their feelings and know where these end, and the patients' or clients' begin. They know their own strengths and limitations and have some appreciation of the impact of what they have to say on others, remembering the caveat, however, that being more self-aware only allows an individual to be more aware, and in touch with people like themselves.

Stereotyping and so-called unconscious bias can, however, remain (Heffernan, 2011; Kahneman 2011). Corrective adjustments to such bias require 'self-regulatory' effort, which according to Wagner and Heatherton (2011, p55) requires circulatory blood glucose and oxygen.

The next important facet of self-leadership is self-compassion.

Self-compassion

Self-compassion is crucial, for when we are able to be 'gentle with ourselves', we are 'more likely to reach out, connect and experience empathy' and be able to be compassionate towards others (Brown, 2012, p75). According to Neff (2011), self-compassion is about *self-kindness*, *common humanity* and *mindfulness*.

- *Self-kindness* means 'to stop the constant self-judgement . . . it requires us to understand our foibles and failures instead of condemning them . . . to clearly see the extent to which we harm ourselves through relentless self-criticism . . . ending our internal war' (Neff, 2011, p42). 'Self-kindness' creates brain activity associated with positive emotions and compassion; it allows an individual to feel secure, to be able to 'respond to a painful experience', so that he or she can operate from a better place (Neff, 2011, p49).

- *Common humanity* is a 'recognition of the common experience . . . the interconnected nature of our lives', that we all experience feelings of personal inadequacy and 'that human experience is imperfect' (Neff, 2011, p62).

- *Mindfulness* is about not over identifying with thoughts, especially negative thoughts, or exaggerating our feelings. 'It is clear seeing and non-judgemental acceptance of what's occurring in the present moment' (Neff, 2011, p80). It is being in, and creating mind clarity in, the now.

In support, Farb et al. (2012, p1) suggest that increasing momentary awareness, for example, has been found to reduce automatic negative self-evaluation and helps to engender self-compassion and empathy. Furthermore, Neff's (2011, p255) research confirmed that individuals who exercised self-compassion also experienced more 'positive emotions' and 'optimism' and were able to deal with problems better. She also proposed that individuals with self-compassion 'can more easily find inner courage when hard times hit' (Neff, 2011, p256).

In addition, Neff (2011, p275) reminds us that we define ourselves from 'thoughts about who we are' – rich or not rich, successful or not successful, attractive or not attractive. We equate ourselves with the job we do, but no one is their job (or job title); they have simply become lost, and have stopped 'being' who they really are, their perceived self-concept being confused with their actual 'self'.

Senge (2006, p160) importantly reminds us that compassion is grounded in 'awareness' and further suggests that, as individuals appreciate 'more clearly the pressures influencing one another, they naturally develop more compassion and empathy'. Appreciating all that we are, and acknowledging our vulnerabilities without numbing or hiding them, allows us to be more compassionate (Cashman, 2008; Neff, 2011; Brown, 2012). Indeed, 'when we feel compassion, we are in a healthy state of mind' (Pransky, 2001).

Leading self and leading others

The above factors, *self-observation*, *self-regulation*, *self-management*, *self-awareness* and *self-compassion*, determine how individuals manage themselves. According to Goleman

(2011), 'self-awareness and self-management' are the fundamentals of 'self-mastery': 'awareness of our internal states and management of those states'. As Atkins (2014) suggests, however, there is no 'I' without 'you', and therefore self-leadership is as much about self as it is about others.

Importantly, Goleman et al. (2013, p39) would add 'social awareness' and 'relationship management'. 'Effective communication' in the fullest sense (non-verbal, verbal and written) is the eighth facet the author would also include.

Invariably there is the distinction between the facets relating to *leading self* and the linked facets that involve *leading others* (see Table 2.1). *Social-awareness, relationship management* and *effective communication* are integral and worthy of further defining and discussion. All three concepts are obviously interlinked.

Table 2.1 Leading self and leading others

Leading self	Leading others
Self-observation	Social awareness
Self-regulation	Relationship management
Self-management	Effective communication
Self-awareness	
Self-compassion	

Social awareness

Social awareness includes empathy and being tuned into how someone else feels in the moment, which has particular and important neurobiological implications that will be discussed further in Chapter 5, in relation to 'driving resonance', connecting and leadership (Goleman et al., 2013, p30). Briefly, however, someone who can show empathy will attune better and produce a positive rather than a negative reaction in others. As Brown (2012, p8) reminds us, 'Social work is all about leaning into the discomfort of ambiguity and uncertainty, and holding open an empathic space so people can find their own way.'

Empathy is a crucial concept to social awareness as it allows us to connect. It is thought to strengthen team and working relationships, to enable better understanding of each other, and to help resolve conflict (Pavlovich and Krahnke, 2014). A socially aware team is able to notice both individuals' and the group's collective emotions, allowing these to be expressed appropriately, to increase affiliation and mutual appreciation.

Self-leadership, therefore, is not simply about listening and fine-tuning the self. It is about really listening and appreciating as fully as possible another person's perspective. This would manifest itself in being able to better grasp a sense of the emotional impact of words used, for you cannot fully know, one hundred per cent, exactly how the words chosen will impact another individual. This is about getting as close as is reasonable to one hundred per cent. As Phillips (2006) writes, we cannot truly appreciate with absolute understanding the so-called side effects of our words.

Self-leadership is not about acquiescing (trying to please everyone), but is about creating a relationship with others that allows rapport to occur. Rapport is the capability of being able to see each other's point of view, to connect, to appreciate the feelings of others and to be appropriately responsive. An individual does not need to agree to be in rapport with someone else. Being in rapport is an important aspect of good relationship management. The provision of personal information or information not requested importantly indicates the presence of rapport. Being able to be in rapport, however, is a primal ability that will be discussed more fully in Chapter 5. Linked to rapport is relationship management.

Relationship management

Relationship management is created when the individual combines self-awareness, empathy and self-management to interpret, appreciate and handle 'other people's emotions' (Goleman et al., 2013, p51). Creating good working relationships therefore stems first from individuals developing their own emotional balance achieved through the right state or presence of mind.

For people often leave their jobs because of the relationship, or perceived lack of relationship, with their managers. Often, if the individual works on themselves first, the relationship with the manager automatically changes. This is the same for all relationships and can be as simple as letting go of the thoughts, labels and judgements we have created in our heads, for these are not physically real; they have been given attention, and exist, through conscious thinking. The more attention given to this type of thought the more preoccupying it becomes.

Leadership is about relationships that require attention and development. Kouzes and Posner (2002, p258) stress the importance of 'face to face' interactions to maintain and manage such relationships.

Successfully interacting with individuals and teams, in any leadership dynamic, involves appreciating emotional responses in others and being able to interact appropriately for the best outcome. Pransky (2001) reminds us that when individuals have an insecure state of mind they demonstrate this through counterproductive behaviours that can impact others. This is true, particularly in managing conflict and difficult conversations. As Goleman et al. (2013, p51) identified, at the centre of relationships between individuals is someone's 'emotions'. Being tuned into your own emotions and being in the right state or presence of mind, being authentically yourself, is an important starting place for any difficult conversation. For, when in the right state of mind, an individual is more cognisant of the emotions at play. Being able to interpret these is an integral part of effective communication.

Effective communication

The impact of communication is best seen as a consequence of two extremes of a continuum. When there is evidence of exquisite communication, effectiveness and clarity are the by-products; with bad communication, the opposite impact is obvious for all to see. Responding with ability (response-ability) is part of the tapestry of effective communication. To do this, many of the above facets need to come into play, particularly self-observation and self-awareness – being in the here and now, in the moment, and therefore more capable of interpreting and hearing what was said, or not said.

A significant part of communication is the non-verbal components: body language, voice tone and rhythm, interpersonal contact and gestures. As Argyle et al. (1970) propose, non-verbal communication is vital in establishing and maintaining interpersonal relationships, while the spoken words simply convey external information. Facial expressions, in particular, are described by Ekman (2003) as universal in nature, and are dictated by seven corresponding and basic emotions (sadness, joy, disgust, anger, contempt, surprise and fear). These, he suggests, provide an insight into what someone has on their mind and are automatic, part of the unconscious system (Ekman, 2003).

Frith (2007, p143) advises that we can see two-millimetre eye movements when standing up to one metre away from someone. He proposed that this sensitivity to eye movements is to better understand where someone might be looking, to provide clues as to what they are interested in, or to catch their attention when communicating (Frith, 2007).

Gladwell (2005, p14) talks about what can be seen, or not seen, within the blink of an eye, and states that individuals can make 'snap judgements', intuitively right or wrong decisions, within seconds. Effective communicators are therefore able to appreciate in all their fullness the language, the feelings and the non-verbal representations of what is being conveyed.

Team communication is vital within the professional practices of Health and Social Care, and this means being able to match the communication requirements of a vast range of public service users and coordinating across many different disciplines. This range of communication capabilities requires significant presence and ability.

Hersey et al. (2013, p219) described a study by Paul Cameron, involving students in a lecture, a significant number (88 per cent) of whom were not listening; instead, they were preoccupied with their own internal self-talk rather than the lecture. This introduces an important component of silent communication – what is not said, but what is actually happening on the inside. Someone who is preoccupied in his or her own head cannot really fully hear what another is saying and is unable to convey being fully present, a crucial and essential part of feeling listened to and communicating effectively.

The author suggests that a better state or presence of mind would act as a precursor to being more socially aware, and able to manage relationships and communicate more effectively. For state or presence of mind is the fundamental foundation of self-leadership and of all of the above facets. Chapter 3, and specifically Chapter 4, are dedicated to the discussion of how state of mind is so very central to everything explored so far. The Appendix provides a more detailed elaboration about state of mind by Dr Aaron Turner.

It is important, however, to first consider and examine the context. This is not about changing the leadership style to match the situation (which has been established as too unrealistic and complicated in Chapter 1), but to advance why self-leadership as an approach is of its time, and therefore is progressed within this text. The author will argue that the current contextual and disruptive dilemmas impacting Health and Social Care ensure that self-leadership provides the right paradigm shift, the right focus, to help individuals to adapt, to be resilient and to be the very best they can within each moment, and within each interaction.

The next section examines some of the contextual influences within Health and Social Care to further build the case for self-leadership.

The case for self-leadership

In Chapter 1 we examined the many different historical theories of leadership to emphasise that no one approach or paradigm currently satisfies today's requirements. In this section evidence is also provided that, while leadership development remains popular, both in the public and the private sectors thus far, it has not produced the leaders or leadership to satisfactorily tackle the current complex dilemmas, and therefore something different is required.

Self-leadership as an approach is about both leaders and leadership, and therefore concerns individuals being in the best state of mind to interact with others – interactions that concern teams, organisations and service boundaries.

The context

Although the context is arguably an 'outside' rather than an 'inside' dimension, the relevance is important to consider in terms of 'the why of self-leadership'. The following areas have been examined: the current landscape; reviews that point to ineffective leadership; concerns for quality (also an international feature); a preoccupation with general leadership at the expense, arguably, of developing the best professional leadership; and a perceived lack of compassion and the real concept of compassion fatigue. However, integrally there is a fundamental need for change, and The King's Fund supports integrating services as a necessary and compelling transformation agenda (Ham and Walsh, 2013).

The current landscape

An unprecedented financial squeeze on the public services, and vast and disruptive changes particularly for the Health and Social Care sectors, have daily ramifications for all concerned. This has further compounded the conflicting demands of the public, a demographically ageing population, with the impact of expanding numbers of people with one or more long-term conditions, government policy and the increased focus on scrutiny of all services.

There has been constant restructuring, problems with recruitment and retention of the right staff, continued bureaucracy, elevated levels of uncertainty about the correct involvement, with risks in social work, both in intervening and not intervening, working across boundaries with no line management, a lack of professional supervision, and high-profile tragedies leading to micro-management and knee-jerk responses, with the resultant loss of both professional autonomy and decisions based on professional underpinnings and values (Holroyd, 2012). Central control and the political nature of the public services, especially in the NHS, ensure that it suffers the ramifications of being 'a rather toxic and brutal environment' for leaders with 'an extensive interference in the operational management' (Brookes and Grint, 2010). Edwards (2014, p2) writing for The King's Fund, highlights not only the frequency of restructuring but the fact that this has 'often been poorly thought through and not always skilfully executed'.

The Chartered Institute of Personnel and Development (CIPD, 2013) reported that 63 per cent of staff surveyed from the public sector (base 465) stated that their workload had increased in the last 12 months, while 60 per cent described an increase in stress in the same time period. Furthermore, 40 per cent of staff reported working longer hours, with 46 per cent identifying an increased pressure to meet targets (CIPD, 2013).

The consequence of pressure within the public sectors has been apparent failings within the system. These have sparked a number of publicly high-profile reviews leading to questions about leadership, capacity, capability and strategic development.

Reviews that point to ineffective leadership

A barrage of reports and reviews form a key and influencing background for all individuals working within the Health and Social Care systems. Some of the most recent reports are highlighted in Table 2.2. Leadership is identified as a key denominator across all the reports, whether as lacking, in terms of quality care, transparency or poor systems, or as a recommendation for improvement. Indeed, many more reports and evidence not alluded to here paint a picture of organisations in crisis, and of services lacking fundamental self-leadership.

Table 2.2 Reviews that point to ineffective leadership

Review or report	Date published
The Victoria Climbié Report of an Inquiry, by Lord Laming.	Jan 2003
The Protection of Children in England: A Progress Report, by Lord Laming.	March 2009
The Protection of Children in England: Action Plan. The Government's response to Lord Laming, Department of Children, Schools and Families.	May 2009
Building a Safe and Confident Future: One Year on Progress Report, from the Social Work Reform Board.	December 2010
The Munro Review of Child Protection: Final Report: A Child-Centred System, by the Department for Education.	May 2011
Transforming Care: A National Response to Winterbourne View Hospital. Department of Health Review Final Report.	December 2012
Report of the Mid Staffordshire NHS Foundation Trust Public Inquiry, chaired by Robert Francis QC.	February 2013
Patients First and Foremost: The Initial Government Response to the Report of the Mid Staffordshire NHS Foundation Trust Public Inquiry.	March 2013
Review into the Quality of Care and Treatment Provided by 14 Hospital Trusts in England, by Professor Sir Bruce Keogh.	July 2013
Independent Report: *Berwick Review into Patient Safety. A Promise to Learn – a Commitment to Act: Improving the Safety of Patients in England*, by the National Advisory Group on the Safety of Patients in England.	August 2013
Hard Truths: The Journey of Putting Patients First. Response to Mid Staffordshire by the Department of Health.	November 2013

This is self-leadership based on everyone exercising a better state of mind, being able to be both self-aware and socially aware, and able to exercise the qualities of self-observation, regulation and management and, most importantly, self-compassion. This means remaining so, even under pressure, short staffing levels and busy workloads, and being able to manage relationships and communication effectively. Most importantly, it means continuing to follow best practice and, if this is not possible, being able to appropriately raise concerns and to act – this vital concept of being able to stand back and really see what is in front of you.

Certainly, if everyone is exercising self-leadership, the often unconscious dynamics at play within organisations will be evident. This will in turn prevent individuals from consciously and unconsciously colluding with habitual ways of doing things, often the unsaid 'this is how we do things around here'.

We can all remember starting a new job in a new place and seeing things done for the first time, noticing different practices, which might be more or less effective, relationships, dynamics that, with the passing of time, become less distinct, more familiar, mainstream and unconscious. Self-leadership is about having access to those 'fresh eyes' every day, and the ability to really see what is being played out in front of your eyes. Relationships based on self-leadership allow and support challenge.

Indeed, in Figure 2.2, common themes have been identified from the above-mentioned reports, together with how self-leadership can provide an antidote. Common themes in terms of concern for quality, and the emphasis on leadership development being seen as the solution, are not unique to the UK.

Common themes	Self-leadership antidote
Missed opportunities to really see what was happening.	Being fully present in each moment allows everything to be seen fully.
Lack of communication both within and across sectors.	Better able to relate to others.
A lack of leadership based on integrity.	Leadership based on self-integrity.
The wrong focus.	Able to see what is relevant in each interaction.
Too much bureaucracy.	Capable of spotting what is important.
A lack of professional judgement.	A clear state of mind allows professional expertise to inform judgements and decisions made.
Individuals turning 'a blind eye'.	Breaking habitual thinking and subsequent behaviours. Seeing what matters and being able to express this in a way that is heard.
Losing the person in the patient/client user.	Greater connection and authenticity is possible, and with it a culture based on relating better, as a primary focus.
An absence of openness and transparency.	Enhanced and more open communication, even in complex situations.
A lack of compassion, dignity and respect. (Poor-quality services.)	A quieter, clearer mind creates the abilty to resonate empathetically, to be compassionate and respectful.
Things had to go seriously wrong before problems in the system were detected.	Self-leadership is about everyone reaching the very best of their potential.
Stressed and busy staff.	A strong sense of inner resilience and well-being through a better state of mind.
No evidence of the impact of leadership investment.	

Figure 2.2 Common themes from reports

Concerns for quality – an international feature

Concern for quality care and services has not been restricted to the UK, for Barnett et al. (2004) talked about the international interest in America, Australia and New Zealand. All these countries, together with the UK, produced reports identifying the need to concentrate on 'leadership for quality' and to provide 'supportive organisational' environments in order to secure better-quality care (Barnett et al., 2004, p1). However, almost a decade later we have déjà vu, for this continues to be a repeated, and unchanged, priority. Arguably, traditional models of leadership have failed to deliver.

Self-leadership provides a focus on what Pransky (2003, p13) would suggest is working from the 'inside-out': 'a recognition that true change can only come from within – through a shift in perspective that leads to a change in consciousness'.

Instead of justifying a particular perspective or blaming, for example, the environment, a particular staff member, a boss, the bad traffic, which are implicitly outside-in influences, it points to a more helpful interpretation – that individuals can choose, implicitly, their internal sense of wisdom and how they can react about the situation. In other words, they need to be self-observant and self-aware of when their thinking is less than helpful and potentially faulty. Cashman (2012, p13) would describe it as an 'inner knowing' – an inner wisdom to guide our responses that is so often missing in daily interactions, the essence that creates quality interactions and produces quality care.

A preoccupation with general leadership

This preoccupation with leadership as the solution to cure all ills continues to flourish, evidenced by the fact that, if you typed 'leadership books' into Google in 2012, there were 84 million hits (Snook et al., 2012, pxi) and, more recently, 453 million (Google, 2013). It is big business with billions paid in the commercial arena, and millions consumed in the public sector. Significantly, £1,515 per manager is spent on leadership development in the public sector per annum (McBain et al., 2012), ironically with little evaluation of value for money, other than the usual 'happy sheet' (Brown et al., 2008; McAllan and MacRae, 2010; Hafford-Letchfield and Bourn, 2011). Despite this faith in leadership, Boyatzis (2012) would suggest that 70–80 per cent of managers and leaders could be removed from their roles and the systems would run more smoothly. In the study he is referring to, which examined leadership across 94 countries, it was thought that 50 per cent of people in leadership and management add no value, while only 20–30 per cent add value in only one person's view.

Leadership development, however, has been a central tenet of the government's reform policies for the NHS since its inception (Brookes and Grint, 2010). Models borrowed from industry, the private sector, across the water and elsewhere appear to have not delivered the outcomes hoped for.

In the social services sector, leadership has been based predominantly on a generalist managerial business school model. This potentially loses the importance of the professional values underpinning all development and with it a loss of what really matters – a focus and distraction away from the importance of human exchanges and the impact of intervention, to a rigid focus on targets and stifling over-bureaucratic processes.

In healthcare, leadership development has concentrated primarily at the top with a trickle-down effect, when actually the people who probably need it the most, especially self-leadership, individually have had less provision, both in resources and quality. The best leadership for the top makes no sense. However, this is not about providing the most expensive courses, but about teaching individuals to understand how their state of mind impacts everything they do, every interaction and every encounter. A bottom-up intervention and emphasis therefore is of paramount importance, particularly when considering that services will only be as good as each interaction at the very front end.

This, however, is not exclusively a public sector conundrum, for the private sector is questioning the 'failings of the business school educational model' in producing the right type of leadership (Chadwick, 2013, p5). Leadership development mirroring an outside-in intervention rather than an inside-out self-leadership fundamental process may have resulted in this described lack. Professional leadership advanced from the inside-out from self-integrity, authenticity, self-regulation and self-compassion is what has arguably been lacking within Health and Social Care.

Notwithstanding, there has been some genuine concern about standards of care, with reports of a lack of respect, dignity and compassion and a real sense that things have gone so terribly wrong. Having the right calibre and numbers of staff certainly has been a key feature in nursing (Aiken et al., 2014). One area that has been discussed specifically has been compassion.

Perceived lack of compassion or compassion fatigue

Showing compassion to others is a key aspect of Health and Social Care, prompting the introduction of the documents *Compassion in Practice* (Department of Health, 2012), and *Delivering High Quality, Effective, Compassionate Care* (Department of Health, 2013). In social adult care it forms the meaningful values of the National Skills Academy for Social Care's (2013) document, *Leadership Starts with Me*.

Compassion in healthcare is defined simply as 'a deep awareness of the suffering of another coupled with the wish to relieve it' (Chochinov, 2007, p186) and, in social care, 'being caring and valuing of all people' (National Skills Academy for Social Care, 2013, p14). 'Compassion is our innate interpersonal lubricant' (Pransky, 2001).

Bornemann and Singer (2013) importantly suggest that, while compassion is rooted in the motivational system of care in society, there has been a clash between care and achievement. Implicitly focusing on achievement has created a gap in compassion as the two work in opposition in the brain. Halifax (2013, p209) also reminds us that a focus on 'curing without caring causes not only patients to suffer, but clinicians and family members as well'.

Listening to accounts of abuse and horrific depravity, and dealing with traumatised individuals when illness erodes the person, disintegrates who individuals are and have been. Repeated exposure in human services is the 'unconscious at work'; it catches up and potentially makes its mark; Moylan (1994, p51) describes this as the 'contagion' effect. Feelings of helplessness and hopelessness can result, and be replaced by a protective numbness of disconnection. This can be coupled with extraordinary working conditions, of gaping holes in staffing, horrific environments and no time for breaks, not even toilet breaks. Other pressures are ensuring the paperwork is completed without making the practitioner vulnerable to criticism or disciplinary action. Making certain targets are met buttresses against the real nature of human suffering, providing a contrast, a juxtaposition and artificialness that is hard to rationalise.

Both health staff and social workers are exposed to individuals who have suffered the above traumatic events, resulting in the potential for 'compassion fatigue'. Compassion fatigue, as distinct from burnout (although both can co-exist) is described as the 'natural consequent behaviours and emotions resulting from knowing about a traumatizing event experienced by a significant other, the stress resulting from helping, or wanting to help, a traumatized or suffering person' (Figley, 1995, p7). This can be the result of one event, or accumulative in nature. Burnout is more of a progressive process, often associated with increased workload, institutional stress and person–job mismatch (Sabo, 2011).

This is part of the context and, just as it is hard to relate to whatever someone else is feeling, the impossible wish to 'walk a mile in my shoes', it is difficult to really understand or appreciate 'compassion fatigue' in its fullness, or the above impact on individual workers in Health and Social Care. This is why self-leadership is so very important – the facet of self-compassion to counterbalance, to create the right state of mind to be able to be compassionate in these extremes without feeling a victim, or having to 'switch off' to get by. Neff (2011, p192) confirms that individuals who are able to be self-compassionate are less likely to experience 'compassion fatigue'.

This is about changing the way we think, being more resilient and self-compassionate, and being there fully in every exchange no matter what is happening in the environment. This is what self-leadership is about.

The next important context issue is linked to connection, and invariably discusses what happens when there is a lack of the right connection and engagement.

Lack of engagement

Here are some interesting and illuminating facts: less than 20 per cent of staff in most organisations are engaged, while 65 per cent 'just do the job', with 15 per cent negatively impacting (Corporate Leadership Council, cited by Roebuck, 2011, p6). A recent American Gallup (2013) poll would suggest that 30 per cent are engaged, with 20 per cent actively disengaged; a staggering 70 per cent are therefore not actively participating. Success starts with the leaders (Gallup, 2013).

In addition, 65 per cent of transformation programmes produce no improvements and some (20 per cent) actually result in worse outcomes (Wagner, 2013). The influence of the leaders is identified as the key feature; the author would go further and propose that self-leadership has an integral role to play in changing this status quo.

Roebuck (2011, p5) suggests that 'good organisational culture is vital in getting high performance from staff at all levels', implicitly to change the above figures of disengagement. If the right culture is created, effective communication increases by almost 30 per cent, together with reputation of organisational integrity, culture of innovation and flexibility, customer focus, equity and recognition, culture of risk-taking without blame, community involvement and the overall success of the organisation (Roebuck, 2011, p6). He further suggests that, for staff at operational level, if they become engaged they can reap performance improvements of 57 per cent (Roebuck, 2011, p7). According to Roebuck (2011, p7) these data are based on identifying 'the top 300 drivers of employee engagement from 50,000 employees in 50 organisations, 27 countries, and 10 industries'. He additionally states (Roebuck, 2011, p8) that, of the leaders in organisations:

- 5 per cent are of a good quality;
- 25 per cent are competent;

- 60 per cent are less than competent;

- 10 per cent are counterproductive.

Furthermore, he stipulates that the challenge for the NHS is 'exactly the same as [for] commercial organisations . . . to move average quality leaders from the less than competent to good, or at least, competent' (Roebuck, 2011, p8).

Self-leadership is primarily and instinctively about engagement and implicitly being in the right state of mind to engage at the very best level possible. Self-leadership is therefore crucial if the changes required, outlined next, are to be achieved.

Fundamental change is required

There are 300 million yearly contacts between the public and NHS practitioners – all opportunities to 'make positive changes to their lifestyle' (Naylor et al., 2013, p2). The Health and Social Care systems, however, are described as failing to meet the current demands, with the increasing complexity, greater co-morbidities and person-centred care (CQC, 2012), prompting the suggestion that the 'delivery system is broken' and requires 'fundamental change' (Ham et al., 2013, pvii).

Extraordinary monetary pressures affecting the whole of the public sector, particularly Health and Social Care, mean that incremental adjustments, according to Ham et al. (2013), will no longer be sufficient; instead, unprecedented change is the suggested way forward. Their report (Ham et al., 2013, pvii) states that there needs to be a greater emphasis on:

- preventing illness, helping people to stay in good health;

- supporting people to live in their homes, offering wider options of housing in the community;

- providing better primary care;

- making more effective use of community health services and related social care and ensuring these services are available 24 hours a day;

- using acute care and care homes only when people cannot be treated anywhere else;

- integrating care around the needs of people and populations.

Interestingly, there is nothing so very new or dramatic here, for integrating care and supporting people to live in their homes has been a prescribed focus for some time, with 'care closer to home' introduced in 2006, in *Our Health, Our Care, Our Say: A New Direction for Community Services* and, more recently in 2009, *Transforming Community Services, Ambition, Action, Achievement: Transforming Services for Acute Care Closer to Home*. However, the Royal College of Physicians (RCP, 2012) would remind us that there is no categorical proof that savings in providing care closer to home can be made.

Furthermore, since the 1980s there has been a trend towards integration with 'coordinated' care, 'interagency working' in the 1990s and 'inter-professional working and whole systems' in the 2000s (Shaw et al., 2011, p4). However, it is clear that there is no room for duplication and therefore real integration, rather than tinkering at the edges, seems the contextual 'must-do' for Health and Social Care and requires all the facets of self-leadership (leading self and leading others) to successfully achieve the required outcomes.

Integrated models of care

The King's Fund supports the case for integrated care, suggesting that 'the current fragmented services fail to meet the needs of the population and that greater integration can improve the patient experience and the outcomes and efficiency of care' (Ham and Walsh, 2013, p1). They propose that the main benefits are derived not as a result of organisational integration but 'from clinical and service integration' (Ham and Walsh, 2013, p5).

Brookes and Grint (2010, p17), however, advise that 'the NHS . . . could easily be seen as actively discouraging cross-boundary leadership, or at least making its achievements rather difficult'. Storey and Holti (2013, p136) concur, however, and they also provide some examples of achievements across networks of 'high impact cross-boundary clinical leadership'.

'Whole-system working' is advocated by Ham and Walsh (2013, pp3–4), who recommend that this means the following.

- Organisations may have to share some of their 'sovereignty' through establishing shared reasons for reducing the divisions between services and developing integrated approaches instead.
- Developing a shared narrative to explain why integrated care matters.
- Developing a persuasive vision to describe what integrated care will achieve.
- Establishing shared and collective leadership (to be discussed further in Chapter 3).
- Creating time and space to develop understanding and new ways of working.

Self-leadership and the foundations of self-leadership are key and crucial to achieving many of the identified suggestions.

Summary

A catalogue of reviews evidencing system and people failings, with suggestions of compassion fatigue and a lack of engagement, provides some of the context. Despite this, leadership development has remained the perceived solution with significant investment and expenditure, arguably without the reciprocal successful outcomes. Leadership development to date fits an 'outside-in' solution, often deemed only for the few with the title – a top-down precedence. The author argues that what is missing is the 'inside-out' approach of which everyone is capable.

In the face of mounting challenges, diminishing resources and the subsequent risk of being distracted away from what should count (something that is unlikely to get any easier), a focus on implementing self-leadership is, therefore, vital in the Health and Social Care fields. It is an ability to appreciate and leverage capability to its fullest potential, in order to sustain effective interventions when it counts, in the moment. Implicitly, therefore, this should ensure that a person's best potential ability can be drawn out in the worst of circumstances, making them able to perform regardless of the challenges they face.

This relates to an inside-out process of self-leadership rather than the outside-in leadership development that has dominated for decades. The facets of self-leadership have been identified as two integral influences on both leading self and leading others. The individual facets of self-observation, self-regulation, self-management, self-awareness and self-compassion have been explored, together with the important influence of social awareness, relationship management and effective communication. These form eight essential facets of self-leadership.

The context of self-leadership provides an important discussion to further build the case for why self-leadership is an essential approach. The next chapter explores the fundamental foundations of self-leadership, implicitly outlining what is important for self-leadership to thrive.

Chapter 3
The foundations of self-leadership

Introduction

In Chapter 2 the eight important facets of self-leadership were introduced and some critical context dilemmas within Health and Social Care were presented. This chapter will examine the foundations, the supporting underpinnings, for self-leadership development.

It will be established that the fundamental footings, or building blocks, on which self-leadership development can thrive include four key aspects: *state of mind* as a central concept; the importance of *everyone counts (self-leadership for all)*; the need for *devolved coordinated structures*; and the importance of *evaluating impact* as a mechanism for understanding and continuously improving (see Figure 3.1).

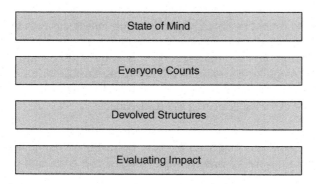

Figure 3.1 The foundations of self-leadership

The case will be presented that, in order to realise the full potential of self-leadership, the supporting foundations need to be in place, particularly for sustained and consistent impact. And just as the foundations for a house need to be built on solid structures and not sand to sustain the weathering of time and changing environmental conditions, so the foundations of self-leadership are about creating resilience and consistent sustainability whatever happens.

In terms of the foundations for self-leadership, therefore, these four underlying aspects will be discussed further within this chapter. The case for each foundation will be presented, but first we need to discuss what we mean by foundations.

The foundations of self-leadership

Foundation as 'an underlying basis or principle' (Oxford Dictionaries, 2013) will be the emphasis throughout. These would represent the roots of a tree, the secure footings of a building, or the basis upon which self-leadership can thrive, integral aspects therefore to the concept and advancement of self-leadership. For leadership development and the focus on leadership theories have often been about singular dimensional aspects, for example traits, behaviours, styles and situations or contingencies. Less attention has been focused on 'what' allows leadership and specifically self-leadership to thrive. Self-leadership, it is suggested, is a fluid phenomenon potentially, not a static concept. Just as leaders do not always exercise leadership in all that they do, self-leadership can 'flux'.

Ideally individuals would want to overcome this flux, this variability, and be the best of self in each moment. The foundations therefore support maximising potential and reducing this variability.

Self-leadership as an approach therefore requires foundational principles. The most significant and integral feature, and the most important foundation of all, is state of mind, for in order for self-leadership to be more of a constant feature and less amenable to dissipation and 'flux', state of mind is a foundational imperative, a crucial concept, that within this book is one of the main features explored.

A better state of mind, for example, will lead to an improved resilience and sense of well-being, together with greater presence, dignity, respect and capacity for compassion, all of which will create a better working culture.

The second most important foundation is about self-leadership being exercised by everyone to maximise its impact and to develop individual potential that is based on inclusion. The practice of leadership cannot be about relying on single individuals with the powerbase, for it will be argued that this excludes everyone from counting, a particular imperative with leaner and highly accountable service organisations. It is not about having the day off because someone else is in charge, or perceived as ultimately responsible for decision(s), and it is not about burying heads in the sand hoping and willing that things will miraculously change somehow. It is about everyone exercising self-leadership.

Furthermore, the best environment to allow self-leadership to thrive is in devolved structures that support self-leadership from the very front, the exchange area of interaction – the very place where the service and its impact begins and ends, and ultimately what it is all about.

A more decentralised, devolved approach, which is coordinated, in order to avoid the 'no one in charge' criticism, will, therefore, be the emphasis. For hierarchical organisations this would represent a distributed model, and for networks of integrated provision, a shared or collective coordinated approach.

Evaluating impact of any leadership development is integral to the concept of a learning culture, continuously improving the potential of all individuals to impact daily the quality of their interventions with others. Too much leadership development has been about input rather than assessing the impact and learning from and further adapting and improving. The importance of impact evaluation will therefore be a foundational aspect of self-leadership.

The first foundation and perhaps the most important and radical in terms of leadership development is state of mind.

State of mind

State of mind is at the centre of self-leadership – the two are inextricably linked. In the next chapter the importance of state of mind will be further discussed and one approach outlined, with additional information provided in the Appendix.

In Chapter 1 it was established that earlier leadership theories focused almost exclusively on external differences, for example traits, behaviours, competencies, situations and circumstances, with only a more recent, but limited focus on cognitive theories in terms of intelligence and experience. State of mind is the missing essence that so fundamentally impacts the outward discernible results of leadership. Banks (1998, p3) would describe it as the 'missing link', Kline (2009, p21) as 'a way of being in the world' and Siegel (2010, p109) as the 'inner sanctuary of clarity'.

It is, therefore, proposed that a leader's state of mind has a direct correlation with her or his potential to lead well. For example, an agitated, angry team leader who frequently becomes overwhelmed with hair-trigger, explosive outbursts of snappiness has a different quality of thinking and subsequent interaction with others. Unconsciously such leaders may feel aggrieved by the excessive weekly extra hours worked to keep on top, with an underlying and paralysing fear of failure that drives their daily actions and reactions. An awareness of this can provide a temporary, fleeting redress, an attempt to consciously rebalance, to gain a better perspective. However, the unconscious, background activity of the amygdala can easily, especially if there are repetitive stressors and habitual overthinking patterns, play havoc with the state of mind and the resultant ability to gain perspective.

This is not about having skills and competencies; it is about what happens when under pressure and the ability through a clear state of mind to manage and direct ourselves effectively. Pransky (2003, p71) refers to it as an 'internal resilience' that we all inherently have. Being able to draw on this natural internal resilience, the body's inbuilt innate system of re-balance, is what we are talking about.

For example, an experienced health worker with proven excellent communication skills can find themselves grappling with situations they normally find straightforward. The result: miscommunication, distress and upset. Most incidents of poor practice are from professionals who are not only trained appropriately, but are capable of knowing when their state of mind is adversely impacted. Stress and distress are states of mind; unidentified emotional shifts not only affect the individual, but can also affect so significantly the health and well-being of others around them (Goleman et al., 2013). The neurobiology of this will be discussed further in Chapter 5.

It is about becoming aware in the moment; self-leadership, and specifically state of mind, is appreciating when this is happening and not just observing self, but how to transcend, regulate and change. The premise is that changes in the way an individual feels are the discernible elements, the actions we see, and are a direct by-product of a shift in the state of mind. For example, when an individual's feelings change everything else about his or her mind does too; this shift is described as a 'state of mind'. The individual feels, thinks, sees and reacts differently depending on his or her state of mind. The way people feel will always indicate the quality of mind and therefore the abilities they possess in any moment (Pransky, 2003).

Turner (2014; see the Appendix) emphasises the important implications of this variability of an individual's state of mind, in that 'stress and poor performance go together'. The experience of returning to work following a holiday, the fresh perspectives and clarity of thought, initially a stark contrast often replaced with distracting busyness as time passes, provides an example of an initial positive state of mind that we can relate to. We have all had the experience of forgetting someone's name or something perceived as important when put on the spot, only later when in a different state of mind to remember exactly and with ease.

State of mind as a concept allows us to refer to the way every aspect of the mind shifts: the emotional experience, resilience, well-being, volatility, clarity, memory recall, creativity, clearness of perception, the ability to focus and to be compassionate, respectful and present, and everything else about the individual and her or his interaction(s). In the moment a person's state of mind is obvious to everyone around, for the non-verbal clues spill out into conversations and exchanges with others. It therefore impacts profoundly how the individual relates and interacts, whether they are fully present in each exchange and whether there is dignity, respect and compassion. We would suggest being in the right state of mind allows all these states to be achieved with ease.

Figures 3.2 and 3.3 capture both the evidence of a poor state of mind and the reality of an improved state of mind. These are all patterns of a state of mind. It is not an exhaustive list but a sample of what it can look and feel like. The state of mind, therefore, arguably can govern what an individual is capable of doing in any given moment and is a significant concept in terms of leadership. The ability to 'navigate the state of mind' in order to maximise an individual's potential is what self-leadership is about (Turner, 2014; see the Appendix). The 90:10 rule described by Evans (2011) would be an example: implicitly 10 per cent is what happens, for example someone is given a difficult diagnosis; it is the 90 per cent concerning how a person responds to this that counts, that is, what they choose to do with the information – their state of mind.

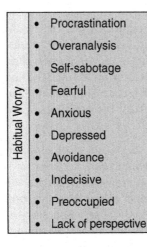
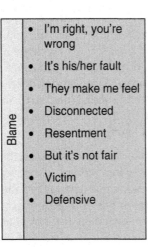
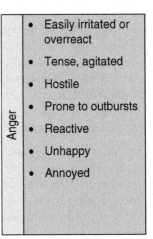

Figure 3.2 Evidence of a poor state of mind

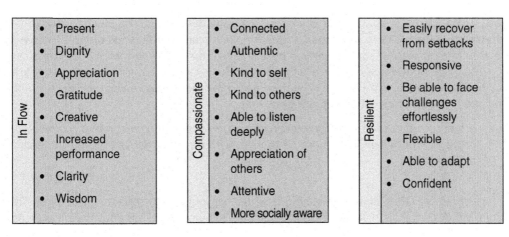

Figure 3.3 Evidence of an improved state of mind

When discussing state of mind there are a number of concepts that deserve additional attention and these include resilience, well-being, being present, dignity, respect, compassion and the important impact on the working culture.

Resilience

Resilience, for example, is explicitly about state of mind, and is referred to earlier as the ability to recover easily from setbacks. Pransky (2003, p17) asserts 'that stress is caused by the way we see the outside world from within' and 'to realise the amount of stress we have is completely determined by our own stressful thinking; that our stress level shifts when our thinking shifts'.

This realisation allows individuals to recover more quickly, and to stop dwelling on and regurgitating worry or anxiety-provoking thoughts. This is not about more thinking, or about how to control thought with thought, but to recognise it for what it is, just thought. An important part of resilience is exercising self-compassion in our thinking.

Letting go of unhelpful thoughts will allow the innate inner resilience to naturally emerge. As Bohm (1996) suggested, 'we often perceive a difficulty to originate outside ourselves when in fact it is primarily a construction of thought'. He also comments that, 'we haven't paid much attention to thought as a process', but have instead concentrated, and have been distracted by, the 'content of thought' (Bohm, 1996). As human beings we feel our thinking, for thoughts manifest in chemical by-products and markers creating emotional responses and reactions – as the mind and body are so intricately connected.

Well-being

Related to resilience is well-being. Neill (2013, p67) reminds us that 'connection, presence and well-being are a part of our factory settings'. The default mode we all have access to, he calls 'innate mental health' (Neill, 2013, p67). Pransky (2011a, p155) suggests that 'People will increase their well-being to the extent they understand that their problems, difficulties and stress never come from the outside world but only from how they use their thinking'.

McGonigal (2013) supports this notion. Implicitly she describes the results of a study that tracked 30,000 adults in the United States for eight years, the findings of which showed that 'stress makes you sick' only if you believe it will, for 'how you think about stress can change your body's response to stress'. If individuals can view their responses to stress as helpful, they will tap into their 'built in mechanism for stress resilience', which is also related to human connection. She suggests that:

> When you choose to view your stress response as helpful, you create the biology of courage. And when you choose to connect with others under stress, you can create resilience.

(McGonigal, 2013)

She also advises that 'chasing meaning is better for your health than trying to avoid discomfort' (McGonigal, 2013). Part of meaning and being connected is about being present.

Being present
Remaining curious creates the space for the connection of being in the moment and able to appreciate, rather than being preoccupied in thought, amnesic and disconnected; it means feeling our way instead of thinking and overanalysing. This is something akin to Scharmer's (2009, p8) 'presence' and 'sensing', or 'presencing', which is 'to tune in and act from one's highest future potential – the future that depends on us to bring it into being'. He suggested that successful leadership is contingent upon the quality of the attention and intention the leader brings to bear on each situation (Scharmer, 2009).

Williams and Penman (2011, p43) remind us that 'we *re-live* past events and *re-feel* their pain, and we *pre-live* future disasters and so *pre-feel* their impact'. Instead, being present is about the here and now and seeing what unfolds in each moment (Kabat-Zinn, 2012).

The importance of being present in Health and Social Care interactions is evident in the impact it has on others and the quality of the exchange. And as Solomon (2010, pxxx) states: 'your impact is one of the only things that you are totally and completely in control of', therefore being present and responsible and accountable for your impact in each moment is what we are talking about. This links with the concept of dignity.

Dignity
The Royal College of Nursing (RCN, 2008) defines dignity as 'concerned with how people feel, think and behave in relation to the worth or value of themselves and others'. The Social Care Institute for Excellence (n.d.) suggests 'dignity is about seeing the individual person and respecting their own space and their way of life'. The importance of dignity was first discussed within the White paper, *Modernising Social Services* (Department of Health, 1998), and Skills for Care (n.d.) stated that 'dignity must be at the centre of everything we do'. The author would contend, however, that starting with the right state of mind is so very fundamental to dignity and that the right state of mind will naturally result in dignity occurring in every exchange.

'I just wish he would give me his whole mind just once', the words of Anatole Broyard, former editor of *The New York Times Book Review*, were captured by Chochinov (2007, p184) in his article on 'Dignity and the essence of medicine'. Broyard is writing about being a patient and the uniqueness of illness to each individual. When dignity is absent in Health and Social Care, the individual practitioner is absent, and his or her right state of mind is absent too.

Being in the right state of mind allows connection on a deeper level, with minds connecting with minds, and is interlinked with respect and compassion. Dignity is more than the right words and appearing to listen; it is a felt experience we all know. Brown (2012, p2) would describe it as willing to be fully vulnerable, 'daring greatly', as Health and Social Care workers, 'to show up and let ourselves be seen'. It is being able to appreciate that many manifestations of behaviours are about state of mind, and being willing to see people and the person in front of you with empathy, as someone who is worthy of connection, is to treat someone with dignity.

Respect

Respect, particularly in relation to leadership, is a concept often associated with needing to be earned. The type of respect we are referring to, however, is universal, unconditional – there no matter what. It is the type of respect that is accompanied by deep listening – being fully present, listening to pick up what is felt, using intuition to tune in, being curious, and listening beyond the words. Pransky (2011a, p112) would call it 'extreme listening'. This is not over-listening, but being more appreciative, being in the moment, not holding on to any judgements, and being fully engaged.

Respect within Health and Social Care has been discussed recently and prolifically written about in terms of its lack in caring interventions. The author would argue that, when you have to remind practitioners to be respectful, this is a clear indication that it is a state of mind issue and that practitioners need to start with improving their state of mind. For as soon as this occurs, respect will automatically result in all exchanges. No prescriptions of how to show respect, or respect frameworks, would be required. An associated concept is compassion.

Compassion

Barack Obama in 2010, cited by Pavlovich and Krahnke (2014), suggests that the world has an 'empathy deficit'. The NHS and the world of Social Care would describe it as compassion fatigue. The right state of mind is key to being able to be compassionate, for if someone is unable to be fully present with the right state of mind they will be unable to express compassion. This is often evidenced by preoccupation, disconnection, withdrawal and detachment.

Compassion, as highlighted earlier, is as much about being able to exercise self-compassion. This is the ability to see that state of mind and the resultant way we feel is transient, a part of reality we create that is part of the mind, thought and consciousness. Being aware in the moment of this ability to be in a better state of mind creates options to see, be and react differently; to get out of our own way and to be fully there for someone else.

Remarkably, recent science shows that 'human connection' and 'caring' actually have an inbuilt mechanism for stress resilience and that connection rather than disconnection is what is required (McGonigal, 2013).

Impact on working culture

A team of individuals exercising an awareness of the role of their state of mind has the ability to create something more than the sum of each individual – a connection and an environment of individuals who are able to function to their better, fuller potential. Surowiecki (2005, p11) would describe it as the ability to be 'collectively smart'.

We all know the impact of someone in a negative frame of mind, and the influence her or his mood can have on the collective. A better state of mind instead can have a ripple effect, a positive contagion.

This is about changing habitual work behaviours with a better state of mind; it is about changing habitual thinking patterns that create the behaviour and the daily work culture that becomes the accepted norm. And it is explicitly about including everyone, rather than a select few with the title of leader, who are often perversely relied upon and expected to change culture.

This section has provided an introduction to the concept of state of mind; the next two chapters will explore this in more detail. Self-leadership as a concept is not governed by job titles and therefore everyone can benefit from a better state of mind and being more effective, whatever their role. Self-leadership for all is therefore a fundamental foundation and is about ensuring everyone counts.

Self-leadership for all (ensuring everyone counts)

With the unprecedented financial squeeze on the public sector, with leaner structures and more emphasis on integrating services, self-leadership as an approach becomes an obvious need to ensure everyone counts. Self-leadership for all is the second and fundamentally integral foundation. Supported by Brookes and Grint (2010), the importance of leadership at every level is stressed. It is not about one individual leader needing to engage, persuade or influence; this is about leadership coming from within each individual.

The fact that we all lead ourselves, and will inevitably lead others at some point, suggests that leadership is not limited, or exclusive, to individuals with the 'proper background, income level, or education' (Johnson, 2005, p6). This is not leadership by title. Indeed, there is a lack of research evidence supporting the single leader, the charismatic leader having the significant impact frequently proclaimed (Thorpe et al., 2007). Leadership, Grint (2010, p65) instead proposes is more 'collective', suggesting that no one single individual has the 'knowledge or power to lead effectively'. As Crosby and Bryson (2005, p29) state, 'potential for effective leadership lies alike with those who do, and do not have formal positions of power and authority'. Smart (2013, p215) suggests that we all have the 'innate capacity for leadership'.

Indeed, pushing the 'one person in charge' and the 'leader by job title' model arguably excludes potential and, worse still, precludes a level of responsibility each and every individual could bring to every exchange – to be the very best they can be, and taking accountability for all interactions and their impact. It is therefore about the practice of leadership, based on self-leadership for all.

It is important to remember that 'it is from the Self that all behaviours come; and it is only in the Self that effective change happens' (Brown and Brown, 2012, p35). Self-leadership is therefore a model that necessarily involves starting with the self and including everyone. This reiterates Kouzes and Posner's (2002) concept and the crux of leadership being about individual relationships.

Self-leadership therefore challenges the concept of developing the 'talented ones', of spotting the 'talent' and treating them differently; if we did this in schools there would be an outcry. It should be about providing opportunities for all, matched to ability and capacity, but most importantly with an explicit emphasis on a responsibility to lead self and to start with a better state of mind; and everyone is capable of this.

Truly, this is an 'inside-out' model of leadership development and accountability that starts with a fundamental focus on our state of mind. This contrasts with a historical legacy of an 'outside-in' approach to leadership development, which arguably has been based upon assumptions that a certain set of traits, competencies and styles of leadership, once role modelled or mastered, would always provide the right and appropriate leadership.

Self-leadership, instead, is about being able, in the moment, to experience 'innate health' or 'internal resilience' (Pransky, 2003, p71). Judith Sedgeman of the West Virginia University Medical School is cited by Pransky (2003, p89) as defining this 'as an inborn capacity of people to see things for themselves and redirect their energy of life' – a moment by moment capability available to everyone.

The author would therefore assert that bestowing leadership on to a few individuals excludes the benefit of involving the many. Indeed, arguably it gives the many permission to step back, rather than step up to fulfil their full potential. Leaning back into the concept that someone else is in charge, someone else is responsible, makes 'me' in some way less responsible and not only creates a chasm of missed opportunity for further development, but also reduces individuals' competence to respond with a fuller ability.

In large organisations you cannot fixate on one leader or the heroic model of leadership, as they achieve via many leaders. As Spillane (2006, p5) would suggest, organisations succeed through significant interactions and the 'practice of leadership'. In addition, with complex problems, it is less likely that one individual leader will have the ability to solve these challenges. Waiting for fewer leaders to make decisions is not tenable in fast-paced environments. A new approach is, therefore, needed – inextricably, self-leadership.

As Bradford and Cohen (1998, pvii) state, 'Central to the model is the belief that managing is the responsibility of everybody in the unit, not just the designated leader.' It is 'a multi actor process that is manifested in and enacted through relationships with colleagues and partners' (Brookes and Grint, 2010, p16). Individuals are expected to lead from the front and 'do the right thing' (Zheltoukhova, 2014, p3). Self-leadership is about increasing leadership capacity and capability. It is not about senior management descending when there is a risk that targets or clinical guidelines are going to be missed, and forcing short-term knee-jerk responses, forged out of panic and pressure, which adversely impact quality. This is about creating the capacity in each individual to be functioning in a better state of mind, more capable of producing proper sustained and owned responses.

Zheltoukhova (2014) suggests that the continuous nature of change requires leadership from the very front to enact and own the organisation's agenda. This is particularly true when working across organisational boundaries, where there is no line management leverage and appropriate professional judgement is required.

It would not take too much imagination to realise what an incredibly different environment this could create within Health and Social Care, starting with each individual being in a better state of mind, rather than one or two leaders trying to be role models. It makes no sense to rely on one or two individuals trying to succeed in transforming the many different and unique personalities.

In addition, this would not end with self-leadership development just for staff, but conceivably for the public to grasp and realise this innate potential for resilience – true leadership for all in the widest possible sense. Understanding what determines the state of mind and therefore the ability to change the outcomes of this, even in the most difficult of situations, is a universal possibility for all. This potential for effective leadership and the ability to influence others is discussed further by Turner in the Appendix.

Interestingly, Northouse (2013) would suggest that leadership that focuses on teaching people to lead themselves is not considered a part of leadership within the definition that he uses within his discourse. However, as Johnson (2005, p6) states, 'the fact that the vast majority of us will function as leaders if we haven't already done so means that leadership is not limited to those with the proper background, income level or education'. Indeed, leaner organisations as a result of restructuring in the public sector ensure that everyone needs to count.

Professional leadership is an important associated concept to discuss in relation to leadership for all, particularly within Health and Social Care. For these public sectors, however, there has debatably been a crucial underachievement in extrapolating the best of professional leadership.

A lack of professional leadership

This lack is compounded by the historical notion that professional leadership has an inappropriate powerbase, which is something that should be reduced or dismantled, particularly for medical professionals (Brookes and Grint, 2010), rather than something to be celebrated. However, this demise and a focus on general leadership models fails to work to the very best of professional experiential and operational know-how. Including, rather than excluding, leadership based on the fundamentals of professional judgement and decision making is therefore crucial for the very important and integral roles of:

- safeguarding;
- professional not paternalistic values;
- being the right advocate when needed and promoting independence;
- living and breathing the code/constitution of the professions and therefore not accepting any behaviours that cause harm to others.

Professional leadership is poorly defined within the different sectors of Health and Social Care, yet professional leadership is enacted on a daily basis, and is not singularly exclusive to the named leaders by title. Non-professional managers do not really understand it, and professional managers find it difficult to describe to 'non-practitioners'. Yet it is not elusive or elite, as some might think, but integral to excellent practice, like Blackpool rock, with the letters running right through the centre, still there no matter which way the rock is split or broken. When barriers are overcome, professional leadership truly makes a difference (Storey and Holti, 2013). Implicitly it saves lives.

Professional leadership: towards a definition

In the NHS professional leadership might be alluded to as 'clinical leadership', which would include all groups of clinicians, medics, nurses and allied health professionals. For Social Care it would include all qualified social workers.

A number of recent policy documents have supported the important notion of professional leadership as key to successful quality provision (Darzi, 2008; Department of Health, 2009; Munro, 2011), for importantly professional leadership is integrally linked to practice based upon evidence, expertise and experiential know-how.

There has been a real move away from professional silos and boundaries, to working across new networks based on whole-system approaches. Arguably, however, to get the very best from the so-called professional is to celebrate what is, in essence, the unique experiential expertise that must always feature at the table of improved quality provision. Storey and Holti (2013, p26) talk about clinical engagement and the importance of ensuring that clinicians are involved in decision making. The same emphasis is evident within the Social Care arena, with professional judgement a key component (Munro, 2011).

Anyone who has truly worked at the operational end of services realises that the individuals at the cutting edge are the very people who impact daily, and who know actually what is needed if they were supported in the right way. As Hackman and Johnson (2009, p268) suggest, 'lower level leaders can deal more effectively with local problems'.

However, in terms of professional leadership, Matthewson (2007, p38) makes the distinction between immediate line management and an 'opportunity for the exercise of expert power and informal strategic influence'. Arguably, both operational and strategic know-how and engagement are required for professional leadership to be impactful, rather than focusing on particular powerbases, which have proved an unnecessary distraction away from what matters.

Not including the professionals in the business of leading creates an abdication of potential responsibility, permission to disconnect in the name of the profession, and a separation of the front service delivery from the organisational priorities. Some would argue that this disconnection is a necessary evil; however, the gap it creates allows services to fall between the craters produced, with staff just doing their jobs, as the best of professional autonomy is lost.

Brookes and Grint (2010) talk about the notion of public leadership and define it as:

> *A form of collective leadership in which public bodies and agencies collaborate in achieving a shared vision based on shared aims and values and distribute this through each organisation in a collegiate way which seeks to promote, influence and deliver improved public value as evidenced through sustained social, environmental and economic well-being within a complex and changing context.*

They focus on the collective need and nature of leadership within the public sector and draw distinct attention to moving away from what can be counted to 'counting what counts' (Brookes and Grint, 2010). This is an explicit feature of professional leadership and, as the psychoanalyst Wilfred Bion (cited by Stokes, 1994, p19) would suggest, it concentrates on the 'primary task' (the service business), the why we are here, implicitly for the provision of quality human services, rather than being distracted by unconscious group dynamics, which play out when individuals are side-tracked away from the 'primary task', for example a perverse concentration on specific targets. This can manifest itself in three different ways (Stokes, 1994, p21):

- '*dependency* which inhibits growth and development', as managers try to protect staff with paternalistic behaviours;

- '*fight–flight*', where 'there is an enemy which should be either attacked or fled from', with a focus on 'worrying about rumours', the shadow side of the organisation, when a heightened sense of threat preoccupies and distracts from the main task and groups within organisations 'fight' and compete instead of concentrating all their efforts on what matters;

- and, finally, the *'pairing assumption'*, believing that, no matter what, there will be someone, or some connection with perhaps an external person, a saviour in the future, and a sense of hope in terms of being rescued from it all. Living for the future creates a here and now burying of heads in the sand.

All the above can create their own dysfunctional self-fulfilling cultures without the fundamentals of professional leadership. For true professional leadership, exercising professional values and standards would keep these at the forefront of all human services, stopping the distraction away from the 'primary task' (the why we are here). For services based on professional values and standards that are truly integral (like the letters in Blackpool rock) will not disintegrate into poor practice. Instead, a focus on the quality of work and patient and client/service users' outcomes would be at the centre. In nursing, for example, it is known that professional practice enhances patient outcomes (AACN, 2002) and reduces mortality rates (Aiken et al., 2014).

Despite the rhetoric, Lansley (2011) suggested that there should be prominent leaders in every professional clinical role. The evidence indicates that the approaches to date are making it difficult for individuals to succeed in these remits (Storey and Holti, 2013). Moving away from compliance to using professional judgement is also a key emphasis within Social Care (Munro, 2011). However, with a dominant legacy focused heavily on processes, this experiential art of professional leadership may be rarer than hoped. In addition, certainly, the more diluted professional standards and values based on outcomes become, the more difficult it is to keep these as an integral part of the 'primary task'.

Indeed, Thorpe et al. (2011, p243) allude to the importance of professional leadership counterbalancing the 'dominance of managerialist values' and of 'promoting the profession itself'. And leading the profession is a key role of leadership (Lawler, 2007). Yet both Health and Social Care have witnessed a dominance of top-down managerial changes that have failed to win the hearts and minds of those at the front (Attwood et al., 2003), arguably an ongoing legacy mixed with fear and policies written by people either too far away, disconnected or never connected in the real world of front-line services.

A fundamental and poorly understood concept is professional experiential know-how; while not an exact science, this creates an untapped reservoir of intuitive wisdom, surrounded by dry lands of failed managerial fads. For most industries would acknowledge that the individuals at the front operational end understand the business so well, and given the right support would solve, and champion, the necessary changes required without unnecessary prescriptive, paternalistic control and interference. The science irrefutably supports the notion that any hint of control destroys intrinsic motivation (Deci and Flaste, 1995; Pink 2010) and impacts the brain in the same way as pain (Rock and Cox, 2012).

'Leaders are formed in the fire of experience' (McCall, 2010, p679), for experiential knowledge, understanding and its application undoubtedly create powerful levers for operational success. Certainly, as discussed in Chapter 1, the research suggests that in stressful environments and under pressure experience triumphs over intelligence in ensuring that better decisions are made (Caughron, 2010). Collins' (2001, p20) research supports the notion of great leaders having 'professional will' as a differentiating factor of their success.

Tapping into professional experiential leadership is therefore a vital, arguably underutilised, component of the public sector that should be celebrated and capitalised upon. This is not about working in silos, or protecting remits, but expressing what is uniquely different between professions to ensure precious resources are appropriately matched, and the very best of professional leadership is available and exercised.

Indeed, Clinical Leadership networked models have proven to be successful, despite the barriers presented (Storey and Holti, 2013). Too much of a focus on breaking professional elitism, with managerial elitism, negates capitalising within public services on experiential know-how and ensuring everyone counts (and not just in terms of the rhetoric) for real quality impact.

The author, therefore, suggests that self-leadership offers a different approach; instead of an outside-in model, it affords an inside-out approach, which importantly accommodates the best of professional experience (innate wisdom) with self-integrity and resilience.

Furthermore, within professional leadership there must be an ability to make an accurate professional decision, using knowledge, experience and appropriate expertise, and the right state of mind is integral to this. All the facets of self-leadership are crucial in helping individuals focus squarely on the 'primary task', to remain routed in the best of professional practice.

Self-observation and self-awareness, for example, allow the individual to be conscious in the moment of their interactions, actions and reactions, and with this awareness to be able to recognise, appreciate and understand any unhelpful emotions, faulty thinking or prejudgements, which develops an intuitive and emotional intelligence moment by moment. We must also remember that stress depletes the important prefrontal cortex areas (of blood supply and with it essential glucose and oxygen) necessary for very rounded decision making.

Linked to this concept of leadership for all and a specific focus on self-leadership for professionals is the next vital fundamental foundation, the importance of the right structures to achieve this – devolved models.

Devolved models of leadership

It will be argued that the current preparation for leaders has been based on a flawed model, a hierarchical central approach that 'undermines front-line leadership' and 'collaborative working' (Zheltoukhova, 2014, p6). The 'us and them' inference, which potentially negates the 'benefit of workforce diversity', can no longer prevail (Zheltoukhova, 2014, p6). To deal with huge disruptive changes instead requires a totally fresh look and a different way of ensuring all individuals are responsible. Typically, under pressure, individuals adopt a command and control style, yet importantly this is about engaging all individuals. The NHS Confederation (2014) suggests that 'There is evidence from the NHS and other industries, including the oil industry that top-down command and control cultures are the worst kind of culture for quality and safety.'

Splitting the strategic from the operational potentially creates gaps in reality and awkward surprises. Alimo-Metcalfe and Alban-Metcalfe (2011, p11) allude to a 'culture of genuine engagement'. It is proposed that self-leadership as a model would thrive within devolved structures. The following distributed, dispersed and shared (collective) types of leadership represent the different devolved models.

Distributed, dispersed and shared (collective) leadership

All individuals, without the formal position of leader, have the ability to influence others; this is part of being human, whether this is an interaction with a distraught mother, an ill patient or a colleague. Team members can also influence each other and in doing so exercise leadership. This section discusses the leadership models or structures that best facilitate a process of leadership that is not just about single individual(s). This type of leadership is achieved through *distributed*, *dispersed* and *shared* (collective) leadership rather than formal leaders.

Arguably, individuals in organisations do not operate in isolation; they often function in teams, working collectively to achieve organisational outcomes (O'Connor and Quinn, 2004). Gordon (2008, p3) would suggest that with these approaches there is a shift in emphasis from 'the leader to the process of leadership' – a shift from domination to empowerment. All these concepts represent a sharing of power, decentralised approaches and, as Thorpe et al. (2011, p239) advocate, a move away from 'the limitations of top-down models and the limitations of leadership when the unit of analysis is a single individual'.

When 'change and improvement' are required, these models are particularly important and are currently crucial in Health and Social Care (Currie and Lockett, 2011, p287). The first model is distributed leadership.

Distributed leadership

Mumford (2010) describes 'distributed leadership' as 'leadership where responsibilities are not held by one person, but instead are held by multiple individuals'. It is 'an emergent property of a group or network' (Bennett et al., 2003, p7), with professional roles lending themselves well to distributed leadership (Thorpe et al., 2011).

Specific conditions facilitate this approach, for example a shared endeavour, working together on a project, social support and having a collective voice (Shipman, 2010). In Western's (2013, p244) case, this is about 'Eco-leadership', which relates to how leaders conceptualise organisations as networks of connections instead of 'closed systems'. 'Eco' here refers to natural, technological and human/social aspects and is part of all leadership rather than specific to 'environmental leadership'.

Distributed leadership is characteristically the pooling of expertise where the overall output is greater than the individual contributions (Bennett et al., 2003). Brookes and Grint (2010) suggested it is about 'vertical leadership' within the organisation, which is both 'creative and adaptive to the circumstances . . . [and] deals with uncertainty' (see Figure 3.4).

'Leadership practice' is therefore the focus rather than the leader and this is why this model is suggested as a more effective and sustained approach (Spillane, 2006, p89). Currie and Lockett (2011, p290) describe two forms: a top-down distributed model, which requires a hierarchal leadership framework, and a bottom-up trend.

Buchanan et al.'s (2007, p1065) 'nobody in charge' is one example of the latter. However, they were referring to 'nobody in charge' in terms of resisting the temptation to appoint a project manager for change projects, instead allowing for a more fluid approach with less dependence and more involvement and collaboration (Buchanan et al., 2007, p1086).

Gardner (1990) believed that the distributed model was vital to the well-being of any complex organisation. Certainly in the public sector there has been an emphasis on both policy and practice to promote distributed leadership 'from apex to frontline' (Hartley and

Allison, 2000, p39), even though in reality hierarchical models of command and control still preside. And invariably, as Martin et al. (2009) would remind us, however, the limits for this type of leadership will always be set by those individuals who are responsible by title. Western's (2013, p245) emphasis on moving away from a top-down focus to concentrating on 'nurturing' and not 'controlling' is the advocated decentralised approach.

Shipman (2010), importantly, identifies two distinct forms of distributed leadership: *distributed-coordinated* and *distributed-fragmented*. The distributed-coordinated leadership approach involves both a formal and an emergent informal leader, the two working well together. Some have named this 'leader plus' (Spillane, 2006, p6), or leadership coupling, or partnership (Gronn and Hamilton, 2004). This is the most common format, rather than all the individuals in the team being equal leaders (Shipman, 2010). The important nuance is that both leaders accept each other's role either as spontaneous collaboration, or as an intuitive understanding gained over time (Gronn, 2002, p627). In the distributed-fragmented format the leaders do not work well together (Mumford, 2010).

When the team has a distributed-coordinated leadership approach, however, research validates that the team performance increases (Shipman, 2010). Mumford (2010) also confirms that distributed-coordinated leadership is more productive than the traditional leader-centred team structure represented by one official leader. Another decentralised model of leadership is the dispersed approach.

Dispersed leadership

Bolden et al. (2003, p17) refers to a 'dispersed leadership' model, which closely resembles an informal or emergent approach. The premise that individuals at many levels of the organisation are capable of exercising leadership moves away from a hierarchical model, where only leaders with the title can enact leadership. Indeed, Politis (2005) showed that dispersed leadership increased both creativity and productivity – essential requirements within the public sector to enact the changes required in terms of integration and transformation.

Distributed and dispersed leadership are terms used interchangeably; dispersed as an approach is mentioned within the military, the police, education and the NHS. In the military, for example, if the commanding officer is injured or fatally wounded, this approach allows for other leaders to emerge to ensure that the operation is completed.

Dispersing or dissolving traditional organisational boundaries could be described as a feature of a dispersed leadership strategy, with individuals leading themselves and being responsible for their own management and coordination. Therefore, instead of a traditional leader–follower dimension with a reciprocal power relationship, the power is shared between leaders and followers (Gordon, 2008). Again, the focus is specifically on the process of leadership rather than one individual leader. A similar concept, 'shared leadership', is discussed in the following paragraphs.

Shared leadership

Shared leadership is described as leadership that is 'broadly distributed among a set of individuals instead of centralised in the hands of a single individual who acts in the role of superior' (Pearce and Conger, 2003, p1). This description is similar to both of the models above. Brookes and Grint (2010), however, would make the distinction that, with shared leadership, it is more about 'horizontal leadership and beyond the organisation', implicitly 'how we lead when we are not in charge', for example in a network or working collaboratively within a partnership arrangement.

Alimo-Metcalfe and Albin-Metcalfe (2011) would add that it surfaces when people work effectively together. Often there is a cross-functional group who might have a traditionally appointed leader who does not have line authority outside this environment – an expert who often represents only one of a number of specialisms within the group (Pearce and Conger, 2003). Clinical networks and integrated models of care would therefore be examples of shared leadership as an approach to bring about change across traditional boundaries. Bradford and Cohen (1998, p57) described this as an 'elixir for better performance'.

Brookes and Grint (2010), however, would advocate 'Collective Leadership, which is both horizontal, shared between organisations, and vertical, distributed throughout each organisation' (see Figure 3.4).

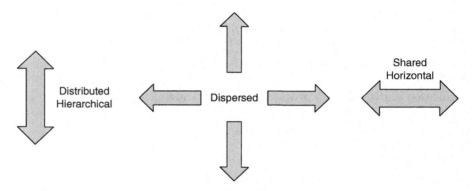

Figure 3.4 Distributed, dispersed and shared leadership

In all of the above models, even if there is an intention to share, distribute or disperse leadership across a number of individuals, in practice this may be more difficult, because of the concept of power and previous expectations and relationships with the identified leader and how much implicitly they are able to legitimately and personally let go to subordinates. Despite this, Currie and Lockett (2011, p292) point out that in the NHS the government has continued to 'seek to distribute leadership to frontline clinicians', although they go on to suggest that:

> *professional hierarchy and traditional power relationships, combined with a strong centralized performance regime, will act to stymie policy-makers' aspirations for enacting distributed leadership [and] as such, the health and social care context creates a paradox for distributed leadership.*

(Currie and Lockett, 2011, p295)

However, re-examining a collective approach, both horizontal (shared) and distributed (hierarchical), within Health and Social Care provides a more effective infrastructure for a process based on leadership rather than individual leaders. Within leaner, restructured organisations this would appear the essential format and, as Zheltoukhova (2014, p7) suggests, when distributed leadership is discouraged it can also slow down collaborative working and decision making.

Important concepts such as distributed, dispersed and shared leadership were examined and, while the distributed-coordinated model has been shown to increase productivity and despite the public sector courting this model, full integration remains aspirational.

Indeed, with the current financial focus, a centralised hierarchical hybrid is arguably damaging much of the progress made.

Paradoxically, the need to reduce spending, and with it layers of management, means that devolved structures are even more important to getting the practice of leadership right. Self-leadership as an approach in itself would also negate some of the identified dilemmas: the concept of power, expectations and relationship issues. Self-leadership is about recognising individual potential and the enacting of leadership as an activity. With thinner structures this means everyone needs to count and devolvement is a format that can allow it to happen. The author would suggest, however, that self-leadership as an approach can happen regardless of the structures, though to be more effective devolved environments would enhance the impact of self-leadership.

Knowing how leadership investment is impacting at the front end of services and to the bottom line in terms of outcomes has been an under-researched area. Despite the significant investment in leadership (discussed in Chapter 2) and the preoccupation with leadership as a 'cure all ills' concept, the evaluation of its impact has been lacking.

The final foundation of self-leadership is the important role of evaluating the impact of leadership development.

Evaluation of impact

The evaluation of leadership development impact, other than the so-called 'happy sheet' (suitableness of the venue, delivery of the course and general administration) is rare (Mitchell, 2001; Draper and Clark 2007; Hafford-Letchfield and Lawler, 2010; Nohria and Khurana, 2010). Yet, as established in Chapter 2, there is a significant amount of money spent in the public sector on leadership as continuous professional development (McBain et al., 2012). The evaluation of impact is, therefore, an integral foundation of self-leadership.

The evaluation of impact arguably is closely connected to professional accountability, governance, best practice and ethical public service delivery. Evaluation is described as fundamental to identifying if there has been sustainable organisational change (CIPD, 2012). It provides not only the evidence base to justify investment but also the information to build on and further adapt.

Once commissioned, however, it is often assumed that leadership development will automatically achieve what is required. When such development is competing in a financially constrained environment for the same resources, programmes need to be able to satisfy value for money (CIPD, 2010). Being able to measure impact is therefore crucial (Carpenter, 2011).

There has, nevertheless, arguably been a preoccupation with cognitive rational knowledge, increasing the so-called body of knowledge, rather than with really understanding the true dynamics of a change in practice, and a change in behaviour that impacts the service user, the individual, the team and the organisation(s). One important theme is that organisations need to measure the impact of learning and development in terms of transformation, rather than purely the acquisition of knowledge.

Evaluating impact not only provides a quality assurance, a framework to work with, but also supports the reality of creating organisational learning (Hafford-Letchfield, 2007) – a 'learning culture' (Munro, 2011, p9). It therefore becomes an integral part of any organisational learning cycle and is crucial in demonstrating not only that an organisational learning culture exists but also the extent to which it is embedded.

Testing assumptions about impact, and adjusting any programme, is also key as part of continuous improvement. New knowledge learned and shared is potentially captured. Sustained changes and long-term impact and the ability to track investment become important elements. Evaluation also provides a measure in relation to return on expectations, 'a focus on assessing the extent to which the anticipated benefits of learning investment have been realised' (Anderson, 2007, p38), and the metrics to communicate the specific value of planned development, including the impact in terms of operational effectiveness, together with an appreciation of what might be the organisational barriers to incorporating learning.

Effective learning evaluation, the author proposes, is a process that necessitates a whole-system approach, from establishing the metrics required, to the relevance of the learning, to meeting organisational priorities, and to delivering a return on investment and expectation (Anderson, 2007). It provides the details to communicate the explicit benefit of planned development: not simply that the individual understood what was taught but could actually apply it at the right level; and the programme achieved its intended outcomes, implicitly the learning governance (O'Driscoll et al., 2005).

Kirkpatrick (1959) arguably provides the most popular and widely used model of evaluation. It specifies four levels of outcome:

- learners' reaction to the development;

- learning (knowledge and skills);

- behavioural change;

- results (effect on environment).

A fifth level was added by Phillips (1994) to include a return on investment – 'the ratio of money gained or lost (whether realised or unrealised) on an investment, relative to the amount of money invested' (Kirkpatrick and Kirkpatrick, 2010, p66). Brown (1996) adapted this model to fit the world of social work, and provided a focus on the actual impact in terms of job performance, and the strategic link with the organisational impact. Carpenter (2005) added a more defined focus on benefits to users and carers. Table 3.1 depicts a combination of some of the above features and provides more detail.

The Chartered Institute of Personnel and Development (CIPD, 2010, p8) has challenged the 'overuse' of Kirkpatrick's approach, suggesting that the levels 'don't relate to each other, or amount to a taxonomy ordering system'. Collins and Holton (2004) would also suggest that Kirkpatrick's model takes no account of the state of the systems within an organisation.

Importantly however, very few studies go beyond attitudes and perceptions, and even fewer move to the assessment of impact, discernible at levels 3, 4 and 5, yet these are the levels that Chief Executives most wanted information about in relation to impact of learning (Patel, 2010).

Impact in this instance is about having a 'marked' or 'strong effect or influence on' (Oxford English Dictionary, 2011, p713), in this case the individual, others and their practice. It occurs when the learning is applied and contributes to enhancing performance, which makes a beneficial difference to practice, with self-leadership identified in Chapter 2 as the 'ability to bring out the best in individuals in any circumstances for the ultimate outcome of providing better services'.

Impact evaluation in this case is about measuring how self-leadership development has influenced the individual's behaviour, and been applied to practice to achieve beneficial

Table 3.1 Evaluation outcome levels example (adapted from Kirkpatrick (1959), Brown (1996) and Carpenter (2005))

Level	Focus	Questions
Level 1	Learner's reaction to the development	The learner's reaction. What did the student think about the training?
Level 2	Learning attained	Learning attained during the period. Did the student learn what was intended? Did he or she demonstrate newly acquired skills?
Level 3	Behavioural change at work	Job behaviour in the work environment at the end of the training period. Did the learning transfer to the job?
Level 4	Impact at team, departmental and organisational level	Effect on the learner's organisation. Has the training helped organisational performance?
Level 5	Impact on users and carers	Has the development improved services, and is there any evidence?

outcomes. Hersey et al. (2013, p291) would remind us that 'changes in behaviour are significantly more difficult'. 'Behaviour means our action or reaction to something . . . what can be observed rather than what can be speculated or assumed' (Joseph, 2009, p2). It is proposed that self-leadership when exercised, however, will create significant behavioural change. There are therefore four specific areas to evaluate in terms of impact.

- Was there deep transformative self-learning?

- Was there a change or changes in behaviour?

- Were there changes and improvements in practice?

- What was the impact on services users?

Deep transformative self-learning is about promoting a change of perspective and understanding about self, which brings about changes in behaviour. This might be related to realising limiting assumptions and beliefs about self, developing instead self-confidence through new perspectives. Indeed, McEwen et al. (2010, p37) suggest that:

> At the core of transformative learning theory is the process of 'perspective transformation' . . . Clark (1991) identifies this process to have three dimensions: psychological (changes in understanding of the self); convictional (revision of belief systems); and behavioural (changes in lifestyle).

The important foundation therefore of impact evaluation in terms of self-leadership is suggested by the author as a key prerequisite and means of matching and meeting ongoing organisational and service user requirements. Evaluation creates organisational buy-in, support and accountability.

Summary

Figure 3.5 provides a graphic summation of the foundations of self-leadership. It has been established that state of mind, and specifically the right state of mind, of moving from amnesia into the now of being fully present, of being fully self is, however, the most important and integral foundation of all.

Involving everyone in self-leadership development nevertheless is key to realising the full benefits of resilience, well-being, creating the right working cultures where dignity, respect and compassion flow naturally and thrive, and being fully present in all exchanges as the norm and not the exception. And while self-leadership can succeed in any structure, inclusion of everyone is most amenable in devolved environments.

The different theoretical structures of devolvement have been explored, and it has been identified that two specific arrangements work for hierarchical structures (distributed-coordinated) and network (shared or collective) approaches. This is a leadership process that focuses on all individuals, with no exclusions, allowing everyone to benefit from self-observation to become more self and socially aware in each moment, and to be able to consciously regulate and self-manage their state of mind, in order to effectively connect, relate and communicate – this is what self-leadership is about.

Evaluating impact, like all the other foundations (see Figure 3.5), forms an integral unit surrounding the benefits of state of mind. Establishing whether deep transformative self-learning and beneficial changes in behaviour and practice have occurred, and what the real effect has been on the service user, is the identified impact to be evaluated. For without impact evaluation, accountability for investment in leadership and the adaptive learning required is potentially lost.

The foundations identified, therefore, form the fundamental underpinnings of self-leadership. In the next chapter and within the Appendix is a fuller examination of the most important feature of all – state of mind.

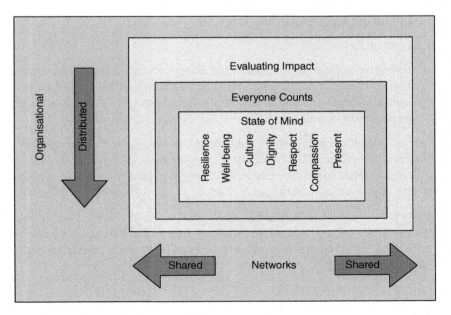

Figure 3.5 The foundations of self-leadership

Chapter 4

What determines state of mind?

Jane Holroyd, Keith Brown and Dr Aaron Turner

Introduction

This chapter proposes not only that state of mind is a central feature of self-leadership, but also that being able to influence state of mind is key to improving leaders' abilities, implicitly maximising the quality of all their interactions. Understanding, however, how state of mind functions is integral to this process. This information ensures that a person can navigate his or her own state of mind in any area of life, not just at work.

This chapter will explore state of mind, three key principles (Mind, Consciousness and Thought), its sometimes invisibility, commonly held misunderstandings of the mind and new counter-propositions. The importance of a quiet mind, for clear thought and good decision making, will be stressed. The challenge for the reader is to explore the way a person's state of mind can influence all they do, appreciating that this may well be a new learning edge.

The key challenge

Everyone has a unique experience of life, with its own tapestry of encounters and inter-pretations of experiences, whether or not, most importantly, this has been recognised as such. Certain writers have identified that individuals use this foundation to determine 'in the now' conclusions (Dispenza, 2007; Frith, 2007; Kahneman, 2011; Merleau-Ponty, 2012). So, whether known or not, an individual may already have lots of preconceived ideas of what determines state of mind, just the same as what makes an individual feel great, and what makes them feel miserable, or what they are good or bad at, and why. These ideas do not have to be right for a person to be convinced about them. They are usually based on personal experience and are therefore convincing.

Knowing one's mind in this way can lead to individuals dismissing some form of activity or challenge, with '*I know I cannot do this . . .*'. Convinced about these ideas, the ability to reconsider state of mind and its potential can be limited, and therefore, arguably, the capability to make improvements in state of mind will also be limited.

Think of the social worker who has a confident state of mind with clients, and in the workplace, but is nervous with the idea of presenting at a conference. Some people think the experience of nerves means that they are not, and could not be, confident, capable presenters: *'I'm just not that kind of person. Talking to lots of people makes me nervous.'* Assume for a moment that it is possible for this person to be at ease and comfortable talking to a large group. The person has no idea that this is true, so this personal belief therefore limits them, and they are unlikely ever to discuss this about themselves. They either:

- stay away from presenting in order to avoid discomfort, and in the belief that it is not for them anyway; or

- if they do have to present, they tend to accept the nerves as an unavoidable, understandable part of the endeavour.

These ideas camouflage the underlying thought or idea in them that *'I cannot present to large groups of people'*; perhaps they believe they are going to stutter or make a fool of themselves. These ideas are treated as fact, and therefore it can be hard to challenge them; however, loosening their status as fact would allow for another perspective, other possibilities. This willingness to be open about assumptions and experiences frees us up to reconsider any conclusions made, to see other possibilities and create new understandings.

This is a willingness to consider that there might be value and validity in perspectives that are outside, or contradictory; indeed, that the social worker can present well at a conference. It is not about learning new skills, for individuals have all the skills they need to have a better state of mind. It is how these skills and the mind are used that makes the difference. Self-leadership relies on being aware of the subtleties of the mind and the effect it has on us. The goal, therefore, is to achieve some insight into how it works, and in-the-moment realisation of the impact. Competence in this area is therefore based on understanding.

For example, someone may be aware that their thinking is no longer clear and they have written a report, and have checked it over and over; however, when reading it days later (when in a better state of mind) they spot the most obvious and glaring errors. Being able to do this in real time is what is being referred to here and three important key principles are at play.

Three key principles

State of mind as lived moment to moment can be understood according to these three internal elements, or 'principles' (to indicate their inherent presence in our experience[1]) (Banks, 1998, p21):

1. Mind

2. Consciousness

3. Thought.

There is a potential for well-being, resilience and highly clear, productive and responsive thinking to be built into the mind. This potential is accessed through the capacity of thought.

This capacity, in turn, is the source of moment-to-moment awareness of life, and experience of reality through the element of awareness, or consciousness, a completely internal system creating an individual's state of mind. 'Thought and consciousness are as inseparable as a light switch and light' (Pransky, 2003, p81). This perspective points to an unlimited potential for people to have a quality about their state of mind, in every moment, and in any circumstance (Turner, 2014; see the Appendix).

State of mind – the invisibility

Before discussing the three principles that determine state of mind, it is important to appreciate why state of mind is so invisible. Although it is the driving factor behind an individual's capability, and the quality of their life and relationships, it is something taken for granted and relatively unappreciated. The mind, however, impacts dramatically, but yet avoids being identified as the cause. This happens through two generally less well understood facts about the mind: our emotions come from our minds, and emotions are not separate from thought (Damasio, 2006).

Our emotions come from our minds
People's minds are used as if they are reliable information processors. People assume the mind relays exact information from the world, much in the same way as a window. This simple view, that we extract information from the environment in some ways much like a computer, arguably therefore leads to many interpretative problems. An individual might not trust what he or she sees, thinks and feels if recognising this lack of neutrality.

If a person is happy they accept there is something out there to be happy about. If they are stressed they presume the mind is providing reliable information about external factors that are creating the stress. If an individual is angry, they believe that their mind is responding effectively to some external stimulus. So when stressed an individual might say, '*I have too much on my plate*', or '*the deadline is too tight, I feel stressed*', or '*my boss is putting pressure on me*'. You can see in these statements the confidence that whatever is being felt is coming from a verifiable external source, and is an appropriate, unavoidable experience of some external factor. In fact, some people would even say, '*If there was nothing "out there", (like a deadline) I would not feel the stress.*'

The same is true of anger and satisfaction. If an individual feels anger, their knee-jerk response is to assume that something '*made*' them angry. In terms of satisfaction, if someone is unhappy at work, the common response is to suggest leaving. The idea that external factors are responsible for how we feel is so commonly accepted that there is no debate. Among friends, if someone says they are looking for a new house, or a better job, or a different partner, in order to have a better life experience, the conversation usually accepts the assumption, and takes it for granted; external factors will make them happy.

This is not about the merits of right and wrong, or accuracy, but a common assumption. Behind this assumption is the idea that the mind is inherently reliable in terms of providing information about circumstances and appropriate feelings and actions. This understanding of the mind offers very little room for self-leadership. Because experiences such as stress or anger are assumed to be somewhat unavoidable, as responses to things outside an individual's control, like their circumstances, their personality and what life has given them, there is anger management, stress management or stress reduction; all these approaches accept the unavoidable reality of anger or stress and set about trying to limit or control the effects.

The mind, instead, is playing a much bigger role in creating these experiences than is accepted. Moreover, if the role of the mind in creating these experiences is recognised, new options for assessing the reliability of the mind in the moment, undermining sometimes unproductive anger and paralysing stress, can emerge.

If the role of the mind is not identified, options for better states of mind in the same circumstances, although present, remain unavailable to the individual. This limitation is a result of the person's understanding, not their inherent potential. Just recognising the role of the mind in creating an experience gives an individual better access to the inherent potential of an improved state of mind in any given circumstances. A second invisibility is the presumption that emotions are separate from thought.

Emotions are not separate from thought

Individuals assume that most of the time their feelings remain constant and they think logically. However, they do not realise the true influence of emotional changes on their thinking, and how this impacts the ability to reason and see clearly.

Fluctuations in individuals' emotions, therefore, signal overall changes in their minds. The suggestion here is that the quality of the mind, and everything it does, is varying moment to moment. The clarity with which we see, think, process and have ideas is the product of the variability of state of mind. This is why intelligent, well-prepared students fail exams. When a student's stress level is high enough, it does not matter how intelligent or well prepared they are. If they cannot think distinctly, they cannot remember clearly, and they cannot focus properly. This is an example of an unavoidable pattern in human functioning.

A more pervasive, yet subtler example is conversation. If a person is tense or self-conscious in a conversation, their ability to hear what is being said and to think clearly and fluidly deteriorates. It is always afterwards, when they are less tense or insecure, that they realise *'that is what I should have said!'* Over the course of a person's lifetime, the decisions or actions they most regret in hindsight are usually the ones that occurred to them in a state of relative tension, stress, insecurity or upset. The decisions or actions that they are usually most happy with are those that occurred to them in a state of clarity of mind, one that had a relative absence of tension, stress, insecurity or upset.

The two key presumptions, therefore, that have been challenged here are:

1. that our minds accurately reflect the environment (reality); and

2. our emotions remain separate from thought.

Instead, it is proposed that changes in emotions are the symptom of larger wholesale shifts in the quality of state of mind. Emotions change everything about the mind, including the way someone deliberates and their ability to think productively. The two are inextricably linked (Damasio, 2006). Most importantly, however, this is all generated from within (inside), rather than from the outside (Banks, 1998; Pransky, 2003; Neill, 2013).

The components from within, responsible for an individual's current state of mind, are the three principles listed earlier: *mind, consciousness* and *thought*. These will be examined further in relation to the concept of self-leadership.

Mind

There is no end or limitation, nor are there boundaries, to the human mind.

(Banks, 1998, p35)

Mind is a way of discussing the source of thought and the nature of the mind: the energy in the system. It is a way of discussing the potential of the mind – the feeling that there is a limitless possibility to thought, to creativity, to an ability to have new thought. Instinctively we all know that there is a potential to the mind that outstrips our use of it, that we do not use the full limit.

As a principle, mind is also a way of discussing the intelligence that is observable in the mind, and in life generally. This is not straightforward to pin down either, but is easy to point to. It is observable in the way our minds gravitate to happiness, clarity and well-being without our efforts. This is easiest to see in toddlers, because their use of thought is much less complex and habitual than that of adults (Blakemore and Frith, 2005). But this can also be true for adults. Whenever they are not actively using their minds to think, there is an automatic drift to calm, clarity and well-being. It is why, when we stop trying, the name we were struggling to remember comes clearly to mind. It is why many people have their best ideas just before they fall asleep, just after they wake up, in the shower, or while running and walking – all times when they are not actively thinking, or trying to control their minds.

Mind is also a way of discussing the energy running through the human system – the animating substance of life. Although this seems like a vague concept, it can be measured in brain and cellular activities. This leads to the second of the three principles, 'consciousness'.

Consciousness

Consciousness is the gift of awareness.

(Banks, 1998, p39)

Consciousness in the moment is *awareness*. It describes the ability to have a sense of things, a feel for an experience, and is the ability to feel, see, sense or be aware.

The three principles (mind, consciousness and thought) together help us to understand reality as a moment-to-moment creation, a momentary manifestation of a vast potential in the form of thought brought to life as a sensory experience. This can often be seen most simply in dream life. When dreaming it is obvious that all of the experience is coming from the mind. We are not experiencing the bed, or our room, but whatever our mind is doing. Yet we have a sensory experience of whatever reality we are thinking – falling feels just the same as though we were awake.

The quality of experience is so similar to the waking experience we cannot generally tell the difference, no matter how unrealistic or unlikely the events and environments. The reality in the mind is the only reality experienced. Even if you left school decades ago, while dreaming this fact is forgotten. The experience of failing the same exams, passed 20 years earlier, feels real.

The sensory experience is as tangible as the waking experience, because it is being created in exactly the same way from a potential for thought; the thought created is experienced as a sensory reality through consciousness. The fact that the degree certificate is hanging on the bedroom wall is no match for the feeling of being late for that same exam during a dream. It feels so real that this reality is not questioned in the moment, even though later we *know* it cannot be real.

From this perspective, any particular experience, perception, sense of things, thought, feeling, or any aspect of experienced reality, is just a momentary manifestation of a much larger potential through thought. It only appears to be solid and limited, but is essentially one thought away from a completely new version.

> *Consciousness is more than just the ability to be aware and to experience life but is itself a force that in its purest form contains wisdom.*

> (Pransky, 2003, p87)

This links to the third principle, 'thought'.

Thought

> *Thought is not reality; yet it is through thought that our realities are created.*

> (Banks, 1998, p49)

When discussing thought it is not simply the intellect, or the thoughts seen; the focus is on something much more general – that the energy in the human system is manifesting as something psychologically. This is called 'thought', the formation of which generates an individual's experience of life. It is through the generation of thought that an individual is able to have perception, and to have awareness consistent with the thought that is formed. As Neill (2009, p123) suggests, 'Every emotion you experience is a direct response to a thought, not to the world around you.'

For example, a family are out in the snow, all of them in the same temperature. It is so cold that one of the parents retreats and goes home. The other is keeping an eye on the children; the feeling of cold comes and goes as their thinking shifts between monitoring the children, to see if they are in danger, and how they themselves are feeling. All of the children's thought is focused on the thrill of the snow, and while they are biologically colder than the adults, their skin colder to the touch, and they have been handling more snow and rolling in it, they have absolutely no conscious awareness of the cold.

'*How are you doing?*' asks the incredulous parent, '*Are you cold?*' '*No,*' is the reply. '*Are you sure?*' asks the parent in disbelief. But you can see that, compared to the parent, clutching a coat around them and shivering, with shoulders slightly hunched, the children are not feeling any cold, and they run and scream and roll around with ease. Suddenly one child goes from happy and relaxed to crying, '*I'm cold, I want to go home*', and cries with cold until they get home. This was not a result of temperature change, but a change in thought. It is only through thought that an individual is able to be aware of anything. So if the children are running around shouting and annoyed, thought creates a reactive experience of it, and loving thought creates an appreciative experience of the same circumstances, whereas distracted thought prevents any experience of it at all.

Thought, therefore, produces something that appears to be real, to be outside. As Bohm (1994) suggests, thought creates something and then says 'I didn't do it, it really exists out there.' Thought is a way of discussing the mind's ability to create a form to our experience. It could be seen as the moment-to-moment manifestation of the potential of mind.

- *Thought is the way we gain access to the potential of the mind*. In this sense, thought is a vehicle. It is the way we access our potential for feelings, perception, ideas, learning and intuition.

- *As a manifestation of a much larger potential, thought is always incomplete*. Hence, there is always more to learn, more to experience and any single experience is singular, and limited, relative to the potential range of experience; so even someone's best idea is only their best idea to date. Implicitly, a great idea does not exhaust the potential for new ideas.

- *Thought is not real like an object*. What is felt, however, is very real to the individual. But the reality of thought seems to be more of a feeling; because presumed to be reality, many of the clues are missed as just passing.

The essence of the mind is therefore its potential to create thought; the thought it creates determines the nature of experience moment to moment; and the form of that thought determines the reality seen, and experienced from moment to moment. Never transcended, this is the system an individual lives in.

This is visible in problem solving, working on a problem and gaining little ground despite the time spent. At some later point the solution, however, becomes simple and evident, and the problem is solved. In these cases, it is common that the solution to the problem is preceded by a completely different view of the situation: an 'Aha!' moment.

This common occurrence points to the way an individual's experience is determined by her or his mind through the function of thought. Stepping back to look at this neutrally makes it easier to see the patterns that are common to all; all personal experience is an example of this more general process, no matter what those particular experiences might be – the human experience.

The human experience

An ability to understand the mind is limited by misunderstandings of it. The four most significant commonly held misunderstandings of the mind are listed below.

1. The way that an individual feels and thinks is determined/affected by external factors.

2. Thought is real and needs to be 'dealt' with.

3. Individuals are the victims of something.

4. A person needs 'to do' something to feel better, or think more clearly.

1. The way that an individual feels and thinks is determined/affected by external factors.

This assumption is so common that people often feel it is ridiculous to even question it. The following are examples of individual assumptions:

'You hurt my feelings.'

'Public speaking makes me nervous.'

'I have a stressful job.'

'My life is stressful at the moment.'

'I am doing well considering (considering the circumstances I am in).'

'Anyone in this situation would feel this way.'

'I would be less stressed if I was more financially secure.'

'It's all right for you. You have . . .'

This supposition links states of mind to certain circumstances; in making this connection, it:

- undermines the freedom of state of mind and, hence, the ability to have free and effective self-leadership;

- creates predictable patterns in state of mind, and in so doing reduces the freedom of self-leadership.

This is discernible with stress; for example, an individual can take thought for granted as reality, for when stressed an individual's thinking is not as clear as it could be. Dispenza (2007) and Kahneman (2011) both write about the ability of the brain to make associations and patterns and they suggest that this pattern processing continues potentially in default mode, identifying in the environment supporting evidence for a person's current thinking. When stressed there is potentially no override, or appropriate adjustment, resulting in what often happens, which is that 'we get the wrong end of the stick'. As Kahneman (2011, p85) states, an individual operates 'as a machine for jumping to conclusions'. Misinterpreting and going off on entirely the wrong tangent are examples, which some writers suggest become more permanent beliefs (Dispenza, 2007; Kahneman, 2011). As Stephenson (2009, p91) states, 'A belief is a thought you've convinced yourself is true. In other words . . . A belief is just a thought that you've made real.'

Victor Frankl's experience in a concentration camp alludes to this ability to react in different ways to the same situation, for he states: 'I understood how a man who has nothing left in this world still may know bliss (Frankl, 2004, p49). And, as William Shakespeare suggested in Hamlet, 'there is nothing good or bad but thinking makes it so' (Hamlet, Act 2, Scene ii: 1136, Shakespeare, 1987). Indeed, Banks (2003) states that 'All life experiences from cradle to grave are psychological experiences.'

Most people know that past encounters, expectations, prejudices and filters all affect the way things are seen, and the way reality is interpreted and experienced. Seeing things outside our own perspective can seem very difficult (Borg, 2010). The mind creates a person's experience of the world around them, their sources of reality (Dispenza, 2007; Frith, 2007; Borg, 2010). So any perspective that explains experience or state of mind, by pointing to situations and circumstances, completely overlooks the role of the mind in generating the person's grasp and experience of those circumstances. For example, if an individual does not like the colour green, trying to explain it by pinning the problem on that particular shade of green would be fruitless. It is not green's doing. You would be better off trying to understand what happened in the person's mind that made green an unpleasant colour. Here, a clear distinction is made between:

- an individual's experience: how things look and feel; and

- what is generating this experience; where this experience is coming from.

Within an experience, we feel like the external world is affecting us. This feeling is part of the experience the mind is creating. So, although it is the sense an individual has, it is not a useful explanation. Experience feels influenced by circumstance because of the creative power of the mind, through 'thought', brought to light for us by our senses. An individual, therefore, might feel that the sun is making them feel good, or the wet winter is making them feel bad, or long slow queues and traffic are annoying. This is what it feels like, that certain external factors create certain kinds of experiences. What is less visible is that what things 'feel' like is the result of what the mind is doing.

Part of this 'feel' is the impression and sensation that external factors have something to do with our experience. On closer inspection an individual can see that they only appreciate the beneficial influence of the sun when they are feeling good. There are many more times in life when, out in the glowing sun, an individual is oblivious to it, or even in a bad mood: frustrated, depressed, stressed or annoyed. If distracted an individual might not notice the sun at all, and if stressed only notices how much needs to be done, and that it is annoyingly hot.

In the supermarket queue, the slowness is frustrating, and by the time the front is reached and it becomes obvious that the friendly checkout person is talking to each customer, mild irritation becomes a rage of indignation, and '*How dare they waste my time in small talk*'. But this is only the case when someone is impatient. Another time this does not have the same impact, and the wait is hardly noticeable.

An individual's experience can therefore change independent of the particular external factors. Parents might say to their children: '*Stop doing that, I hate it when you do that.*' This same behaviour on another day is experienced as exuberance with: '*Isn't it cute how excited the children are.*' The fact that experience is created by the mind means that there is a vast, and underappreciated, potential for a range of experiences in any circumstance, an individual already having some range of these experiences in the same circumstances but tending to overlook them. The mind therefore has an unlimited potential to create experience.

In response to this common misunderstanding, that the way an individual feels and thinks is determined/affected by external factors, a new proposition is suggested:

> **Experience is therefore a product of the mind. An individual is experiencing nothing but his or her mind.**

This leads on to the second of the common misunderstandings.

2. Thought is real and needs to be 'dealt' with.

The idea that thought is a key variable in an individual's experience and their effectiveness is common to a whole range of approaches, for example cognitive therapy (Beck et al., 2007), psychodynamic therapy (Summers and Barber, 2010), cognitive behavioural therapy (CBT) (Beck and Beck, 2011) and neuro-linguistic programming (NLP) (Tosey and Mathison, 2009). So the relevance of thought to experience is not a new idea. There are, therefore, numerous methodologies and techniques that focus on the importance of thought.

It is crucial to remember that thought is not reality. It sounds strange to say that the variable creating experience is not real. There is no doubt that the results of thought – sensory experiences – are real to an individual and feel emotionally and viscerally tangible. It is often the substantive quality of this experience that leads people to assume that there is something of substance behind it, and they accept that thought is real, like a 'thing'.

The concept of thought as real, like a 'thing', an object or entity, is behind any approach that 'deals' with thought by doing something to it, or with it. If I have a table I do not want, I have to treat it like a thing to deal with. If I do not move that table, it will stay where it is, and nothing will change. That is how entities behave; for they have a life of their own, independent of our attentions. So to deal with an object, an individual has to do something to it, or with it. To get rid of the table, a certain amount of time and energy is required to move or destroy it, and until this is achieved it will stay the same as it is now.

Many of the approaches to and understandings of thought, identified above, treat it as if it is like a table, an object, and as if something needs to be done with it, for example trace it back, uproot, reframe, do battle, analyse and discredit it. All of these approaches have in common the fact that they deal with thought as if it is an object, with a life of its own, that someone needs to do something about. Indeed, Seppala (2012) cites Norman Farb's findings from the University of Toronto, suggesting an individual cannot stop racing thoughts, anger or in fact any thoughts, for 'we cannot control our mind with our mind'.

The idea of thought as a thing has been extended to the notion of different 'kinds' of thoughts. From this understanding comes the concept of more and less powerful thoughts, and more and less fundamental kinds of thought. In line with the idea that these thoughts are different, assorted approaches are developed for different types of thought. There can be diverse kinds of thought, however; the basic fundamental nature of thought trumps these differences.

Just as someone can mould many different objects from clay, there are many varieties of thought. But all objects made from clay, whether they are cars, people, flowers or birds, behave and react the way clay does. An understanding of clay as a substance would help someone, more than an understanding of the object it is moulded into, when dealing with that object. So an expert on cars is less equipped to deal with a clay model of a car than an expert in the properties of clay who knows nothing about cars.

Seeing thought therefore as real, like an object that needs to be addressed and dealt with, is a misunderstanding of the nature of thought and, therefore, a misunderstanding of how best to 'deal' with it. The proposition here is that the nature of thought is a constant and shared fundamental quality of all types of thought and, therefore, all kinds of human experience.

Many individuals have had the experience of being either very urgent or very upset about something. On some of these occasions they may feel differently later. Once the upsetting thought is gone it is not only hard to relate to the feelings they had before, but sometimes it is even harder to relate to why they felt so badly about it all. Dispenza (2007) states that, if you look carefully you will see that:

- when thought changes, someone's whole reality changes automatically;

- thought is not self-sustaining; without attention thought automatically changes.

Someone can be celebrating their birthday with all their dearest friends, and yet be preoccupied and worried with what has happened at work; everyone around them is happy, however the individual can feel miserable, lost in thought.

When people are upset, if they do not ruminate, or focus on it, they feel better. Even if they are trying to remember something, if they do not keep it in mind it will disappear. This is what is meant by thought not being like an object. Thought comes and goes and none of it has a life of its own. It lasts as long as someone thinks it and when it is gone it leaves no trace. An individual can have between 60,000 and 80,000 thoughts in 24 hours (Borg, 2010). If thought had an existence of its own, it would just be a matter of time before storage space would disappear.

The confusion about the nature of thought comes because thought responds to the way it is treated. If someone has a thought that they believe, they are affected by the thought and respond to the thought *as if* it is real. When attention is paid to a thought it gains more significance, and becomes bigger and all-consuming, as with an obsessive worry, for example, about finances. This makes it appear to have a reality of its own. Someone, however, is only burdened by these concerns to the extent they think about them. In contrast to this, if a person realises a certain experience is just a thought, and sees that it has no life or relevance of its own, it will come and go and not appear to have much effect. The following examples illustrate this further.

Example 1:

Public speaking has been mentioned, and is a good example of how the same thinking can appear real or irrelevant. Everyone has experienced to some extent nerves about public speaking. If a person believes that the nerves are a real thing, that they have to somehow address or deal with them, the nerves not only affect them, but even seem to become a more significant problem. In some cases the person is thinking more about the nerves than the topic of the presentation. This is because, unbeknown to the person, by believing in the reality of the nerves they are accepting the thought behind them as a reality (rather than just as a thought), and hence giving it attention. This amounts to fuelling the thought, or the reality of the thought. This, in turn, makes it appear to have an existence of its own.

In contrast to this, if a person sees the nerves as an irrelevant fact, they essentially leave the thought alone, and will find that the nerves dissipate on their own, without any impact other than giving the person an occasional uncomfortable feeling. The following is another example.

Example 2:

Everyone has experienced meeting someone they do not like. According to the propositions discussed so far, this would just be an experience created by thought; so why is it so difficult to overcome? Again, it is the belief and endorsement of the belief and experience by the person themselves that makes the difference. Generally speaking, if someone has a momentary thought, that they do not like their friend, they let go of it, and end up continuing to like them.

This comes from having a new thought after the dislike or temporary irritation of thought. With people not liked, the individual may never let go of that thought. The most extreme version of this is the way people get over their thinking of annoyance with, and dislike of, their toddlers. Very often it does not matter how upset the parents get, they completely get over it, without effort, in a relatively short period of time. It is usually because they do not want to dislike their toddlers, so when they do, they treat it with less relevance and it passes.

To illustrate how this is happening in the mind of the parent, it is important to say that it is not conditional on the children, or anyone else. That is why people have different propensities to like, and dislike, others. They treat their experiences of dislike differently. If they tend to see it as important, or relevant, they will be making use of that thinking and hence it exists longer. If they treat it as less relevant, like the toddlers' parents, they will have new thoughts sooner, and hence feel better and see things differently.

These examples point to the way thought responds to how someone pays attention to it. All thoughts are equally real, and equally unreal. If a person can see this they no longer need to feel victimised by their thinking. Whenever someone does not, they feel like they are facing a substantial challenge, whether real or thought-created. At this point they have already lost the ability to self-lead, because they have accepted that it is difficult, or impossible, to have a new thought, and hence a new state of mind in that situation. This is why realising the illusory nature of thought is central to empowered self-leadership. Being illusory means it always feels real and acts as if it is real, but it is actually just a formation of thought that has no substance, dissolving naturally in the absence of belief and attention.

In response to this common misunderstanding, that thought is real and needs to be dealt with, a new proposition is suggested:

> **All thought is the same – it is the mind's ability to create detail/content, but it is never real like an object.**

Now we come to the third common misunderstanding.

3. Individuals are the victims of something.

This common misconception comes from the fact that individuals often blame something external for causing their suffering and stress. It feels as if it is originating from somewhere beyond a person's influence. People explain this experience in many different ways: suffering circumstance, past experiences, personality, DNA (genes), conditioning from the past or force of habit. What all these things have in common is that they are all perceived as relatively real, and outside a person's influence, and therefore not much can be done.

People explain their suffering and limitations in these terms, as if they are the victims of something, with relatively little influence over it. If this were true, an individual would have little scope for improving their state of mind, responses, patterns and capabilities. Patterns and experiences, it is acknowledged, feel like they are real, and there is little ability to influence them; this, however, is a misunderstanding of the actual situation, for it is more of a perception than a reality.

At a theme park someone might go on a space ride that looks and feels exactly like riding through space. This perceptual experience obscures the fact that they are in a shaking metal box, watching a large video screen. The perceptual reality covers over the mechanics of how that experience is created. Just as in the theme park, being aware of the mechanics might spoil the perceptual experience of the reality of the ride; understanding the mechanics of how they come to feel, and experience what they do, undermines the reality of that experience. Whereas, at the theme park, that would not be a good thing because it spoils the ride, in terms of our mental life, understanding the mechanics enables someone to feel less victimised by their feelings, patterns and experiences, and more able to use a fuller potential of the mind. This can be summarised as follows.

- The feeling that individuals are being affected by forces outside, or beyond their control, is deceptive.
- An individual is merely being affected by changes in thought.
- Thought is not real but a temporary formation within the mind that passes automatically once attention drops.
- The essence of mind is a constantly emergent potential for new thought.

An individual is therefore continuously one thought away from a new thought and hence a new state of mind. This potential is never absent, no matter how absent it feels, so nothing stands between an individual and the potential for increased clarity and well-being.

On the experiential level, this does not seem to be true, for stress feels real and unavoidable, but it always passes easily, without notice, when not focused on. This explains why, no matter how troubled a person is, they will get over these feelings and come out of their current state of mind, unless they do not let go of it. Think of holding a grudge: it lasts as long as an individual holds it, and disappears as soon as they do not.

In response to this common misunderstanding, that individuals are the victims of something, a new proposition is suggested:

> There is freedom and potential in every moment and only beliefs in thought/ experience stand in the way (an illusory barrier).

Now we come to the final misunderstanding.

4. A person needs 'to do' something to feel better, or think more clearly.

When you ask people about the times when they have felt happy, or in love, or inspired, or had their best thinking, there are a couple patterns that emerge.

- Everybody can clearly identify these times. They are visible and present for everyone, and this points to the universal potential of clarity of mind and the potential behind thought.

- No one can tell *how* they did it, or how they got there.

They have suspicions; so, for example, they think it was something to do with being on holiday, or exercising. But there is never a one-to-one relationship between these places and activities and these experiences. In fact, there is always some variation for any given person on where and when, what and how they had these experiences. Remember the number one common misunderstanding, that our state of mind is determined by external factors.

The reason people cannot explain, or control, these kinds of states of mind is because they are the result of a natural, emergent, default of the mind. They are states of mind that an individual falls into, not states that are created. This is why 'positive thinking' helps but does not make an individual actually happy. Happiness is a default, emergent state that occurs when minds are free. So positive thinking helps an individual feel better, but does not tend to lead them to be actually happy.

When people are happy they usually have no idea what they did to bring it about. They often say they just found themselves happy or it 'just happened'. Usually, people's best thinking comes when they are not actively thinking. This pattern of not actively thinking can be generalised to cover all the higher functions of the mind and points to a pattern in the way state of mind works.

It is akin to John Keats's writings about 'negative capability' in a letter to his brothers, George and Tom, in December 1817: 'When a man is capable of being in uncertainties, mysteries, doubts, without any irritable reaching after fact and reason' (Nagar, 2005, p269). He is referring to the removal of the intellectual self. There is, however, nothing you need to do mentally or physically to have a better state of mind, to feel better, or to think more clearly. It is already happening. The real challenge is that individuals are thinking in ways that are counterproductive, and interrupt this inherent, fundamental function of the mind.

In fact, you could argue that it is 'doing something' – thinking about things when in a certain state of mind that prevents it changing automatically. We have all experienced the overthinking associated with analysing a decision, which in turn produces a stuck, procrastinating feeling and a resultant indecision. This 'overdoing something' hinders a natural process and makes something so innate seem so very difficult.

This is quite often perpetuated in groups when they attempt to produce a list of solutions; overthinking, especially if the group is feeling pressured, can result in reinventing the same solutions, or being distracted by too many proposals. These faulty thinking traps are commonly experienced by managers who may feel too close, and that they must make a decision as the most senior on duty – an explicit and implicit expectation.

This pressure and the associated thinking can prevent someone from being wise, or even responsive, in the moment. Getting caught up in all sorts of ways in the moment prevents individuals from tuning in to a deeper clarity of mind. This concept is linked to having the internal resources to effect change, whether these are thoughts, feelings, beliefs or behaviours, and everyone has this propensity.

Therefore, in response to the common misunderstanding, that a person needs 'to do' something to feel better, or think more clearly, the following new proposition is suggested:

There is an inbuilt fundamental but non-personal intelligence in the mind.

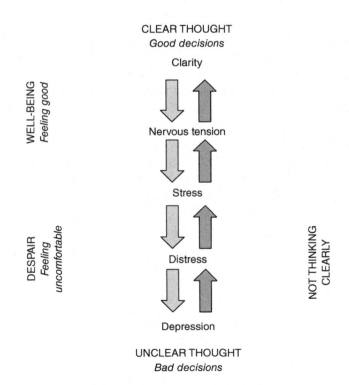

Figure 4.1 Thought

The above is best summarised as shown in Figure 4.1. The quieter the mind, the clearer the thought, and the better the decisions made will be. With it a sense of well-being, feeling good, is evident. In contrast, as the mind gets busier, nervous tension builds into stress, and thinking begins to deteriorate, gradual uncomfortableness is apparent, and bad decisions and unclear thought are the result.

Summary

This chapter presented 'the key challenge' to a better state of mind in the form of thought and feeling masquerading as reality and the resultant reinforced beliefs, for example *'I cannot achieve this . . .'*, *'I cannot do this . . .'*. It introduced three fundamental principles: Mind, Consciousness and Thought. That the concept of our emotions comes from our minds and that these are not separate from thought was discussed. Two commonly held presumptions that our minds accurately reflect the environment (reality) and are steady and separate from thought were therefore challenged.

Mind creates thought, our thought creates feelings, however thought runs its course and is replaced by new thought. Focusing on thought and giving attention to it will keep it in existence longer, when in fact, thought when left alone will simply disappear like clouds. Quite simply we are only dealing with the result of thought and, hence, are free to relate to it however we like. It is this freedom to change our relationship to our experience, state of mind/thought, that allows access to new potential, to escape the momentary limitations of any given experience, or state of mind.

It is the simplicity that is both enabling and fascinating, the challenge hinged, or unhinged, on an ability therefore to see:

- the role of state of mind;

- that the thought creating it is not real;

- that there is an underlying emergent clarity of mind; and therefore

- an individual is one thought away from a clearer mind (an automatic shift of mind).

The human experience and four common misunderstandings were also explored. The assumption, for example, that external factors govern how we think and feel, and that we have no choice, instead is replaced with the powerful notion that experience is a product of the mind, and that individuals experience nothing but the mind.

The second misconception is that thought is real and needs to be dealt with like a 'thing', or an object, and the third is that individuals are therefore the victims of something, when all it is, is thought, and with it the freedom and potential in every moment to change. The final misunderstanding, that a person needs 'to do' something to feel better, or think more clearly, is replaced with a reminder that there is an inbuilt fundamental, non-personal intelligence, or wisdom, in the mind that operates as an innate default setting, or inner natural resilience.

Note

1. The term 'principle' is used to denote characteristics that are fundamental and irreducible aspects of something; the term is not being used to denote any ideological or ethical position.

Chapter 5
Self-leadership: neuroscience implications

Introduction

This chapter examines some of the significant neuroscientific research findings and their implications for self-leadership. All eight facets of self-leadership (self-observation, self-regulation, self-management, self-awareness, self-compassion, social awareness, relationship management and effective communication) will also be cross-referenced throughout with the key identified themes.

The discovery of mirror neurones, for example, and the primal instinctive ability individuals have to naturally achieve rapport (which unfortunately is undermined by busy and judgemental minds) will be presented. We will also examine the important role emotions play in effective communication and how understanding our emotions, our 'hot buttons', can make us better communicators; for instance, being more mindful, fully aware in the present moment, reduces unwanted emotional responses.

We explore Daniel Kahneman's two thinking systems (fast and slow) in detail and how being prone to certain unconscious biases impacts our thinking in a number of undesirable ways. The brain–body connection and the importance of brain plasticity in changing self will be examined, together with leadership blind spots, the negative impact of multitasking, the very caustic implications of adversarial stress and the vital role of self-awareness in self-management and resilience. Mindful interventions will be proposed and reducing meandering conversations into more productive, brain-oriented, effective communication will be outlined.

Emotional intelligence and the consequences of resonant and dissonant leadership approaches will be investigated. The role of empathy in our thinking and the need for both cognitive reasoning and empathy to make more rounded decisions will also be further discussed.

David Rock's SCARF model, developed from extensive neuroscience research in the field, will be examined in the context of change. The threat impact on the brain, in particular of change, and how to reduce the adversarial consequences and become more resilient by using the SCARF model will be presented.

The importance of mirror neurones

Giacomo Rizzolatti, Vittorio Gallese and Leonardo Fogassi, as part of a team of Italian neuro-scientists from the University of Parma in the early 1990s, discovered mirror neurones. This was a watershed moment, described by the neuroscientist Vilayanur Ramachandran as comparable to the discovery of DNA. The Italian team identified mirror neurones quite by accident while observing monkeys' brains. They noticed that, when a monkey watched another monkey or scientist reach out and grab for a raisin or nut, the same areas in the brain responded. In other words, they reacted in the same way in their brains as their counterpart picking up the food. They found that this intentional action by one monkey produced a mirror response in a second monkey – that in certain brain regions 'doing and seeing, may actually be the same' (Keysers, 2011, p14). Invariably, understanding inten-tion in another has important social and learning implications. The discovery of human mirror neurones soon followed (Rizzolatti et al., 2002).

This impressive anticipatory reaction when observing somebody else has powerful implications. Mirror neurones allow us to 'mirror the behaviour and emotions of the people surrounding us' (Keysers, 2011, p10), which assists in the extraordinary capac-ity humans have for empathy (Ramachandran, 2011; Lieberman, 2013), with empathy being the 'ability to appreciate others' points of view and share their experiences' (Ward, 2010, p351).

The moment someone sees a person's pain they share it; 'a little bit of you becomes me, and a little bit of me becomes you' (Keysers, 2011, p221). Ramachandran (2009) describes the impact of watching someone being touched on the arm and the mirror effect this can have. He suggests that the receptors in our skin detect that we are not actually being touched; implicitly we can be empathetic but not actually experience the touch. However, if our arm was anaesthetised so there were no sensations, and we watched someone being touched on the arm, we would feel the touch.

He goes on to propose that all that is separating individuals is essentially their skin; if you removed the skin, you would experience that person's touch in your mind, dissolv-ing the barriers 'between you and other human beings' (Ramachandran, 2009). If some-one is poked on the thumb with a needle, the anterior cingulate region (an area near the front of the brain that responds to pain) of the other person watching will react, and the observer neurones in this area will also fire – but only a subset of approximately 20 per cent (Ramachandran, 2009, 2011).

Ramachandran bases this understanding on neuroscience and studying phantom limb pain and described the impact of touch. If an individual has lost an arm and experiences phantom pain, and then observes somebody else being touched on the arm, the individ-ual will feel it in their phantom limb. If, in turn, they massage another person's arm, it can relieve the pain in their own phantom limb.

Indeed, Ramachandran (2009) would go as far as to say we are 'connected not just via Facebook and the Internet', but 'actually quite literally connected by our neurones', and there are whole chains of neurones surrounding us, talking to each other. 'Thus the response properties of mirror neurones disregard the distinction between self and other' (Ward, 2010, p165). However, it is thought a deficiency in mirror neurones may be linked to autism.

What are the implications for self-leadership?

Lieberman (2013, pix) suggests that 'we are wired to be social', and that mirror neurones create connection and mutual dependence (Iacoboni, 2009). 'Empathy neurones' has become the associated term, and they mediate 'our capacity to share the meaning of actions, intentions, feelings and emotions with others' (Pavlovich and Krahnke, 2014). This is an unconscious reality, a natural response. What gets in the way is us, our busy mind states of preoccupation, irritation and stress, as examples. The importance of self-observation and self-regulation as facets of self-leadership is appreciating in the moment when this may be occurring, how we are responding and adjusting as appropriate.

Much has been made of the importance of rapport building in terms of the resultant effectiveness or otherwise of communication (Hayes, 2006; Wake, 2010), with rapport described by Knight (2009, p379) as the 'ability to relate to yourself and others in ways that create a climate of respect, trust and cooperation'. Brooks (1989, p19) associates rapport with the concept that 'people like people who are like themselves'. However, to be in rapport does not mean you have to agree with someone. An indication of being in rapport is that the individual provides information that can often be personal information, which was not originally requested.

Artificially matching someone's body language and deliberately mirroring their posture and gestures have been suggested as the remedy for creating excellent rapport in all aspects of communication. Significantly, however, the important message is that rapport is a natural unconscious default mode we can easily slip into, and therefore this is about simply tuning in, relaxing and being open without the preoccupation of judgement or self-importance getting in the way.

In Chapter 3 we highlighted McGonigal's (2013) focus on the specific importance of human connection and its role in supporting resilience. Oxytocin is the neuropeptide involved, and Zak et al. (2005) have shown that, when someone receives an intentional and perceptible signal of trust from another, the brain automatically releases this chemical. Oxytocin not only makes an individual more willing to help and support others, but it also has a restorative impact on the body, specifically the cardiovascular system, protecting it from the effects of stress as it strengthens the heart (McGonigal, 2013). It also has a natural anti-inflammatory effect, helping blood vessels to stay relaxed during stress. Connecting with others when under stress, McGonigal (2013) suggests, will actually help someone to recover faster from its effects. Creating trusting connections with others is an important feature of self-leadership and, in turn, has a symbiotic influence on the facet of self-management, being able to self-regulate against the effects of stress by tapping into an inbuilt resilience.

The discovery of mirror neurones, therefore, links to the importance of connection, the need to be able to appreciate and anticipate what others are experiencing. Like mirror neurones, our emotions play an important role in how we interact with others.

The role of emotions

This section will demonstrate that emotions perform an integral role in shaping our social interactions and the way we self-lead. Emotions can have an impact both consciously and unconsciously. Subjective feelings are the result of conscious awareness of emotions, while threats are detected more quickly on an unconscious level. Damasio (1999, p42) makes the distinction that the term 'feelings' ought to 'be reserved for the private, mental experience of an emotion', while 'the term emotion should be used to designate the collection of responses many of which are publicly observable'. He states: 'Emotions are complicated collections of chemical and neural responses, forming a pattern; all emotions have some kind of regulatory role to play' (Damasio, 1999, p51).

The emotional network within the brain is called the limbic system, with the amygdala, an almond-shaped mass of grey matter, a particularly important area in the system involved in fear management. Like the hippocampus behind it, the amygdala is believed to play a significant role in the emotional content of memories (Richardson et al., 2004). The limbic system as a whole determines how we feel in each moment, playing often an unconscious role in our behaviour (Rock, 2009).

Mood, in contrast, arises as a result of 'situations in which a particular emotion occurs frequently or continuously' (Ward, 2010, p337). When a mood lasts longer it becomes a 'temperament', which produces habitual expression of an emotion that lasts for weeks or months and can eventually turn into a 'personality trait' (Dispenza, 2012, p89).

Dolan (2011) suggests a hierarchical system and talks about low-level emotions such as 'fear and disgust', to the more complex emotions of 'regret and pride'. Ekman (2003) identified seven universal emotions and their corresponding facial expressions:

- anger
- sadness
- contempt
- surprise
- disgust
- joy
- fear.

These seven span all diverse cultures and are detectable often as micro-expressions that cannot be disguised (Ekman, 2003). By the age of seven most children are able to determine unconsciously other people's emotions (Keysers, 2011). Being human is about recognising emotional states in the faces of others. However, approximately 10 per cent of the population suffer from a condition called alexithymia, which is characterised by difficulties in interpreting emotional expressions in self and others, including people's faces. Serani (2014) calls it 'emotional blindness', which can also feature a limited, or rigid, imagination.

Damasio (1999, p36) reminds us that we are not always conscious of all our feelings and provides the examples of suddenly becoming anxious or angry, or bursting into tears. He makes three distinctions in terms of emotions and feelings (p37), processing along a continuum:

1. a state of emotion – which can be triggered unconsciously;

2. a state of feeling – which can be represented unconsciously;

3. a state of feeling made conscious.

In other words, we cannot always feel our emotions consciously and some feelings are also not consciously discernible. However, Ekman (2003) would remind us that these leak out as external markers in voice tone and non-verbal expression.

Repetition creates 'cognitive ease' and a 'comforting feeling', according to Kahneman (2011, p66). He also reports that, in experiments to determine intuitive performance, if individuals were asked to think of happy events in their lives before a test, they more than doubled the accuracy of their responses: implicitly, when in a good mood individuals become more intuitive (Kahneman, 2011, p69). Dr Mark Beeman, cited by Rock (2009, p80), also suggests there is a 'strong correlation' between emotional states and insight, specifically, 'increasing happiness increases the likelihood of insight', while anxious states have the opposite impact. Interestingly, Rock (2009, p81) reports that Beeman was able to identify in his experiments those individuals who had more insights as people who had an increased 'awareness of their internal experience', that is, an ability to observe their own thinking, changing how they think and being able to quieten their minds when required. Insights are an important part of problem solving, especially in finding creative and innovative solutions.

People also use their emotions in judgements, in reasoning and in decision making (Damasio, 1994). This has important implications, which will be discussed in the next section in terms of the two systems of consciousness and unconsciousness (or non-consciousness).

We all have our own 'hot buttons that can trigger limbic system arousal' (Rock, 2009, p107). These have been created through life experiences; flagged as dangerous, they provide an alert response, but over-arousal for either real or imagined dangers results in the limbic system responding, which can actually impair the brain from functioning. Rock (2009, p108) provides the example of an increase in adrenalin as the result of the limbic system being activated unconsciously. This might make someone feel focused and potentially more confident in their decision making, when in fact their ability to make good decisions has actually been downgraded.

An over-arousal of the limbic system reduces the resources available to the prefrontal cortex (Rock, 2009; Kahneman, 2011). This means that all functions – the ability to comprehend, to memorise, to learn, to decide – are impeded. According to Rock (2009), it is remarkably easy to arouse the limbic system. He cites a study which demonstrated that even seeing smiling faces versus frowning faces impacted the prefrontal cortex performance, with smiling faces positively improving functioning (Rock, 2009, p108).

Once an emotion is in your conscious awareness, Rock (2009, p111) suggests, we have three options:

- express the emotion;

- suppress the expression (holding the feelings in);

- cognitive change.

Expressing the emotion in its fullness, for example crying with rage or upset, would not be conducive to work interactions, particularly with service users.

With the second option, Rock cites the work of James Gross from Stanford University. Gross found that people who tried to suppress a negative emotional experience were unable to do so; invariably 'trying not to feel something doesn't work'. Worst still, when someone tries to suppress an emotion, their memory of the encounter becomes impaired, and furthermore any witnesses seeing the occurrence experience a rise in blood pressure and discomfort. 'Suppression' therefore adversely impacts the individual and any observers (Lieberman, 2013, p218).

With the third option, cognitive change, Gross describes two approaches: *labelling* the emotion – (I am angry); and *reappraisal* – changing the interpretation of the event. Increasing the arousal of the prefrontal cortex, by labelling the emotion, implicitly can reduce and calm down the limbic response, for there is a pendulum effect: when the limbic system is aroused, the prefrontal cortex, the cognitive thinking part of the brain, is adversely impacted and vice versa.

Often, talking about feelings is something purposely avoided, especially in the work environment, for talking about emotions can be perceived as 'not the done thing'. The importance here is how this is accomplished; choosing one or two words to express the emotion will engage the prefrontal cortex, rather than dwelling on and debating about it, which can increase the emotional response (Rock, 2009; Lieberman, 2013). According to Lieberman (2013, p219) pre-schoolers who are able to 'describe their feelings have fewer emotional outbursts, get better grades and are more popular with their peers'. This 'affect' labelling therefore 'regulates our emotions and thus appears to be a kind of implicit self-control' (Lieberman, 2013, p220).

'Reappraisal is the more cerebral approach', according to Lieberman (2013, p216), and involves our ability to see things differently, 'to consider a new perspective that changes how we experience something that is upsetting to us'. He quotes Bower et al. (2007), who state that 'our reality derives from the stories we tell ourselves – at least the ones we believe' (Lieberman, 2013, p217). It is about reframing, about standing back and seeing an objective and different interpretation – being the scientist, the observer, asking 'what is missing here for me to understand better?', and remaining all the while curious and accepting.

Farb et al. (2010, 2012) would suggest an alternative approach by focusing on the present-moment experience, getting individuals to put their attention on the sensation, for example, of taking a deep breath and feeling what this feels like, rather than complete any cognitive re-evaluation or intervention. This process engages interoceptive awareness (Farb et al., 2012). Interoception is described by Cameron (2002, p3) as synonymous with a 'sensory-perceptual process for events occurring inside the body', and how we recognise and discern these bodily sensations and feelings. We therefore have an inbuilt capability to quieten ourselves down, which can be as simple as taking a deep breath while being fully aware of how this feels within the body (Seppala, 2012).

What are the implications for self-leadership?

Being able to have a quiet mind therefore further enhances our abilities to deactivate the amygdala, to be able to think clearly. Indeed, Creswell, cited by Rock (2009, p114), found that the 'more mindful an individual is, the more of the brain is involved' naturally in this deactivation process.

Mindfulness in this instance is full awareness ('direct experience') in the present moment, not day-dreaming, which can be the so-called 'default setting' (Rock, 2009, p93). Indeed, Farb et al. (2010, p25) found that individuals who received mindfulness training not only were able to recover from emotional challenges, but also developed an increased tolerance and resilience.

As leaders of self it is important to be able to regulate (self-regulate) our emotions particularly when necessary, not only to influence good emotions to improve our insight and intuition abilities, but also to be able to recover from emotional setbacks. Remember that more insights and creativity occur when we are relaxed and happy (Rock, 2009). Expressing emotion in the form of feeling words not only helps in terms of self-leadership and managing work stressors, but also positively impacts others around. Furthermore, encouraging individuals to express their emotions in one or two words can also impact positively a group or team, thus allowing more creative and fruitful exchanges. Avoiding conflict and suppressing emotion are common features of difficult management situations, and yet these states can ironically unconsciously, and adversely, negatively affect the overall result. Remember, therefore, that trying to suppress an adverse emotional response will only make it worse.

The important facet of self-leadership, self-awareness and the ability to observe and be aware in the moment in an objective way takes some emotional heat out of situations and therefore allows a quicker recovery. Becoming more self-aware lets you deeply understand that 'You are what you are, you are where you are, and you are who you are because of what you believe about yourself' (Dispenza, 2012, p111).

Beliefs are the thoughts we have accepted as true, which in turn impact our version of reality, consciously or unconsciously (Dispenza, 2012). Becoming self-aware of the thinking associated with a particular feeling begins to allow us to understand our actual state of mind and potential habitual patterns of thinking, appreciating whether these are helpful or unhelpful.

Being aware of the thoughts and the attached emotions is as much about realising that many thoughts are simply thoughts that we have identified too much with and paid too much attention to. Being self-aware is 'like being tapped on the shoulder and reminded that we have a choice' (Fenner, 2007, p82) – a choice to let go of the thought and the story we are telling ourselves and with it the impact it is having on our state of mind.

Dispenza (2012, p243) describes 'a repetitive cycle of thinking and feeling, feeling and thinking', which can have a habitual element to it. Regurgitating thought, Begley (2009, p35) cites the Canadian psychologist Donald Hebb, who in 1949 first suggested that 'cells that fire together wire together', which became Hebb's law. This means that, if you keep firing the same neural synapses (nerve cells) through the same habitual ways of thinking and feeling, they will become quicker at firing together and therefore become 'hardwired' (Dispenza, 2012, p45), resulting in an automatic unconscious reactive way of responding. As Chödrön (2001, p57) states, 'most of us keep strengthening our negative habits and therefore sow the seeds of our own suffering'. She advises that:

> It is possible to move through the drama of our lives without believing so earnestly in the character that we play. That we take ourselves so seriously, that we are so absurdly important in our own minds, is a problem for us. We feel justified in being annoyed with everything. We feel justified in denigrating ourselves, or in feeling that we are more clever than other people. Self-importance hurts us, limiting us to the narrow world of our likes and dislikes . . . we end up never satisfied.

> (Chödrön, 2001, p28)

This self-importance and ability to recognise other people's faults rather than our own is captured in the next section, along with the psychology behind thinking biases and how intuition and our very human need to avoid loss can result adversely in mistakes being made in our thinking, judgements and subsequent decision making.

Two systems: a model for understanding thinking

The famous psychologist and Nobel Laureate in Economics, Daniel Kahneman, in his book *Thinking Fast and Slow* (2011), defines two thinking systems, a dual process model. He describes:

- *System 1* – the fast system, which is instinctive, intuitive and based on emotions and habits;

- *System 2* – slower, controlled, rational, analytical and more effortful (see Table 5.1).

According to Kahneman (2011, p24), 'System 1 runs automatically in the background generating impressions, intuitions, intentions and feelings; if endorsed by System 2, impressions and intuitions turn into beliefs, and impulses turn into voluntary actions.'

Table 5.1 System 1 and System 2 (Kahneman, 2011)

System 1 (Thinking fast)	System 2 (Thinking slow)
Effortless	Effortful mental activities
Intuition	Rational/reasoning
Automatic	Deliberate
Patterns	Orderly steps
Threats, esp. in voice tone	Conscious reasoning
Recognises objects	Relies on evidence
Feelings – impressions	Self-criticism
Unconscious	Conscious

Most of what we think and do therefore comes from System 1; according to Kahneman (2011, p13), it is the 'secret author of many of the choices and judgements' we make and is always on. Indeed, System 2 requires more glucose to function and therefore slows thinking down; Kahneman (2011, p21) describes this process as an 'effortful' activity. It is this system that is involved in self-control.

In contrast, System 1 is making decisions unconsciously and quickly based on impressions and emotions; 'it is a machine for jumping to conclusions' (Kahneman, 2011, p85). It can, therefore, oversimplify – 'what you see is all there is'; implicitly, we disregard what we do not know; although able to make some sense from incomplete information, System 1 is bad at dealing with statistical information required to make the right decisions (Kahneman, 2011, p86). Table 5.2 identifies some of the potential biases System 1 is prone to falling foul of.

A loss aversion can mean that we will take even more risks if we believe that there will be a net loss. With a branch of Economics dedicated to Behavioural Economics, it is easy to realise why these considerations in a finance system can make it vulnerable. The work of Professor Laurie Santos with capuchin monkeys has shown that this risk, loss aversion, as a poor strategy, could be 35 million years old. Although we might have these 'biological limitations', what Santos (2010) suggests is that knowing and being aware we have these limitations is an important component in overcoming them.

Table 5.2 Potential biases, System 1 (Kahneman, 2011)

Type of bias	Description and example
Anchoring effect	Making a decision that is actually influenced by recently acquired information.
	Example: judges had been asked to roll a die and then decide an appropriate sentence for a given offender (the die was loaded). The judges gave differing periods related to the number they rolled on the die. In other words the number rolled became the anchor (p125).
Loss aversion (prospect theory)	We fear losing more than winning, so our intuition will guide us often to make the wrong choice.
	Example: 'These negotiations are going nowhere because both sides find it difficult to make concessions, even when they can get something in return'; losses outweigh larger gains (p299).
Sunk-cost fallacy	'Throwing good money after bad'– this is the intuitive decision to invest more resources into a losing situation.
	Example: driving into a blizzard because you've paid for tickets to see a game (p345).
Bias to believe	Believing can often be an automatic response and once someone believes it is much harder to unbelieve. In addition, when System 2 is kept busy, 'we will believe almost anything' (p81).
Confirmatory bias	The tendency to translate information to support preconceived beliefs and ideas.
	Example: we seek information or data to prove what we already believe and have decided (p81).
Affect heuristic	If we emotionally feel a decision is right we ultimately believe it is a good decision.
	Example: 'He likes the project, so he thinks its costs are low and its benefits are high' (p104).
Halo effect	If you like one thing about an individual you are more likely to like everything about them. First impressions therefore can become important.
Optimistic bias	Optimism can be a good thing; however, being overoptimistic can introduce bias.
	Example: 'the evidence suggests that an optimistic bias plays a role – sometimes the dominant role – whenever individuals or institutions voluntarily take on significant risk' (p256).

The 'remembering self' will override the 'experiencing self'. Kahneman (2011, p381) provides the example of someone listening to a long and beautiful symphony on a disc that was scratched near the end – which the listener reported ruined the whole thing, when in fact it was only the end that was spoilt. There are particular implications when making decisions for memories play an essential role in this process. The 'remembering self', however, can distort and exaggerate, and its 'susceptibility to hindsight' can generate altered memories of real events (Kahneman, 2011, p409). Individuals identify with the remembering self and are connected strongly to their stories. Overconfidence and an exaggerated sense of how well we understand the world can be the result. Kahneman (2011, p152) suggests, however, that frowning will alert System 2 and reduces 'both the overconfidence and the reliance on intuition' of System 1.

What of expert intuition? Kahneman (2011) suggests that rapid-feedback environments, together with practice, help to produce expert intuition that could be relied upon.

Firefighters, anaesthetists and paediatric nurses are some examples of those using expert intuition that can be described as reliable (Kahneman, 2011).

What are the implications for self-leadership?

Kahneman (2011) identifies that biases are predictable and therefore importantly, as leaders, we should become more acquainted with our own potential biases. There is also a natural conflict between intuition and logic; however, in order to make more rounded, informed decisions we need to be aware that intuition, especially if we are tired, distracted or lacking blood glucose, will potentially trump logic. Taking breaks and getting enough sleep are obvious remedies, and awareness of what part of the day we function best and dedicating difficult tasks to this time slot is more productive.

Here we really see the importance of self-observation, self-management and self-regulation, for if we focus on one thing, we can become blind to other things happening around us. Remember, just because something has been repeated many times does not mean we do not need to think it through. In busy environments it is important not to make quick decisions, based just on a good feeling about something. It is essential to take appropriate time and not be bulldozed into quick decisions.

Confirmation bias can be the most pervasive in that we can ignore significant information if it does not confirm what we believe. Instead, obtaining as much data, from as many independent evidence sources as possible, will help to negate this potential bias.

Thus, slowing down as a leader, to be in a better state of mind as we have discussed earlier, in order to encourage the rational System 2 to be more involved rather than allowing it to simply accept System 1 thinking, will improve decision-making processes.

While Kahneman's (2011) Systems 1 and 2 are fictitious characters in his book, for there are no parts of the brain labelled purely System 1 and System 2, he shares a considerable wealth of research and evidence base to support a lifetime of work in understanding how we think and therefore make decisions.

From childhood we have had lifetimes of developing beliefs and assumptions that become unconscious patterns that guide us. The next section sheds some light on how this happens and how the brain's natural neuroplasticity and maturational ability is so forgiving. Some of the structural realities that have important implications for leaders will be explored.

The brain

This section will examine briefly the brain and more of what we know about the brain's two functions, which have important implications in terms of self-leadership: the unconscious (sometimes called the non-conscious, or subconscious) and the conscious systems. According to Gazzaniga (2012):

> *The current view of the brain is that its large-scale plan is genetic, but specific connections at the local level are activity-dependent and a function of epigenetic factors and experience: Both nature and nurture are important.*

The brain constitutes 2 per cent of the body's total weight (approximately 3lbs, or 1.5kg), yet consumes approximately 20 per cent of the body's energy in the form of glucose and oxygen, both of which it cannot store. This has important implications in terms of how the two systems have evolved. Concentrating, which is a conscious activity, requires significant amounts of glucose and oxygen, which are carried in the blood. Many responses the brain makes are therefore automatic and unconscious. The brain can live without oxygen for approximately 4–6 minutes; however, 10 minutes results in permanent damage. There are 100,000 miles of blood vessels in the brain.

Today functional magnetic resonance imaging (fMRI) can detect blood flow to the brain. Quite simply blood flows to the parts of the brain that are most active. Positron emission tomography (PET) scans involve injecting an individual with a radioactive substance that attaches itself to glucose, showing specific take-up in the brain. When awake the brain produces enough electricity to power a 12–20 watt light bulb.

The brain is encased by 22 joining bones and is made up of approximately 86 billion neurones (nerve cells) and glial cells, which perform an important role in the homeostasis of the brain. Interestingly, 69 billion neurones are found in the cerebellum, a small configuration at the back of the brain that helps refine motor control (Gazzaniga, 2012). There are reported to be many more glial cells; Birey (2013) suggests 90 per cent are glial cells, which he believes play a special function in mood disorders. According to Birey (2013), less is known about glial cells than neurone activity. These cells, however, play a key role in immune signalling and are implicated in issues ranging from epilepsy through to stress and depression (Dr Mark Hutchinson, cited by McKay, 2014).

Neurones process information and continue to be made throughout life in response to mental activity. Previously, it had been wrongly believed that early in life the brain cells are fixed and that adults lose these cells and experience a deterioration in their function (Blakemore and Frith, 2005; Begley, 2009). According to Ernst et al. (2014), certain neurones in the brain involved in movement and cognition are renewed continuously. The hippocampus is one example: a pair of seahorse-like arrangements in the brain's temporal lobes, importantly involved in the memory and social memory (Hitti and Siegelbaum, 2014).

Keverne (2004) describes the prolonged period of time full human brain development takes as fundamental to understanding individual distinctions. For most of brain development is a postnatal feature, with significant restructuring changes occurring in adolescence and the frontal lobes continuing to develop into early adulthood. The frontal lobes are in control of higher-level activities such as planning and conscious emotional management.

Most of the processing in the brain, however, is occurring 'unconsciously and automatically' (Gazzaniga, 2012). Automaticity can also be acquired, for example, by practising, driving, typing or playing a musical instrument (and soon these can all be carried out unconsciously without thinking); this ability makes us more efficient (Gazzaniga, 2012).

Every time a person has a new thought they are creating connections within their brain and this is a lifelong capability (Blakemore and Frith, 2005; Medina, 2008). It is a myth that we only use 10 per cent of our brains (McKay, 2014). On learning something for the first time new synapses are created, and in order to retain information the synapses need to remain stable for long periods of time, even a lifetime (Meyer et al., 2014).

However, Dennett (2013) cites the work of Mike Merzenich, who sutured together a monkey's fingers and showed how the part of the cortex that represented the two individual digits soon contracted, ensuring that the area could be used for other things. Removing the stitches resulted in a return of the normal function of the cortex. Doidge (2007, p210) refers to the experiments Alvaro Pascual-Leone devised, which involved blindfolding individuals. Within two days the 'visual cortex' began processing 'tactile and auditory signals'. The impact was reversed within 12 to 24 hours following removal of the blindfold. What the experiments show is the versatility of the brain and also the fact that to some extent we must 'use it or lose it' (Blakemore and Frith, 2005, p128).

The ability of the brain to continually adapt has been named 'plasticity' (Blakemore and Frith, 2005; Begley, 2009). '*Plasticity* refers to the brain's ability to change as a result of experience and whilst greatest during childhood, plasticity persists throughout life' (Ward, 2010, p181).

Despite the capacity of the brain to be able to adapt and change (which we will return to shortly), the system is governed by two overarching features: reward and threat. The brain on both an unconscious and conscious level is ever vigilant for threats in the environment, to keep us safe. It is also pleasure seeking; therefore, these two governing aspects dictate the so-called operating system (Gordon, cited by Rock, 2008, p1):

- to move away from threats – avoid;

- to move towards rewards – pleasure.

Therefore, minimising danger and maximising reward are the organising principles especially within the limbic system, constantly making 'towards' and 'away from' decisions unconsciously, approximately 'half a second before you are consciously aware of them, if you become aware of them at all' (Rock, 2009, p105).

Leadership blind spots

Heffernan, in her book *Wilful Blindness* (2011, p17), discusses the development of 'stereotypes' as 'energy saving devices', or unconscious shortcuts – the need to want to belong, to follow a known 'set of rules' and to find 'people who make us feel comfortable, people like us' (Heffernan, 2011, p11). What this does, however, is to potentially exclude others and stop us really seeing what is happening. She quotes an ongoing study, which examined over 4.5 million people and showed that more than 80 per cent of individuals had a bias against the elderly and 70 per cent associated science more with men than women; the study included people from 34 different countries (Heffernan, 2011, p17).

Indeed, Banaji and Greenwald (2013) confirm that research on the unconscious has significantly changed how human behaviour is understood, that we have real 'blind spots'. Heffernan (2011) described the pervasiveness of the familiar, the similar feeling comfortable and most importantly safe. The worst version of it is 'group think', described by Garratt (2010, p44) in his book *The Fish Rots from the Head*. The pervasive nature of this leads to 'a propensity to yield under pressure', not to say, to avoid being the odd one out. Further discussion within this chapter regarding the work of David Rock and his SCARF model will explain the neuroscience of why this happens and the insidious impact of 'in- and out-group' scenarios, which can become leaders' blind spots, and the 'way we do things around here'. Invariably science suggests we are wired to belong, so we do not challenge and we avoid conflict, believing it to be something negative to be averted.

Continuous partial attention

Another significant implication is a concept called continuous partial attention (CPA), a phrase coined by Microsoft executive Linda Stone back in 1998. This describes the all-consuming technological surfing we have become accustomed to within busy environments. This involves simultaneously multitasking, with emails announcing their inbox arrival with the familiar heart-sinking ping, text alerts from phones, on-call bleeps, dual work and personal phones, iPads or similar tablets and duplicate calendars – all possibilities to distract and reduce clear thinking, and which can be taken home to continue the distraction.

Ironically, the more tired an individual is the easier it is to become busy being distracted, sucked into the constant interruptions with the impression of being productive. We feel busy; after all, we are doing something. McCartney (2014, p10) advises us to beware of the busy 'badge of honour' types and information overload, for he argues that success is inextricably linked to our attention capability. Rock (2009, p58) suggests that being always on, connected to others via technology, can drop an individual's 'IQ significantly, as much as losing a night's sleep'.

What we do know is, quite emphatically, it is a myth that the brain can multitask, when it comes to more than one cognitive task. Multitasking hinders learning and has disastrous consequences on retention (Davis et al., 2014). The brain 'naturally focuses on concepts sequentially, one at a time' (Medina, 2008, p84), for 'we are biologically incapable of processing attention rich inputs simultaneously' (Medina, 2008, p85).

What compounds this situation is the over-arousal of the limbic centre, which takes resources, in the form of oxygen and glucose, away from the prefrontal cortex, which is required to think rationally and logically, decide, memorise and not overreact (Rock, 2009). Rock (2009) reminds us, however, that with the limbic system aroused you are more liable to react adversely. He suggests that, while the brain is exquisitely powerful, 'even the brain of a Harvard graduate can be turned into that of an eight year old simply by being made to do two things at once' (Rock, 2009, p4).

According to Hamilton (2008), David Meyer at the University of Michigan has spent the past few decades studying multitasking and he reports that:

> For tasks that are at all complicated, no matter how good you have become at multitasking, you're still going to suffer hits against your performance. You will be worse compared to if you were actually concentrating from start to finish on the task.

This is described as causing 'brownout' in the brain, impacting short-term memory, together with potentially pumping adrenalin and other stress hormones into the system, which would further compound blood supply to the prefrontal cortex and adversely impact an individual's response. 'Brownout' in the dictionary is defined as a partial black-out (Oxford Dictionaries, 2011). Difficulties in maintaining concentration levels and being able to solve complex problems result (Kenner and Poldrack, 2009). Satpute et al. (2012) have demonstrated that anxiety and stress significantly impact the hippocampus, which is vital in memory formation. This leads to the crucial impact of stress on the brain.

Stress

Medina (2008, p169) states that 'stressed brains don't learn the same way', and Ilardi (2013) advises that we have replaced 'face time with screen time', when in fact we are 'born to connect'. There is evidence that the fight or flight response, especially over time, is toxic. A certain amount of stress is an essential response, such as we experience before an important meeting, or presenting; however, this is the type of ongoing stress that results in a deterioration in performance, effectiveness and finally our health. Cortisol and adrenalin are the main perpetrators as they help to redirect blood flow away from the vital neural circuitry of the prefrontal cortex. Ilardi (2013) describes the shocking figures that show the rate of depression in current 18–29 year olds in America is 25 per cent and is predicted to be 50 per cent by the time they reach middle age, with a reported one in nine children over the age of 12 suffering from depression.

Stress depletes the available energy for the prefrontal cortex to make rational, thought-through, logical decisions. Brown (2011, p6) makes an important observation that, if 'An organisation is fundamentally running off fear and in the background possibly anger, then a lot of a person's energy is being used in protecting themselves against the organisation.'

According to Dispenza (2012, p45), a vicious circle is potentially realisable, in that, if we keep firing the same neurones by repeating daily habits of thinking and reacting, we are essentially 'hardwiring' the brain and, worse still, making these circuits not only potentially permanent features, but increasing their speed of response. Habitual thinking patterns are the result, with hair-trigger responses. Dispenza (2012, p104) likens it to drinking a triple shot of espresso, which for some people provides an addiction to their problem thinking and their busy lives.

The hippocampus, which helps to regulate the emotions and is the seat of memory, however, becomes adversely affected. Medina (2008, p178) describes one study in which adults who were stressed performed 50 per cent worse on certain cognitive tests than their counterparts who were not stressed.

This, combined with the unconscious alert system primed to spot negative stimuli within the environment, means that a stressed individual can become a victim of this continual cycle and somewhere along the line lose their sense of perception and themselves. Furthermore, an important area of the brain that is adversely affected by stress is the 'language circuits in the frontal lobes which become less active' (Newberg and Waldman, 2012, p10). According to Newberg and Waldman (2012, p10), research in communication demonstrates that 'stress and tension' show up as identifiable tension in the face and 'voice tone', which can, in turn, create mistrust in individuals. Others would add the ever growing scientific research into the adverse impact on the immune system (Medina, 2008). Although, according to Southwick and Charney (2012, p14), initially cortisol has the temporary effect of 'bolstering the immune system', this, however, may explain why, after weeks of working in a stressed busy environment, as soon as you go on holiday you become ill.

Dispenza (2012), however, suggests that the very neuroplasticity of the brain allows individuals to bring this purposefully into play to change regurgitated and harmful stressful thinking habits. The stress response can be simply switched on by thought alone, for the brain cannot distinguish between a real threat and simply worrying, so potentially it has the same negative bodily consequences. Dispenza (2012, p111) therefore suggests becoming more self-aware to inhibit unwanted states of mind and body. With the ability to observe self we therefore have the capability to decide 'we no longer want to be . . . think, act, and feel' this way, being aware of 'your attention, your unconscious reflexive behaviours and automatic emotional reactions', taking instead conscious control (Dispenza, 2012, p112). You should begin by mental rehearsal of new ways of thinking, of being, which will start to rewire 'yourself neurologically to a new mind' (Dispenza, 2012, p13). As discussed earlier, we have a lifelong neuroplastic capability and all change begins, according to Dispenza (2012, p124), with 'thinking'.

In addition, both Medina (2008) and McGonigal (2013) discuss inbuilt natural systems we can benefit from, to reduce the influence of negative stress. McGonigal (2013), you will recall, recommends connecting with others when stressed and Medina (2008, p179) discusses the 'brain-derived neurotrophic factor (BDNF) as the "Miracle Gro", keeping neurones alive and growing in the presence of hostile action'. However, it is important that not too many stress hormones remain too long in the system, for they will overwhelm this natural defence. In summary, it is not that stress is bad full stop, but too much for too long and negative beliefs about stress can create problems in the long term.

What are the implications for self-leadership?

We were never designed for the sedentary, indoor, sleep-deprived, socially-isolated, fast-food-laden, frenetic pace of modern life.

(Stephen Ilardi, 2013)

The facet of self-awareness is integral to self-leadership and certainly to the four identified areas above: knowing our brain, potential leadership blind spots, the destructiveness of CPA and the very caustic implications of adversarial stress. The purpose of becoming 'self-aware', Dispenza (2012, p112) would suggest, is to 'no longer allow any thought, action, or emotion you don't want to experience to pass by your awareness'.

As leaders we can become fixed in our view that we cannot change; however, as discussed in Chapter 2 individuals who understand themselves better and are able to differentiate their emotional states demonstrate an increased ability to regulate their emotions (Koole et al., 2011) and their resultant thinking and mood. Brain neuroplasticity remarkably allows individuals to change, starting with how they habitually think. Being genuinely happier will improve all aspects of any interaction, including the ability to remember the event more accurately, and also improves the immune system (Lyubomirsky et al., 2005).

Self-management plays an important role, for we know that getting enough sleep has very significant implications, not only in terms of day-to-day functioning and improved memory (Girardeau et al., 2009), but also in terms of long-term consequences relating to mental health (Ilardi, 2013).

Understanding the conscious brain's heavy resource requirements means managing thinking time better, planning and organising, through self-management and self-regulation, and ensuring that as far as feasible and possible your best thinking time is matched to the difficulty of the task. Rock (2009, p18) advises 'scheduling blocks of time for different modes of thinking' and seeing 'thinking as a precious resource'.

Remember that, when tired, individuals become more easily distracted, with irrational thinking, indecisiveness, forgetfulness and procrastination, and these then become the only available resources. Often, however, individuals ignore all the signs and tell themselves they cannot have a break and instead they must push through; and with that decision they have singularly become less effective and productive. This is about sustainability; if we become ill (usually when on holiday) or are less effective, what was the use of taking that extra bit of work home, staying later or going without a break? It makes no sense and, of course, it will always happen to somebody else and not you. Exercising self-compassion is about being at your best potential 'optimal mental and emotional mind-set', to help others in a sustainable way (Neff, 2011, p193). This is saying nothing about the quality of interventions with others when limited resources are unavailable.

Hofman et al. (2011, p219) discuss the important role of the 'working memory in self-regulation especially in terms of attention, thought, emotion and behaviour'. They stress, however, that being motivated to set self-regulation as a goal is fundamental.

Other potential leadership 'blind spots' – the unconscious stereotypes, assumptions, self-limiting beliefs and fears that have been allowed to take root, both consciously and mostly unconsciously – mean self-awareness and self-observation are crucial facets. This includes the importance of diversity and ensuring that, as self-leaders, we are aware of the pervasiveness, particularly in organisations and institutions, of group think and the unconscious bias this can create within any group, being vigilant and self-disciplined to positively search out the diverse. Actively speak to the person who might most annoy you in meetings and remain curious to learn what it could be that he or she can teach you about yourself.

Be mindful of the impact of CPA: what do you regularly put your attention on; are these negative thoughts; does the technology manage you and do you allow it? How can you and your team work together to better manage emails, with the explicit intention of reducing CPA as much as possible for everyone? As a guide, the less we hold in our minds at any one moment the better. Three or four different ideas at once is described by Rock (2009, p31) as the optimal number. Concentrating on one task at a time and not switching between tasks will ensure your limited energy lasts longer. Our attention becomes easily distracted and our minds wander to the default thinking mode; this is the 'lost in thought', unfocused state. Davis et al. (2014, p50) suggests our attention starts to wane and reverts to the default state after about 15–20 minutes and that 'multitasking is the enemy of learning'.

Communication is so fundamental to leadership and effective communication is a clear facet of self-leadership, but, as discussed earlier, stress interferes with communication: 'Language shapes our behaviour, and each word we use is imbued with multitudes of personal meaning' (Newberg and Waldman, 2012, p3). They suggest (2012, p4) the following as strategies of compassionate communication.

- Relax.
- Stay present.
- Cultivate inner silence.
- Increase positivity.
- Reflect on your deepest values.
- Access a pleasant memory.
- Observe non-verbal clues.
- Express appreciation.

- Speak warmly.

- Speak slowly.

- Speak briefly.

- Listen deeply.

Reducing meandering conversations into meaningful 30-second time slots works better for the brain's short-term (working memory), which is estimated to be able to hold 'four chunks' of information for 30 seconds (Newberg and Waldman, 2012, p16). Again, using this as a way to work in teams, starting meetings with each person speaking for 30 seconds, has the advantage of getting individuals to really identify what the key issues are and what they specifically need. Ironically, we can abuse each other's precious mental resources by not being focused and it is so easy for the whole team to fall into this trap. Helping each other in this way will further hardwire this learned approach.

Newberg and Waldman (2012) introduced a technique called the 'breakout principle', used by Herbert Benson of Harvard University, who has spent over 35 years conducting research in the fields of neuroscience and stress (Newberg and Waldman, 2012, p188). Benson (2005, p2) describes this as a 'paradoxical active–passive dynamic', which can regulate the amount of stress and increase performance. This fascinating phenomenon involves pushing yourself as hard as you can on whatever you are doing – immersing yourself in the activity fully, all the time staying aware of your stress levels. As soon as you begin to feel tired, bored, stuck, stressed, angry or irritable, take a break, by doing something completely different, something passive to create a relaxed state. When this occurs it is possible 'to stimulate much higher neurological performance than would otherwise be the case', for activity increases in the areas of the brain associated with 'attention, space-time concepts and decision making' – potentially leading to 'sudden and creative insights' (Benson, 2005, p3).

Individuals can get themselves caught up in trying to be what they think somebody else expects them to be – their boss, colleague, service user, partner or family member. We can end up with many versions of self. However, being our true self takes less energy than trying to be someone we think other people expect us to be.

Neff (2011, p122) discusses the value of being 'aware' of our feelings without being 'hijacked by them'. She talks about the important role of self-compassion and how research shows that the more 'self-compassionate' an individual is the 'more emotionally intelligent' they will be and with it able to maintain 'emotional balance when flustered' (Neff, 2011, p123). This introduces the next section, which looks at the neuroscience behind emotional intelligence and two important concepts for leaders, the resonant and dissonant implications.

Emotional intelligence: primal leadership

The brain is the organ of relationship . . . all effective leadership is about relationship.

(Brown and Hales, 2011, p42)

Boyatzis (2012) and Goleman et al. (2013) talk about the importance of the brain in leadership relationships, implicitly the power of emotional intelligence, and in particular two specific concepts, the resonant and dissonant effects leaders can have on others. This section will explore these concepts, together with the role of emotional intelligence and empathy in leadership. Pavlovich and Krahnke (2014) would suggest that 'empathy commits us to one another through shared connection'. Empathy is further described by Goleman et al. (2013) as a primal feature and something that resonant leaders instinctively achieve, with the ability to tune into others in such a way that makes them feel cared about. There is, therefore, always an emotional component of leadership as a process.

Keysers (2011) would remind us that 'throughout our lives there is virtually no moment in which we don't feel'. We demonstrated earlier the importance of the contagion effect of emotions on an unconscious level and how we naturally 'mirror' these, by feeling sad when with people who are sad, and happy around happy individuals (Keysers, 2011). At work, groups 'catch' feelings from each other in a similar mode (Goleman et al., 2013, p7). Leadership as a process impacts feelings and emotions in much the same unconscious and conscious ways.

When leaders have a positive emotional effect on others, Goleman et al. (2013, p5) describe this as 'resonance', with the opposite defined as 'dissonance'. Having a positive emotional effect on others has clear advantages in terms of productivity, creativity, decision making and even how helpful people will be (Goleman, 2011; Goleman et al., 2013). Damasio (1999) reminds us that emotions and feelings are required to make good rational decisions.

Dissonance, instead, involves leaders using negative emotional influences such as fear, manipulation, a lack of transparency and inauthentic behaviours, for example suggesting one approach for individuals and doing something entirely different. Dissonance is not conducive to good relationships, of bringing the best out of people and teams.

The results of Goleman et al.'s (2013) research studies reveal that the underlying emotional competencies required to achieve 'resonance' are known as emotional intelligence, which is described (2013, p38) as including:

- self-awareness;
- self-management;
- social awareness;
- relationship management.

Self-awareness, as the ability to interpret one's own emotions and their impact, is described as the most important, for to self-manage an individual needs to be self-aware (Goleman et al., 2013, p39). To be socially aware starts with knowing self, and finally to manage relationships with others is based upon fundamentally knowing your impact on others. Implicitly, a 'greater awareness of one's own emotional reactions facilitates access to others' reactions and makes for better empathic understanding' (Kisfalvi, 2014).

Goleman et al. (2013, p39), in terms of social awareness, emphasise the importance of not only empathy but also organisation and service user awareness. What currently are the challenges and what are the needs of these two constituents? Influencing others, developing individuals, being a change catalyst, managing conflict and collaborating are all features of relationship management (Goleman et al., 2013, p39).

Jack et al. (2012) describe the significant impact of the analytical cognitive network, which switches off, to some extent, our ability to tap into our empathetic appreciation of a situation. It is therefore difficult for individuals to be analytical and empathetic at the same time, and vice versa (Pavlovich and Krahnke, 2014). In addition, it is important to remember that emotions are not simply 'fleeting events', for they can be rooted deeply in individuals' personal and early childhood experiences (Kisfalvi, 2014).

What are the implications for self-leadership?

The emotional function of the leader is, therefore, primal and linked strongly to the importance of empathy. Indeed, the title of Pavlovich and Krahnke's (2014) book is *Organizing Through Empathy*, which captures the primary prominence of being able to connect with others through empathy. Empathy not only assists with connecting individuals, it forges effective working relationships in teams and helps to reduce and resolve conflict between individuals (Kisfalvi, 2014).

The author would argue, however, that these capabilities and approaches are integral not just to the single leader but to everyone, as part of exercising self-leadership, being more emotionally intelligent and, with this, demonstrating self-awareness, self-management, social awareness and relationship management. It makes sense for everyone to be exercising in this way, and not simply the leaders.

Being aware that empathetic thinking can switch off cognitive reasoning, and vice versa, is important in evaluating and judging to ensure both are actively considered in order to make better decisions. An awareness of how our emotions can be deeply impacted by our personal formative histories is important in addressing any bias and blind spots we might have in the now. Having this awareness is about being able to address and appreciate more fully habitual ways of reacting to situations.

Lieberman (2013, p4) suggests that the brain 'evolved to experience threats to our social connections in much the same way it experiences physical pain'. This, he suggests, forms a significant evolutionary dynamic by stimulating the same neural network as physical pain: 'our experience of social pain helps to ensure the survival of our children, helping to keep them close to their parents' (Lieberman, 2013, p4).

Rock (2008, p1) describes this as 'relatedness', as part of a model he developed called SCARF (status, certainty, autonomy, relatedness and fairness). The next section will explore the importance of SCARF in how change can adversely impact the brain.

How change can adversely impact the brain

Studies on transformational change suggest that there are poor rates of success; for example, a global IBM study (2008) of more than 1,500 change management executives from 15 countries revealed that the 'majority of organizational change projects fail', with nearly 60 per cent of ventures not meeting the objectives set. This is possibly not surprising if you recollect Roebuck's (2011, p6) paper, discussed in Chapter 2, which suggested that in organisations less than 20 per cent of staff are engaged. Yet another study, Aguirre et al. (2013), found that 84 per cent of 2,200 global participants reported that culture was one of the most important critical success factors in organisational change management. There is something very human about change, for a lot has been written about the latest change processes, and the NHS even has its own change model. However, there seems to be something missing.

Important research in neuroscience recommends that change management should be carried out with the brain in mind (Whiting et al., 2012). They suggest an approach that really gets to the heart of human motivation at both a conscious and unconscious level: the SCARF model. SCARF is a brain-based approach developed in 2008 and informed by neuroscience (Rock, 2008). It was grounded on two important tenets we identified earlier (Gordon, cited by Rock, 2008, p1) that govern our social behaviour:

- minimise threat (avoid);
- maximise reward (approach).

As discussed previously, if an individual senses a threat, it is experienced like pain in the brain, and resources in the form of glucose and oxygen will be diverted to the prefrontal cortex. There are, therefore, fewer resources available for brain activity involving working memory, logical thinking, decision making and also intuition. Rock (2008, p3) suggests that there is a tendency (when the amygdala is activated) 'to generalise more', which increases the possibility of making the wrong connections, and to react 'defensively'. Invariably, any type of change is experienced as discomfort and can help to explain why change is resisted. The brain likes the familiar and takes in information, first cross-referencing it with old familiar experiences/memories.

The 'threat and avoid' response is, therefore, not the best state for collaborating and influencing others; however, during change this is often the default setting within teams (Whiting et al., 2012). Rock (2008) reminds us that the amygdala is more predisposed to respond to threats than rewards and therefore is easily activated.

The 'approach state' is described as more 'closely linked to positive emotions (interest, happiness and joy)' (Rock, 2008, p3). This state is characterised by increased levels of dopamine, wanting to learn, being able to solve problems that require insight, being more able to collaborate with others and, overall, performing better. The brain, for example, responds to being given positive feedback by others in the same way that it responds to financial enticements (Lieberman and Eisenberger, 2008).

The SCARF model includes five domains of human social experience (Rock, 2008, p1).

- *Status* is about the relative importance to others.
- *Certainty* concerns being able to predict the future.
- *Autonomy* provides a sense of control over events.
- *Relatedness* is a sense of safety with others – of friend rather than foe.
- *Fairness* is a perception of fair exchanges between people.

Brain activity gathered by fMRI, PET scans and electroencephalograph (EEG) machines indicates that the neural responses that drive us towards food and away from danger are also impacted in the same way as how we are treated by others. Rock (2008, p1) suggests that the model supports people to more easily remember, and recognise, when these social domains might be adversely impacted. It encourages individuals to be mindful of how their behaviour could be received and interpreted in terms of SCARF. Each of the different domains will be further explored with a particular focus on the impact of change.

Status

Rock (2008, p3) cites Michael Marmot, who suggests that 'status is the most significant determinant of human longevity and health'.

- *Status* is about relative importance in terms of seniority. An individual's status will increase if she or he feels superior to another person. Winning a race, for example, would increase the reward circuitry.

- *Threatened by*: Simply speaking to your manager or someone in higher authority can activate a threat response to status. Being excluded, or being given advice, instructions or simply a suggestion, or feedback can cause a threat response. Appraisals and supervision can therefore generate a threat response.

- *Impact of change*: Senior managers may have more information about planned changes and so feel more comfortable, unable to see why they are impacting on others so adversely. People often do not feel up to speed and therefore their status can be adversely affected.

Certainty

As Whiting et al. (2012, p1) suggest, 'one of the toughest tasks is to maintain employee engagement and motivation in the midst of uncertainty'. In addition, as Rock (2008, p4) suggests, the 'brain's pattern-recognition machine . . . is constantly trying to predict the near future . . . it craves certainty', for uncertainty takes resources to determine what is happening.

- *Certainty* is knowing or being able to predict what the future will be like.

- *Threatened by*: Any form of incongruency creates a certainty threat; for example, not knowing job expectations, with restructuring or potential redundancy as bigger threats.

- *Impact of change*: Any change will impact certainty the most.

Autonomy

Autonomy and certainty can be interlinked, for more autonomy can produce a greater sense of certainty.

- *Autonomy* is having choices and options and being in control of these. It is having the sense of being able to escape.

- *Threatened by*: Simply working in a team can threaten autonomy, according to Rock (2008). Micro-management, directing and telling are all approaches that threaten autonomy.

- *Impact of change*: Not being involved in a change and not being involved in any communication about a planned change impact autonomy severely.

Relatedness

Significantly, but not surprisingly, the brain is influenced by an instinctive need to relate to others. Bosman's *How Your Brain Fights for Social Survival in the Workplace* (2012) captures in its title the essence and importance of a basic social precedence. The current lack of trust in organisational leaders identified by the Chartered Institute of Personnel and Development (CIPD, 2014) threatens both certainty and relatedness.

- *Relatedness* involves deciding whether others belong to the 'in-group' or 'out-group'. A sense of belonging characterises relatedness – friend or foe. We like people who are like us. It involves being safe with others.

- *Threatened by*: Being excluded or not included threatens relatedness. Even not being mentioned at a meeting can evoke a sense of threat.

- *Impact of change*: It can create 'in-group' and 'out-group' biases. Managers can often end up in the 'out-group' as they are seen as belonging to other groups. This adversely impacts relatedness and trust. It can also importantly impact the culture of the organisation, with failed change programmes having an ongoing ripple effect within organisations.

Fairness

Interestingly, it has been found that fairness is an important feature in activating empathy in men, for if someone was perceived to be 'bad', men would respond by being less empathetic towards them, whereas women were more motivated by 'their care for other people' (Lieberman, 2013, p132). Therefore men can be motivated more by justice as a driving force.

- *Fairness* also involves perceived unfairness. Simply a lack of ground rules and clarity about expectations can threaten the sense of fairness. Unfairness is the unfair treatment of others.

- *Threatened by*: Being treated differently is a threat to fairness.

- *Impact of change*: It can create a culture of mistrust where collaboration is difficult. People who feel that someone, or something, is unfair will feel less empathy.

There can be individual differences across the SCARF model; for example, someone may be more impacted by certainty, and another by a strong sense of fairness. Whiting et al. (2012, p5) also suggest counteracting the total threat response across all five domains by 'creating rewards in other SCARF' areas.

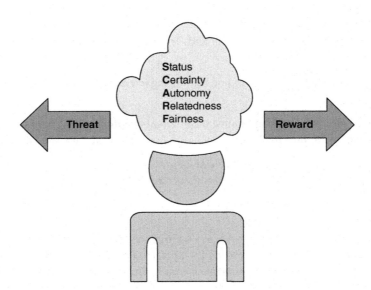

Status
Certainty
Autonomy
Relatedness
Fairness

Threat

Reward

Figure 5.1 The SCARF model

What are the implications for self-leadership?

Knowledge of the SCARF model is clearly extremely useful; especially in change management, knowing the drivers that can cause a threat response is especially advantageous – being able to create 'toward' states in individuals by getting them to 'feel safe enough to think about the future' (Whiting et al., 2012, p2). Rock (2008, p7) reminds us that the 'SCARF model provides a robust scientific framework for building self-awareness and awareness of others amongst leaders'. It helps individuals, therefore, to be able to observe the SCARF implications being played out in meetings and for leaders to understand their own SCARF preferences. Individuals are able to use self-observation and social-awareness facets to appreciate the applicability of SCARF in all activities and how best to respond.

The facets of self-regulation, self-awareness, relationship management and effective communication all have relevancy in terms of the SCARF model. Managing your own state and being aware of the quality of your thinking, particularly when involved in difficult conversations, is an important implication. Being able to better manage the default network (our wandering minds) through improving the focus of our attention will increase each individual's capability to take in more information, particularly potentially difficult news about changes, and to augment relatedness with others. Remember that change can adversely impact and trigger responses in others that actually decrease their effectiveness, efficiency and productivity.

In terms of change and the SCARF model, each of the areas has been re-examined below to improve the five domains, starting with status.

Status
Reducing the impact of a threat on status would be to encourage individuals to provide themselves with feedback (Rock, 2008). Increasing opportunities for others to learn and giving positive feedback will improve status. Including everyone is important in all change. Encourage and facilitate individuals to come up with their own insights in relation to a change (Whiting et al., 2012), avoiding focusing only on the negatives and creating opportunities to praise and reward positive behaviours.

Certainty
Simply breaking things down for people, providing information and communicating are all ways to improve certainty. Making agreements about when to meet, and for how long, will increase certainty. Helping individuals create mental maps of the future with their roles identified will improve the sense of clarity and certainty.

Autonomy
Self-driven learning opportunities and managing their own diaries and duty rotas can improve individuals' autonomy. Involve individuals in compiling agendas and encourage individuals to identify goals in relation to the change and what their specific role might be.

Relatedness
Create opportunities for teams to relate and to communicate, particularly about changes. Encourage individuals to meet face to face, working together as a team and identifying the team's role in the change. Being fully present when talking to anyone about change will improve all the aspects of SCARF, but particularly relatedness.

Fairness

Increase the sense of fairness through transparency. Devolved and dispersed leadership models can encourage a sense of fairness in decision-making processes, particularly in relation to change. Equal time should be allotted for individuals to talk at meetings, setting the ground rules for this before the start, and ensuring everyone receives the same message and no one is unfairly kept in the dark.

Rock (2010) summarises the benefits of understanding this model:

> *When leaders make people feel good about themselves, clearly communicating their expectations, give employees latitudes to make decisions, support people's efforts to build good relationships, and treat the whole organisation fairly, it prompts a reward response. Others in the organisation become more effective, more open to ideas and more creative. They notice the kind of information that passes them by or resentment makes it difficult to focus their attention. They are less susceptible to burnout because they are able to manage their stress.*

Importantly, Rock et al. (2013, p19) stress the significance of ensuring that individuals within organisations believe in the 'growth-mindset concept', that everyone can develop 'at every level'. The important foundation of making sure everyone counts is central here. Rock et al. (2013) demonstrate that allowing individuals to believe they can develop, rather than having the fixed, reinforced view that there are only a talented few, ensures that organisations will benefit from increased performance all round.

Summary

> *Learning about the Brain Changes Everything.*
>
> (Rock, 2013)

This chapter has examined a number of fundamental areas within the field of neuroscience that have explicit implications for self-leadership. The finding of mirror neurones was compared to the significant discovery of DNA. For self-leadership the ability to naturally become in tune (in sync) with someone has important rapport-building and communication ramifications. Connecting and supporting others also acts as a de-stressor and creates resilience as a natural consequence.

The important ability to understand our emotions and therefore to appreciate how these can impact our thinking and reasoning has been explored. Happy states improve intuition, insights, reasoning, problem solving, creativity and, significantly, the ability to remember, but stressed, adrenalin- and cortisol-fuelled decisions are likely to result in overconfidence and poorer decisions being made, as the limbic system robs the prefrontal cortex of essential oxygen and glucose.

Reappraising and reframing provide balance and simply taking four deep conscious breaths (aware in the moment of the bodily sensations of breathing) taps into a natural inbuilt interoceptive awareness that calms the whole system down (Farb et al., 2012). The continuous activation of unhelpful thinking can result in Hebb's law of 'cells that fire together wire together' (Dispenza, 2012, p45). Habitual negative thinking becoming a hair-trigger response can be the unwanted result.

We examined Kahneman's (2011) two systems of thinking to realise the repercussions of bias thinking, for example the natural unconscious aversion to loss fuelling risky decisions. The brains incredible neuroplasticity allows us to appreciate that we can change habitual ways of thinking, and responding through greater self-awareness, and observing in the moment our actions and reactions, becomes an important component of self-management and self-leadership. Indeed, this will help guard against the pervasive impact of 'group think', the leadership blind spot of not saying because it is more comfortable to agree than to disagree.

The poor practice of multitasking and the reality that we can only undertake one cognitive task well at a time was identified. The role of adverse stress and its detrimental effect on the brains of individuals, particularly the language circuits, was explored.

It was established that functioning to the brain's working (short-term) memory, by encouraging individuals to express in 30 seconds the main identified issues, would improve communication and the ability to remember what was said. The important role of emotional intelligence and the preference of a 'resonant' approach were also discussed.

The see-saw effect of analytical and empathetic reasoning as a consideration when making decisions, implicitly each approach potentially switching the other off, was explained – consideration when making critical and balanced decisions.

We explored the important impact of change on the brain using the SCARF model for collaborating and influencing others (Rock, 2008). The two main governing principles the brain works with, avoiding pain (minimising danger) and maximising reward, were therefore explored. It was established, for example, that social rejection is interpreted in the same way as pain by the brain. Knowledge of the SCARF model when dealing with change, therefore, was identified as especially advantageous.

It is important for all individuals to believe in the 'growth mindset' that everyone counts and is therefore able to better lead self. Self-leadership at every level, working with the insights identified from the neuroscience research literature, can make a real difference to every exchange, to the culture and the working environment, to improve compassion through creating resilient leaders.

Chapter 6

Self-leadership and resilience: a key to appropriate professional judgement under pressure

Introduction

This chapter has a closer look at resilience and its importance in ensuring individuals are in the best position 'to do the right thing', in relation to exercising appropriate professional judgement. It identifies from the research what being resilient looks like and what constitutes professional judgement within Health and Social Care. It also examines briefly the specific role of reflection within professional practice.

Southwick and Charney (2012, p6) describe resilience in individuals 'as the ability to bounce back after encountering difficulty . . . and fundamentally related to the experience and management of stress' (p13). It is a form of mental health, and the World Health Organization (WHO, 2014) states that mental health:

> Is more than just the absence of mental disorders or disabilities . . . it is a state of wellbeing in which an individual realizes his or her own abilities, can cope with the normal stresses of life, can work productively and is able to make a contribution to his or her community.

This chapter also examines the role of mindfulness as an effective practice in developing a better state of mind and enhancing an individual's resilience. Indeed, mindfulness as an approach has been identified as conferring many benefits (Farb et al., 2012; Garland et al., 2013). Kabat-Zinn (2012, p1) states: 'Mindfulness is awareness, cultivated by paying attention in a sustained and particular way: on purpose, in the present moment, and non-judgmentally.'

The importance of where we place our attention in relation to thought has been introduced within this text; further exploration and discussion will stress the important tripartite focus of attention as an 'inner, other and outer focus' (Goleman, 2013, p4). Goleman (2013) also argues that we need to sharpen our attention and that, like a muscle, it can be refined and developed.

Resilience has been introduced and discussed in a number of related areas within this text, particularly its importance relative to self-leadership. This chapter affords the opportunity to bring together and further expand what has been discussed so far, with a special focus on resilience, and how to enhance resilience and with it an individual's professional judgement under pressure. Before doing this it is important to first examine what resilience looks like.

What does resilience look like?

Southwick and Charney (2012, p11) found that resilient people took responsibility for their own emotional well-being. They studied why some people are more resilient than others and from their research identified the 10 resilience factors shown in Figure 6.1.

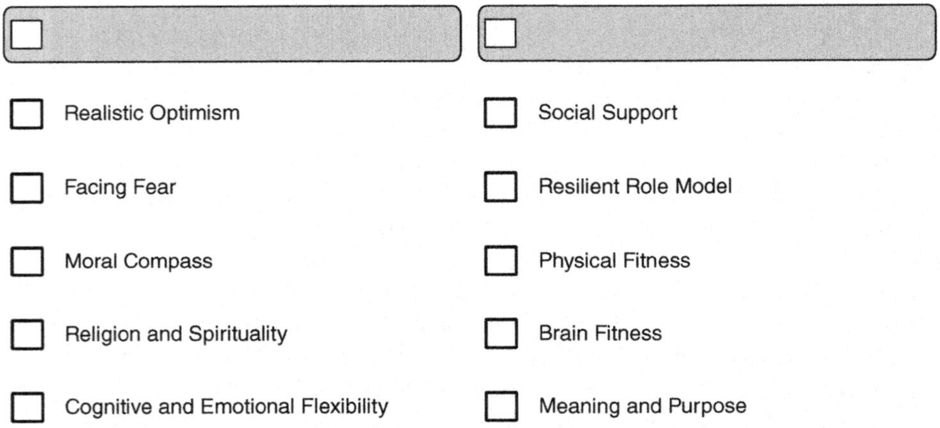

☐		☐	
☐	Realistic Optimism	☐	Social Support
☐	Facing Fear	☐	Resilient Role Model
☐	Moral Compass	☐	Physical Fitness
☐	Religion and Spirituality	☐	Brain Fitness
☐	Cognitive and Emotional Flexibility	☐	Meaning and Purpose

Figure 6.1 Resilience factors (Southwick and Charney, 2012, p11)

They provide the following definitions and explanations for each:

Realistic optimism: pays attention to negative information, but unlike pessimists realistic optimists do not stay fixated on it; and in contrast with over-optimists, they can appropriately estimate and pay attention to risk. When under pressure they are able to increase their capability to 'positively reappraise situations . . . employing strategies to solve problems' (Southwick and Charney, 2012, p27).

Facing fear: Southwick and Charney (2012) suggest viewing fear as normal and more as a helpful guide rather than something to avoid. As Nelson Mandela stated: 'I learned that courage was not the absence of fear, but the triumph over it . . . The brave man is not he who does not feel afraid, but he who conquers that fear' (from *Long Walk to Freedom* (1995), cited in Mandela, 2011).

From a neurobiological standpoint moderate levels of fear can actually enhance the functioning of the prefrontal cortex – too much, however, and the fight or flight response overrides the system and panic sets in, which 'dramatically compromises the prefrontal cortical functioning and rational decision making' (Southwick and Charney, 2012, p48). The author recommends seeing fear as an opportunity to focus, to gather as much information about what is causing the fear, and practising the skills to master the fear, facing the fear with support, and mindfulness can all help. They suggest, 'the best way around fear is through it' (Southwick and Charney, 2012, p53).

Moral compass: 'Doing what is right' – Southwick and Charney (2012, p55) have found that resilient people often follow 'a set of moral principles . . . [which they] strive to adhere to'. They repeat the following questions to ask from Rushworth Kidder's book, *Moral Courage* (2005).

• What are my core values and beliefs?

• And which are the most important to me?

• Am I living by these principles and values?

• Am I falling short, and where?

• Am I motivated to change?

• Do I have the courage to do so?

Religion and spirituality: Southwick and Charney (2012, p78) described resilient individuals as having a 'strength which came from their spiritual beliefs'. They remind us that, of all the resilience factors identified, 'religion and spirituality are deeply personal matters about which people tend to have strong feelings' (p83).

Cognitive and emotional flexibility: Southwick and Charney (2012, p195) advocate meditation/mindfulness for emotion regulation. These activities have also been linked to an enhanced ability to 'focus attention, increased flexibility of thinking, more rapid speed processing of visual information and improved verbal memory as well as greater feelings of psychological well-being' (Southwick and Charney, 2012, p130). They describe the use of humour and cognitive reappraisal, of failure and gratitude, as useful in promoting resilience.

Social support: 'Humans are designed to bond with one another' (Southwick and Charney, 2012, p85). Social support protects against both physical and mental illness and provides resilience to stress. Southwick and Charney (2012) describe giving social support as important as receiving it – for the hormone oxytocin (as discussed earlier) is involved in reducing anxiety by reducing the activation of the amygdala.

Resilient role model: Southwick and Charney's (2012) research found that all the resilient people they interviewed had at least one person they admired as a role model, 'whose beliefs, attitudes and behaviors inspire them' (p97) in their lives. They identified that role modelling as a tool can be used to strengthen resilience.

Physical fitness: According to Southwick and Charney (2012, p109), physical fitness enhances not only mood and cognition but also 'emotional resilience'. They report research findings that confirm the benefits of aerobic exercise to include enhancing the growth of neurones in the brain, and 'anti-depressive, anti-anxiety and stress protective effects' (Southwick and Charney, 2012, p115). The importance of sleep is also identified as key.

Brain fitness: Southwick and Charney (2012, p122) have established that 'resilient people tend to be lifelong learners' and that brain plasticity allows people to improve memory and cognitive performance. They discuss a number of mental exercises identified to improve memory, reasoning, decision making and speed of processing information (Southwick and Charney, 2012, p127).

Meaning and purpose: Southwick and Charney (2012, p158) discuss research studies which found 'that having a clear and valued purpose, and committing fully to the mission, can dramatically strengthen one's resilience'. Indeed, Frankl (2004, p12) states: 'For success, like happiness, cannot be pursued; it must ensue, and it only does so as the unintended side-effect of one's dedication to a cause greater than oneself or as the by-product of one's surrender to a person other than oneself.'

Southwick and Charney (2012) would be the first to suggest that the above list is not exclusive, but that these were the current themes they identified from their own research and other research in the field.

Indeed, resilience is complex and depends on a multitude of factors from our genes (some individuals are more predisposed to stress), early care-giving relationships (family dynamics), environmental factors (social interaction, poverty, stress and drug taking), life experiences, self-efficacy, learned resourcefulness and thinking habits, as part of a much bigger list. Invariably twin studies have shown that 30–50 per cent of most personality traits are genetically transmitted, including optimism, while the other 50–70 per cent depend on the environment (Southwick and Charney, 2012, p32). Furthermore, resilience arguably is a dynamic feature, with the degree to which we are more or less resilient being impacted by the context, timing and the level of adversity. The CIPD (2011) further categorises resilience in terms of individual, team and organisational resilience. The author would suggest that both teams and organisations are made up of individuals and, therefore, will concentrate on the individual as the denominator (entity).

In terms of resilience and its essential impact upon exercising appropriate professional judgement under pressure (a key concept within the discussion of this chapter), it is important to examine from the outset what constitutes an appropriate professional judgement, and to consider the components before discussing how resilience is important to this process.

What is an appropriate professional judgement?

Schön (1991, p21) initially described professional practice in terms of 'professional artistry', which encompasses the intuitive wisdom gained through practical experience, dismissing the idea that practice is merely 'technical rationality' or instrumental problem solving.

As we know, professionals are expected to make difficult decisions, as summed up by Coles (2002, p3):

> [They are expected to] engage in complex and unpredictable tasks on society's behalf, and in doing so must exercise their discretion, making judgments – decide what is 'best', in the particular situation rather than what is 'right', in some absolute sense.

Exercising professional judgement is at the heart of Health and Social Care and is made up of a number of components; for example, the integration of *explicit knowledge* with *tacit knowledge*, with the generation and critical evaluation of options; and making decisions based on appropriate assessment of risk (see Figure 6.2). In a clinical environment, risk would include the consideration of all aspects of clinical governance.

'Explicit knowledge' (knowing that) comprises evidenced-based research, facts, data, related laws, academic information, proven methodology, policies, processes and procedures.

'Tacit knowledge' is practical 'know-how' – not just the practical, technical skill but also intuition, insight, all the information that is hidden, the underlying frames of references, values, beliefs, experiences and personal information. As Michael Polanyi (cited by Smith, 2003) famously stated, 'we know more than we can tell'. Tacit knowledge therefore can be difficult to express and forms instead personal information or knowledge. McAdam et al. (2007, p46) concluded that tacit knowledge is 'knowledge-in-practice developed from direct experience and action; highly pragmatic and situation specific; subconsciously understood and applied; difficult to articulate; usually shared through interactive conversation and shared experience.'

Figure 6.2 *Some key components of the professional judgement process*

Other important sensitivities would include an appreciation of uniqueness, the situational complexity (particularly its instability), ethical and moral considerations. Erik Erikson, the psychiatrist, cited by Schön (1991, p16), describes the distinctiveness of each person as 'a universe of one'. With the absence of an operational manual, it is the complexity of exercising appropriate professional judgements, and capturing this uniqueness in the given context that makes the artistry rather than the science of practice within the Health and Social Care sectors. Indeed, Schön (1991, p45) cites Edgar Schein, who proposes that the hallmark of a professional is the ability to manage, 'convergent knowledge' and tailor this 'to the unique requirements of the client system'.

Two important elements of professional practice, identified in Figure 6.3, are reflection-in-action and reflection-on-action. Both are integral to making professional judgements, with reflection-in-action being described by Schön (1991, p49) as part of day-to-day practice, 'the spontaneous, intuitive performance of actions of everyday life . . . thinking on our feet'. It is the thinking that takes place while doing.

Reflection-on-action, in contrast, is looking back over decisions made, 'in the relative tranquillity of a post-mortem . . . exploring the understandings they have brought to their handling of the case' (Schön, 1991, p61). This could be part of a planned activity, for example critical reflection in supervision or something that occurs closer to the event. It may also feed into reflection-in-action. Both processes contribute to learning, either from the experience as it is occurring, even if this is reinforcement of previous appreciations, or new insights or understandings, both potentially in and after the event. Greenwood (1993), however, would add the important role of reflection before any action, which can be an essential part of the decision-making process and exercising professional judgement. Carroll and Gilbert (2011, p86) would call this 'anticipatory', being prepared by thinking through the potential scenarios and evaluating their impact.

Professional

☐ [ ]

☐ Knowledge

☐ Expertise

☐ Reflection-on-action

☐ Intuition

☐ Beliefs, values, assumptions

Practice

☐ [ ]

☐ Involving the individual in all their uniqueness

☐ Experience

☐ Reflection-in-action

☐ Practice wisdom

☐ Constraints of resources

Figure 6.3 What professional practice involves

Such learning may contribute to increasing the individual practitioner's self-awareness and to the process of lifelong learning. It can also be a solitary activity or involve others. Indeed, individuals are expected to increasingly work across organisational boundaries and work in integrated ways with other professional groupings. Each individual's role within the process of effecting a collective professional judgement becomes an important feature of professional practice.

At the centre of making a professional judgement is the important role of communication in its fullest sense, involving verbal, non-verbal and written formats. The following summarises some of the additional identifiable components that would reflect appropriate professional judgements.

- Decisions impacting individual(s) ensure they are appropriately involved from the outset and kept at the centre of the process.

- Options generated are wide-ranging (before being narrowed), are matched to individual(s) and are inclusive.

- All options are evaluated fully.

- Judgements are informed by the most recent research and evidence-based information.

- They would withstand the scrutiny of peer review.

- Judgements are based on statutory codes of professional practice, national legislation, policies and procedures.

- They take into consideration the situational complexities.

- They have been subjected to risk assessment and management.

- They meet ethical and moral considerations including equality and diversity issues.

- They involve multidisciplinary teams as appropriate.

- They are fully informed in terms of legal and statutory powers and responsibilities.

- They have included, where appropriate, an appraisal of the available resources.

An important feature of professional practice and making appropriate professional judgements in terms of resilience is the essential role of reflection.

The importance of reflection

Finlay (2008, p6) would introduce three central concepts, which she explains are best described as a 'continuum . . . reflection, critical reflection and reflexivity' (see Figure 6.4).

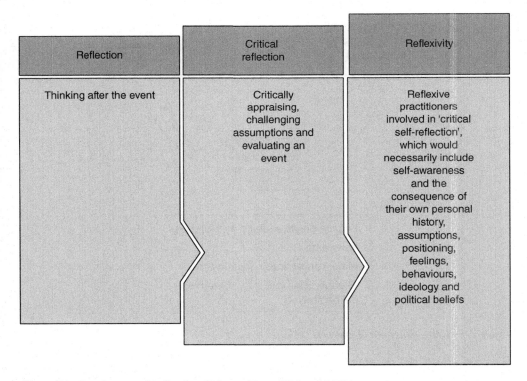

Reflection	Critical reflection	Reflexivity
Thinking after the event	Critically appraising, challenging assumptions and evaluating an event	Reflexive practitioners involved in 'critical self-reflection', which would necessarily include self-awareness and the consequence of their own personal history, assumptions, positioning, feelings, behaviours, ideology and political beliefs

Figure 6.4 Continuum of reflection (adapted from Finlay, 2008)

According to Finlay (2008), all three concepts play an important role in reflective practice. The significance of being able to make consistently good professional judgements is the ability to reflect and learn from practice and experience; as Johns (2009, p3) states:

> *Reflection is learning through our everyday experiences . . . It is a critical and reflexive process of self-inquiry and transformation of being and becoming the practitioner you desire to be.*

This deliberate activity of learning from experience is an interpretative endeavour (Carroll and Gilbert, 2011) – a re-look, an examination that is more than a passive process, but involves action. It is a form of sense making, of exploring an event (or concrete experience), and forms the first stage of Kolb's (1984) experiential learning cycle (see Figure 6.5). Observation and reflection, the second stage, allows for interpretation from many different perspectives; the third stage is the generation of abstract concepts; with these being tested within new situations, learning by doing, as the final fourth stage. To be meaningful all stages of the cycle need to be completed (Kolb, 1984). Reflection as a methodology promotes this learning cycle, helping both to 'deconstruct and reconstruct' (Carroll and Gilbert, 2011, p78).

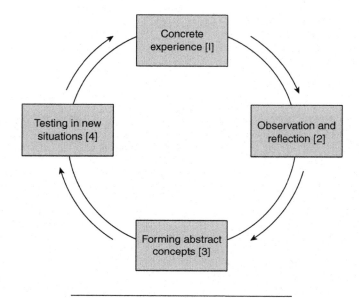

1. Engage practice (doing and leading)
2. Raise data
3. Make connections – gain insights
4. Change behaviour – try something deliberately

Figure 6.5 Kolb's experiential learning cycle

Busy individuals can become trapped in undertaking (1) and (4) with no time for (2) and (3) (implicit reflection). Doing and leading, together with trying something new, without the time to make better-informed decisions, become normal practice.

Reflection with others as a form of supervision requires a number of prerequisites to truly work, for example trust, curiosity, self-awareness, a sense of safety, openness, an understanding of the process, a willingness for self-observation and self-correction (Johns, 2009; Bolton, 2010; Carroll and Gilbert, 2011). For individuals the environment, the context, being fully present, the significance of silence, attention, listening, presence and being aware of defensive behaviours within self and others are crucial components. Carroll and Gilbert (2011, p93) would importantly add preparing for reflection to include not only the environment, but being in the right state of mind ('physically, emotionally, psychologically and culturally'), being prepared for the interaction and 'consolidating motivation'.

Reflection characteristically involves a number of stages, which are best summarised by Boyd and Fales (1983, p101) as:

- a sense of inner discomfort;

- identification or clarification of concern;

- openness to new information from external and internal sources;

- resolution;

- establishing continuity of self with past, present and future;

- deciding whether to act on the outcome of the reflective process.

For reflection is a methodology, a framework to safely and purposefully explore internal thoughts, feelings and actions about an experience that could be either positive or negative. Exploring emotions and feelings is pertinent not only in terms of Damasio's (1994) work in relation to the integral role emotions play in reasoning and decision making, but also in understanding and appropriately expressing these as part of adding to the individual's self-awareness bank. In addition, not getting the feelings expressed, as Stone et al. (1999) identify, can stifle any progress, certainly in terms of learning.

Reflective thinking provides an opportunity to re-examine afresh, to notice and re-evaluate, and to generate new understandings and perspectives of seeing the interconnectedness of things. Although on the surface it appears an 'internal activity' (Carroll and Gilbert, 2011, p85), it is about externalising this thinking and these feelings to take another look.

Reflection with another can also reduce conflict by powerfully filling in the missing perspectives; hugely important when we consider Frith's (2007) and Kahneman's (2011) discussions about how the brain works almost on auto-pilot, with prior beliefs and knowledge, and how specific these are, and so unique to each of us. In terms of words said, reflecting back affords the opportunity to explore, in order to better appreciate the 'deep structure' rather than what was simply said, or the 'surface structure' (Chomsky, 2000, p25).

It supports a process of tuning into 'self' in the now, increasing self-observation, as a crucial dimension to being 'conscious in the moment', in order to realise the things you 'wish you had said' in time to say them (Isaacs, 2008, p399). With practice, tuning in and reflecting in this way, as Gerhardt (2004, p46) would suggest, helps to 'eavesdrop' on what's happening in terms of automatic responses the mind can habitually fall into.

In addition, as Frith (2007, p137) would suggest, 'we don't create in our heads . . . we create by externalising our thoughts'. This can be as an individual, with another or as a group. In terms of groups this can provide an enhanced sense of a common shared purpose, a binding and important feature of groups of professionals working together.

Too much thinking without action, for example, can simply be putting things off, with obsessive ruminating about the future a form of worrying (Carroll and Gilbert, 2011). Other faulty forms of thinking might include the reinforcement of unchallenged assumptions and beliefs.

Reflective thinking can be a painful and uncomfortable process, with individuals opting to avoid in-depth reflection (Johns, 2009) or paying lip service to it (Finlay, 2008). Stressful and busy environments can also cause barriers to reflection (Carroll and Gilbert, 2011), even though the benefits can save time. Motivation may be another challenge and, as Deci and Flaste (1995) remind us, real intrinsic motivation to change can only come from within the individual. People may be willing to change but the organisation is not supportive, leading to 'frustration' and disillusionment (Fleming, 2006, p662).

Fear, anxiety, shame, guilt, unspoken expectations and poor imagination can all negatively impact the ability to reflect (Johns, 2009; Bolton, 2010; Carroll and Gilbert, 2011). There are issues such as 'premature cognitive commitment' (Langer, cited by Carroll and Gilbert, 2011, p87), or in Phillips' (2006, p221) terms, the problem of the 'first impression' being the lasting one that cannot easily be shaken off. Understanding these biases is important in all interactions; reflecting on practice allows a re-look and re-examination to consider whether these instinctive discriminations are adversely influencing the decision-making process and professional judgements. Conflict and a lack of training can undermine reflection, and reflecting in large groups can also be difficult in terms of trust and understanding. Hobbs (2007) would go as far as to say that some individuals may be incapable of critical reflection.

The 'principle of participation' is a term used by Isaacs (2008, p57) to capture the 'essence of the whole'. For Bateson (1972) this was the concept that every experience happens in context. For the author this is more than thinking 'the problem out', as Dewey's 1933 (cited by Jay and Johnson, 2002, p75) interpretation of reflection suggests. This concept of focusing on what went wrong quickly narrows and potentially reduces the breadth and depth of what can be achieved. As we have discussed, any form of judgement, positive or negative, shuts down thinking. Indeed, some would refreshingly suggest going where the 'problem is not' to widen and open up dialogue and thinking (Riggio, 2012, p11).

The importance of reflection and critical reflection to professional practice has been discussed, together with some of the barriers and potential difficulties. The crucial role of being able to both reflect in and on practice in terms of exercising appropriate professional judgement is evident. A closer examination, however, of what resilience looks like in relation to appropriate decision making and exercising professional judgement would be applicable.

What does resilience look like in terms of professional judgement?

Reflective practice is as much a state of mind as it is a set of activities.

(JC Vaughan, cited in Clift et al., 1991)

The important unconscious and conscious roles beliefs, values and assumptions play in decision making have been alluded to within Chapter 5, certainly the biases that can play out. Being tired or depleted in any way arguably would impact adversely professional judgements made as the result of these biases. Both intuitive practice wisdom and tacit knowledge retrieval can be adversely impacted by stress. Reflection provides some balance, an opportunity to look back, to re-examine and to make sense of spotted patterns and potential gaps in information.

Indeed, O'Sullivan (2005, p227) suggests that, in relation to intuition, practice wisdom 'requires a continuous questioning . . . and ongoing examination' in order to integrate this form of knowledge. The resilient practitioner is aware of the interplay between subjective (intuitive practice wisdom) and objective (factual information), but most importantly is self-aware of their state of mind – stressed, relaxed, observing in the now, and able to step back and make sense from a third positional perspective of all the information.

In terms of resilience, operating in multi-professional environments and out of the comfort of uni-professional encounters potentially creates additional stressors, certainly the potential impact of the 'out-group' threat scenario (Rock 2010). As Ratliff and Nosek (2011) suggest, we have a natural, instinctive bias to judge negatively those individuals who are perceived not to belong to our group because the consequences are less grave (implicitly, judging someone as positive and they turn out to be negative). Appreciating the role of increasing relatedness in reducing this unconscious dynamic is an important part of being resilient.

Making sure that considerations of all parties are appropriately heard and communicated in a way that everyone involved understands will improve the sense of fairness and the decision-making ability of all group members. The resilient professional will necessarily appreciate the extra energy requirements of these scenarios and be prepared.

Notwithstanding, additional workloads and the pressures within the current systems to quicken the decision-making processes have potential adverse implications for determining the most appropriate professional judgement. An enhanced self-awareness of when a practitioner is in a better state of mind, or not, is an important feature of resilience.

It is important to address conflict and difficult situations, for as Argyris (2010, p22) suggests, 'we deal with difficult situations by not dealing with them'. Implicitly, we naturally avoid conflict in all its forms, potentially embarrassing, or threatening. Argyris (2010) has identified two operating models, outlined in Table 6.1. He describes Model I as being centred on four values which create defensive 'traps' for organisations, and Model II as far more elusive but dynamic, and is based on productive deduction which shows personal thinking and results in greater openness, transparency and trust. Significantly, like many authors, he stresses the importance of finding the limiting assumptions (Scott, 2002; Lencioni, 2005; Kline, 2009) and challenging individuals who present with Model I behaviours.

Table 6.1 Model I and Model II behaviours (Argyris, 2010, p63)

Model I	Model II
Be in unilateral control.	Seek valid (testable) information.
Win and do not lose.	Create informed choice.
Suppress negative feelings.	Monitor vigilantly to detect and correct error.
Behave rationally.	

Argyris (2010, p65) suggests that the reason 'we create traps for ourselves – is that we espouse Model II reasoning when our actions are in fact based on Model I'. We therefore believe we are behaving in ways that create trust, informed choice based on effective and validated information, but instead we act in ways to protect 'self' by resorting to Model I behaviours, for individuals 'become committed to the status quo', and needing to control situations (Argyris, 2010, p180).

Getting all parties involved in creating options, expanding choice rather than producing these in a top-down process of strategic and operational mismatch, is important. Also essential is being vigilant in terms of reverting back to comfortable Model I behaviours by engaging in dialogue, 'inquiry coupled with advocacy and testing of ideas', assumptions and limiting convictions (Argyris, 2010, p167).

In relation to resilience and professional judgement it is important to explore what we have learnt so far, by bringing it together.

Resilience: bringing it together

Being resilient is everyone's business; an environment filled with resilient individuals will create a whole different culture and with it a significant advantage. Devolved leadership models, based on collective leadership, provide for greater *autonomy*, and an increase in *status*, *certainty* (with a higher degree of transparency), a sense of *fairness* and improved *relatedness*. Observing and evaluating impact routinely allows for further growth and learning as a key focus; with learning being recognised as a reward-activating activity (Gale et al., 2014).

Increasing resilience in the workforce starts with each individual; self-leadership as an approach fosters the development of resilience as its core and integral feature. Importantly, it focuses on emotional intelligence and the significant role of self-awareness, self-management, self-regulation, self-compassion, social awareness and relationship management in building resilience.

In Chapter 2 we examined a number of these facets: the role of self-observation, and of being aware in the moment of our reactions, thoughts and feelings and how this links with self-regulation and management of our emotions, particularly stressful emotions. For as Fredrickson (2001) states, studies have confirmed that when individuals are in a positive emotional state their focus of attention is broader, and problem solving is more flexible and creative than when they are in a negative or neutral state. In terms of exercising appropriate professional judgement it is key to appreciating the impact our thinking, particularly negative thinking, can have on our decision-making abilities.

1	Redundancy
2	Reduction – in resources, pay and support
3	Responsibility – extra accountability
4	Restructuring – change and uncertainty
5	Resistance – passive and challenges to change

Figure 6.6 The top five national key areas of change within the workplace

We have also identified in Chapter 2 some of the current pressures within the working environment. O'Hanlon and Doddy (2013) highlight the top five national key areas of change within the workplace (see Figure 6.6).

They distinguished *work stress*, *change in work role* and *work stress demands* as the top employment-related issues in the UK. The signs and symptoms of work stress were categorised and are shown in Figure 6.7.

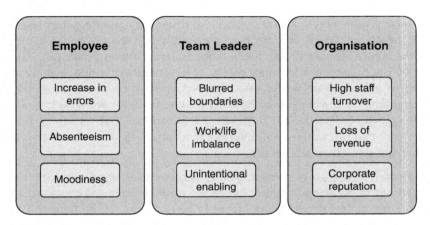

Figure 6.7 Signs and symptoms of work stress (O'Hanlon and Doddy, 2013)

The main factors identified as causing stress have been discussed in Chapter 5, and were highlighted by O'Hanlon and Doddy (2013) (see Figure 6.8).

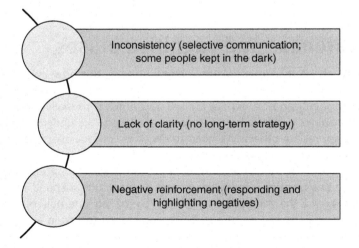

Figure 6.8 Factors that cause stress in organisations (O'Hanlon and Doddy, 2013)

An important feature of managing work and organisational stressors, particularly with reductions in resources and increases in responsibility, is exercising self-compassion, identified in Chapters 2, 3 and 5; that is, implicitly not falling into the trap of working longer hours, especially because of the fear of redundancy.

Self-compassion: working too many hours

Negative thinking, combined with working too many hours, multitasking and being too stressed to sleep, will impact negatively on the decisions we make and the risks we take. Research led by Asebedo (2013) described individuals working more than 50 hours a week as adversely impacting their physical and mental well-being. Her definition of a workaholic was someone who worked more than 50 hours a week. Robinson (2012) suggests that 'one hundred and fifty years of research proves that shorter work hours actually raise productivity . . . and overtime destroys [it]'. She describes research that supports the 40-hour week and anything above this as having negative consequences for health, family life and productivity. Indeed, according to Robinson (2012), after working 60 hours per week for eight weeks, the reduction in productivity is so significant that the average team would have achieved as much completing a 40-hour week. Notwithstanding, following the 60-hour week requires a recovery period, which also impacts negatively (Robinson, 2012). Eurich (2013) confirms that we cannot work excessive hours and that 80 hour-a-week cultures impact adversely, not only on an individual's well-being, but on bottom-line results.

It can become addictive, a team contagion (a way we do things here), with our human fallibility of not being able to realistically see the future impact, the causal effect. People make promises to themselves about work/life balance, but in the here and now they become distracted by the busyness and get swept along with the adrenalin ride, with everything being needed for tomorrow. In the caring professions the cared for become the priority, so skipping lunch, staying later to finish reports, doing an extra shift here and there become the norm. We do not feel the immediate impact of not choosing 'no', for this is an accumulative consequence. Furthermore, when tired we know that our unconscious cognitive biases may have a freer reign.

Self-awareness and cognitive biases

We have learnt about the potential for cognitive biases, but how aware are we of our own biases in thinking? Being committed to exploring is what starting to be self-aware is all about. The significance of developing self-awareness is to really understand our personal reactions, values and beliefs and how we work best. We understand ourselves better in order to appreciate others. We need to check in without overanalysing, to observe our emotions, and see what beliefs are triggered by difficult events. We need to take an observer's position without the emotional judgement and berating ourselves (which can accompany this position), freely let go and purposefully suspend judgement. Also, we need to recognise the sometimes unhelpful role of our internal voice, and how this is impacting our feelings and emotions. Being committed to taking a different position, to reappraise and look with a different lens, and to figuratively stand back and take the slow-motion view, can all be useful strategies. This may be achieved through mindfulness and/or simply tuning in three times a day, practising being in the moment and asking the questions in Figure 6.9.

Stopping the critical voices in our heads, of self and others, can be achieved by imaging dissolving the thought(s), simply letting go or telling ourselves to STOP and changing where we are putting our attention. Writing down why we are making a decision and

Figure 6.9 Three questions to test self-awareness

reflecting later on the outcomes will provide discernible information about the patterns in thinking. Self-reflection can help; however, we can often see others' inconsistencies and mistakes better than our own, and having a neutral coach or mentor can therefore support the process of increasing our self-awareness.

Remaining curious can help to prevent self-anger and irritation with others, for you cannot be angry and curious at the same time. Ask yourself what is missing here, what information do I need, what question would elicit this and what would be a better question, or simply ask yourself, if I had the answer what would it be?

Remember that increasing our self-awareness makes us more aware of people like us. Diversity is key here. Indeed, Roselinde Torres (2013), in studying what makes a great leader, identifies the significance of diversity and proposes three questions to ask yourself (see Figure 6.10).

Figure 6.10 The foundations of great leadership (Torres, 2013)

What a difference compassion makes

Purposefully befriending individuals who are different or deliberately talking to someone who has a different point of view are features of compassion. As Goleman (2013) concurs, for leadership that gets results we need to pay attention to what we are focusing on. We have examined self-compassion in relation to being compassionate to others.

We know from DeSteno's (2012) work that the more we can find similarities between ourselves the more likely we are to exercise compassion. Indeed, he suggests that the degree to which we will be compassionate is governed by 'the individual who is looking'; that is, if they cannot relate to someone then they are less likely to be compassionate. Deliberately finding similarities (if we can see ourselves in others) usually means that we will be more compassionate (DeSteno, 2012). This is about having this in mind and in busy environments to create the opportunity to talk, to find those commonalities. In demanding workplaces this is arguably the first thing that is sacrificed even between each other; with filling in forms becoming more important than finding the person and her or his story behind the name.

Compassion is described as an 'inherent human capacity' and, ironically, the more it is practised the more resilient individuals become (Halifax, 2010). She describes one of the enemies of compassion as being fear, which has a paralysing impact upon our ability to be compassionate. She also suggests that compassion is not draining but enlivening and has the positive impact of both improving the immune system and also enhancing neural integration, connecting different parts of the brain.

The role of empathy as an organising principle

Linked to compassion is empathy. We have demonstrated its importance in creating connections between individuals and the natural nature of this ability, providing we suspend any judgements and are not preoccupied. Atkins (2014) suggests that, for example, if we believe a person is 'personally responsible' for his or her situation, 'we are less likely to experience empathic concern and more likely to experience other emotions such as anger'. In the same way, if individuals perceive others to be 'irrelevant' to their own goals or lives, they are more likely to respond with 'apathy rather than empathic engagement' (Atkins, 2014). And, finally, avoidance occurs in individuals who perceive that they are unable to cope with others' emotions (Atkins, 2014).

Resonant leaders exercise empathy to create a powerful bond between individuals, a capacity to tune in and be able to relate better to others (Goleman et al., 2013). They also recognise the important role social awareness plays in helping individuals within a team to express their emotions, by articulating their feelings in a safe environment, preventing a collision course of suppressed anger or irritation (Goleman et al., 2013). We identified from Lieberman's (2013) work that labelling the emotion in one or two words, or reappraising and reframing the event, are useful in changing the impact. The significance of this is realised in terms of the adverse effects suppressed feelings can have on observers (Lieberman, 2013).

The contagion ripple of emotions can create a prevailing mood for a team, good or bad, as captured in the following:

> *As we let our light shine, we unconsciously give others permission to do the same. As we are liberated from our own fear, our presence actually liberates others.*

> (Williamson, 1992, p190)

Possessing a greater social awareness helps to build and maintain resilience within teams. Having an 'enhanced awareness of empathy means that one is more willing to see other perspectives and to collaboratively engage with others' (Pavlovich and Krahnke, 2014).

However, Atkins (2014) argues that, historically, to improve empathy within organisations there has been a focus 'upon either communication skills or emotional intelligence training', with both approaches presuming that empathy is a matter of improving skills. While this can help, he suggests that there is something much deeper in terms of 'sustainable empathy' and suggests the role of mindfulness.

The new fight or flight response

Fight and flight, we are reminded, have to some extent been replaced by modern-day anger and fear, respectively (Huppert and Baylis, 2004). These authors emphasise our strong inbuilt survival instinct to monitor the environment and be vigilant for negative threats. They cite Randolph Nesse as describing this hypervigilance as a hardwired feature, which can be like a smoke detector set at a level at which it readily activates when there is no real threat. A perpetual stressed feeling causes the brain to 'disconnect more often from the task at hand and we may find ourselves staring at the computer screen, experiencing a momentary state of reverie or trance' (Rock et al., 2012).

This hypervigilance is not just an inherited feature but can be further compounded by the unhelpful thinking habits individuals might have developed. Fear creates anxious thinking and avoidance becomes its hallmark. Overanalysis keeps negative thoughts alive and the amygdala activated, as the individual risks a negative mood prevailing and, with it, a stuck feeling. Individuals often know their problems really well, having rehearsed them in their heads over and over; however, instead of serving to ameliorate, this process feeds them and at the same time fosters a potential growing sense of injustice, right, wrong, unfairness, helplessness and hopelessness, with stressed and tired imaginations potentially running wild.

There are plenty of people who do not get caught up in thinking loops like this. However, from time to time we are all capable of this and different combinations of situations can make some people more vulnerable, especially if there is any form of isolation. Human beings are, however, also innately resilient, with inbuilt systems to encourage stressed individuals to seek out company (McGonigal, 2013). Brain plasticity arguably supports this resilience process.

Neuroplasticity: a chance to change

We established in Chapter 5 that brain plasticity allows, to some degree, the ability to change the firing of neurones within the brain, to break unhelpful, habitual, connective patterns of thinking. It is the change in strength of these connections or synapses that contributes to the concept of neuroplasticity. Merzenich (2013, p48) suggests that such a process can take place 'by internal mental rehearsal' and explicitly does not require external verified practice. Mental internal practice therefore changes the brain in the same way as an external activity; for example, thoughts and thinking can create change (Merzenich, 2014).

According to Merzenich (2014):

> No matter how much you've struggled, no matter where you've been in your life, you're in charge of your life going forward. And you have the capacity; . . . the resources to change things for the better – always have that capacity.

Merzenich (2014) therefore proposes that we 'have the potential to be in a better place . . . the brain is a resource to shape our life' and implicitly to change it. He qualifies this statement by reporting that the brain is not hardwired like a computer, but instead is softwired and thus has a huge capacity to continually change. In agreement is Gazzaniga (2012), who states that 'practice of new tasks promotes dendritic spine formation in adults'.

This ability, however, is about variety, challenging the brain, learning new things and resisting the natural tendency to make everything familiar and safe, getting into ruts and routines. Merzenich (2014) recommends that most physical and functional changes in the brain in old age are 'substantially reversible', but only if we resist the habitual and accustomed by continually exercising the brain with developing new skills, doing things differently instead of in the same way.

The demise of the brain is due to disuse and, therefore, in order to thrive and be resilient we need to make variety and difference our best friends. Taking the easy road to life so that everything is predictable and controlled, therefore, impacts adversely our resilience and functional ability. Merzenich (2014) provides a sobering example of the old person who falls, and begins to change their gait following the fall by walking with a shuffle (in their mind to protect them from falling again); however, by doing so, paradoxically they reduce their mobility and increase the potential to fall in the future. The saying 'variety is the spice of life' really has more to it in terms of resilience than probably we would initially think, for as Csikszentmihalyi (2002, p6) suggests, 'By stretching skills, by reaching toward higher challenges . . . a person becomes an increasingly extraordinary individual.'

Csikszentmihalyi (2002, p4) refers to the important concept of 'flow' and describes this as, 'the state in which people are so involved in an activity that nothing else seems to matter'. His extensive research in this field concluded that happiness is not about outside events, but how these are interpreted; and that the key to more flow in life comes with aligning what we do with what we enjoy doing.

Resilience: a state of mind

We are built to be resilient, so what is getting in the way? Southwick and Charney (2012, p12) talk about the paradox that, in Western society, 'the standard of living in material terms has increased', but the sense of well-being and happiness, however, has declined. They point to a 'me first' culture with a lack of caring relationships, citing Twenge and Campbell's (2009) book, *The Narcissism Epidemic: Living in the Age of Entitlement* (Southwick and Charney, 2012, p12).

There is something more fundamental than the list of external causes of stress, something more innate, and that is self, and the habits of our thinking and thoughts that so severely impact our ability to be resilient. In Chapter 4 we focused on state of mind and the importance of quietening and slowing down to create the space within to listen to our internal wisdom and intuition. Instead, however, the busier we become the more distracted we are, and over time perspective can be lost and replaced by limited thinking.

There are other thinking traps, such as the comparison thinking trap, potentially an innocently learned habit from school and a nurtured competitive streak, for example 'I came first in the race' or 'second to last in the test'. Facebook has produced an internet version of daily reminders of keeping up with the Joneses, a way of feeding the comparison trap with materialistic empty markers of success.

Gleeson and Berman (2012, p58) describe the following as other examples of limited thinking:

'The most I can earn is x . . .'

'You need a PhD for that role . . .'

'I'm not director or chief executive material'

'This is my limit . . .'.

Other limiting beliefs would include:

'I'm not smart enough . . .'

'I'm too old . . .'

'I'm too young . . .'

'I'm too busy to . . .'

'I've tried before . . .'.

All of us have our own specific beliefs that limit and fix our thinking. Gleeson and Berman (2012, p58) state that 'True career resilience and freedom comes when we are aware of the thoughts that bind us . . . [and] when we are aware of our habitual thoughts, we are no longer held and controlled by them.' Ironically, such beliefs and thinking patterns are often developed when we are children, and yet as adults we continue to rely on these perhaps less than helpful ways to respond in the adult world of work (Gleeson and Berman, 2012). Instead of the adult being in charge, potentially the child's thinking habits unconsciously take control – a sobering thought.

The immediacy of the present looms large and distracts our attention, which can impact all good intentions as our self-control is challenged and we put things off until a tomorrow that never comes. Gleeson and Berman (2012) propose that we are born with an innate sense of health and well-being that we have buried, with the busyness of doing, our lives and our thinking habits. They suggest that 'our Inside Job is to learn to trust this innate health', in order to allow it to resurface (Gleeson and Berman, 2012, p68).

Williams (2012) cites Daniel Wegner's experiments on thought suppression, in which individuals were asked not to think about a white bear. This work demonstrated that, when you put your attention on something, you cannot suppress it and instead intrusive thoughts, for example about a white bear, are inevitable; as Williams (2012) states, 'what we resist often persists'. This links to the next section on how we deploy our attention.

Self-leadership: how we deploy our attention

We have discussed the importance of where we place our attention in neurobiological terms, for what we pay attention to grows and has the capacity to change the brain (for example, a worry can become a habitual preoccupation, which in turn becomes a repetitive intrusion in our thinking). Goleman (2013) proposes that, as balanced leaders, we should focus on the three areas shown in Figure 6.11.

Goleman (2013) further suggests that the individual leader who is 'tuned out of his internal world' of self is 'rudderless', the leader who is 'blind to the world of others will be clueless' and those who are 'indifferent' to the larger outer systems will be 'blindsided'. He advocates that the power to change the focus of our attention is a critical feature of 'well-being'.

A failure, for instance, to move freely from inner, other or outer focus can result in an imbalance and, in extreme forms, concentrating on an inner focus may result in depression, with 'helplessness, hopelessness and self-pity' as a feature, or anxiety, with 'panic, fear and catastrophizing' as a trademark.

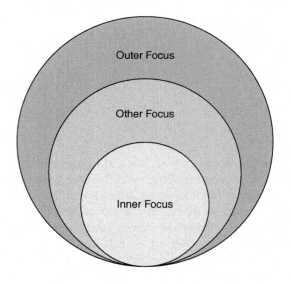

Inner Focus	attunes us to our intuitions, guiding values and better decisions.
Other Focus	smooths our connections to people in our lives.
Outer Focus	lets us navigate in the larger world.

Figure 6.11 Balanced leaders should focus on three areas

According to Goleman (2013), who cites Richard Boyatzis, research suggests that the 'most successful leaders' move back and forth between focusing on the goals of the organisation and 'social scanning', being 'other' focused. Implicitly they are motivated to help other people thrive. He further suggests the following combination of approaches.

- To listen within, being authentic and genuine, and setting out clear expectations.

- To coach others, listening and paying attention to what individuals are feeling and need.

- To listen to others, being 'collaborative' and making decisions by joint agreement when applicable.

- To celebrate successes, recognising the importance of this approach in 'building emotional capital'.

Goleman (2013) highlights two central cognitive ruts that threaten our ability to 'notice our unquestioned assumptions and overly relied-on rules of thumb'. He recommends, instead, that an individual should question and listen carefully, 'probing and reflecting – gathering insights and perspectives from other people'. He cites Ellen Langer from Harvard, who calls this 'environmental mindfulness'.

In group situations, Goleman (2013) quotes Steven Wolff, who suggests that 'to harvest the collective wisdom of a group, you need two things: mindful presence and a sense of safety'. Being fully present allows individuals to be absolutely aware of the emotions within a group and gives individuals permission to express without judgement. The sense of safety is vital in enabling those emotions to surface and, once on the table, they can have very fruitful outcomes rather than being bottled up and unexplored.

Allowing unexplored emotions to be expressed not only builds the collective resilience of the group by addressing and dealing with them, but also provides opportunities for valid reactions to be expressed in a very productive and fruitful way. This provides the opportunity not only to resolve the issues (the elephant in the room), but to explore more fully what are the nuances, what this is telling us. Most importantly, it allows groups the healthy check and balance of being able to 'say' the unsayable.

Other considerations

The importance of mind and body connection

The body, brain and conscious mind are partners in permanent exchange.

(Lieberman, 2013, p104)

Not mentioned so far is the important role of the mind and body connection, for as Lieberman (2013, p93) states, 'a substantial number of experiments show that our bodily state, including our facial expression, can influence our feelings'. He suggests that a 'feedback loop' can ensue, which explains how emotions in a group can 'spiral upward or downward' (Lieberman, 2013, p93). You only have to recollect working with, or meeting, individuals who are excessively negative and seem to drain the life out of you, to relate to this. Being aware of the potential impact and what is happening in the moment is important for both individual and group resilience.

Tone and auditory response, according to Lieberman (2013, p100), can have the same effect; and he provides the example of the auditory sound of someone 'sobbing on the phone' being able to trigger a similar upset response in the listener, albeit somewhat 'weaker'.

It is not all about what people say (the words) that matters, as through the mirror neurone effect we unconsciously mimic their bodily actions and facial reactions. If we put our body or face in a certain position, we can feel the related emotion. Cuddy (2012) reports that, if people are forced to smile by getting them to hold pens in their mouths with their teeth, it makes them feel happy. She further reports that, when individuals posed in high-power positions (made themselves bigger, putting their arms above their heads in a V shape) for two minutes before a job interview, they performed better than the group who posed in low-power positions (hunched up with folded arms).

The importance of sleep and physical exercise

The single most important behavioural experience is sleep (Foster, 2013). Walker (2007) describes receiving adequate sleep as a biological imperative, as it is responsible for restoring the emotional neurobiological circuitry. Rock et al. (2012, p3) describe it as also vital for 'homeostatic restoration, thermoregulation, tissue repair, immunity, memory processing, and emotion regulation'. They would even suggest that 'sleep deprivation can be more lethal than food deprivation' (Rock et al., 2012, p3).

Ilardi (2013) reminds us that stress as a response is damaging and toxic, particularly to the brain over time, and becomes a disease of today's lifestyles. Getting adequate sleep is vital in reducing this impact. Foster (2013) states that good sleep increases your concentration, attention, decision making, creativity, social skills and health. He further suggests that getting good sleep reduces mood changes, stress, levels of anger and impulsivity, and increases our ability to solve complex problems threefold. Importantly, sleep is necessary for memory consolidation, for when sleep deprived our ability to learn is significantly hampered (Foster, 2013).

Physical exercise, especially aerobic exercise and exercise that involves coordination, is particularly helpful for both brain health and resilience (Amen, 2012). Indeed, physical exercise helps to protect the short-term memory structures in the hippocampus from high-stress conditions (Amen, 2005).

Being mindful

The role of the mind

Gazzaniga (2012) states: 'I will maintain that the mind, which is somehow generated by the physical processes of the brain, constrains the brain.' He further suggests that, in neuroscience, consciousness is seen as involving 'a multitude of widely distributed specialized systems and disunited processes . . . integrated by an interpreter module'. According to Gazzaniga (2012):

> The interpreter module appears to be uniquely human and specialized to the left hemisphere. Its drive to generate hypotheses is the trigger for human beliefs, which, in turn, constrain our brain.

The 'interpreter module', he continues, also creates 'the personal narrative, the story that ties together all the disparate aspects of our conscious experience, into a coherent whole'. Pinker (2011, p2) describes the mind as a 'remarkably complex processor of information' and relates the 'quirks of the mind', with what our ancestors needed to negotiate in the world, to natural selection. Dehaene (2011, p224) introduces the concept of consciousness and states: 'the brain can take a pattern of shapes on the retina, and successively turn it into a set of letters, recognize it as a word, and access a certain meaning – all of that without any form of consciousness'. He proposes that:

> Consciousness is global information in the brain – information which is shared across different brain areas . . . What we mean by being conscious of a certain piece of information is that it has reached a level of processing in the brain where it can be shared.

(Dehaene, 2011, p226)

Dehaene (2011, p229) conjectures that a significant differentiating feature between unconscious and conscious awareness is the length of time 'you can hold on to information', for information processed on an unconscious level produces a transitory activation that quickly dissipates. He proposes that, when someone is conscious of information, they can hold on to it fundamentally for as long as they like, implicitly closing the mind to other inputs while they 'play with this mental representation in the mind' (Dehaene, 2011, p229).

Williams (2012) reminds us that the mind naturally makes associations, links and connections and it fills in information gaps. It therefore can generate inferences or assumptions, which is particularly pertinent if we are stressed, anxious or fearful, for these linked associations can create inferences that are less helpful, for example *'she didn't smile at me today – I must have done something to upset her.'* When more resourceful, an individual might automatically think, *'Oh she is preoccupied and hasn't seen me.'*

Williams (2012), therefore, describes the ability we have, particularly when depleted in some way, stressed, rushed, anxious or depressed, to create 'mind knots of our own making'. These can form a feedback loop, for the mind produces thoughts that in turn cause feelings and body sensations that generate a certain behaviour, and this feeds into influencing further thoughts as the loop becomes circular (see Figure 6.12). An example would be catastrophising about a decision made at work – this can produce unhelpful thoughts, such as *'if only I had . . . if only I hadn't'*, and this generates an anxious feeling and sick sensation in the pit of the stomach. Withdrawal, such as not eating (or eating), becomes the result. In turn this produces further ruminating thoughts – *'what if my boss finds out; what will he think of me'* – and this causes a feeling of apprehension (flight) or uneasiness, which as a consequence makes it difficult to sleep.

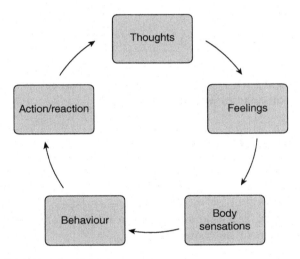

Figure 6.12 Cyclical thinking feedback loop

Williams (2012) reminds us that the mind is multi-layered, for there are:

- the conscious mind moment to moment;
- a past and a future;
- orientation in time and space;
- interactions with others.

Indeed, Siegel (2010, p261) recognises the important role of relationships and connections with others as a distinctive feature of well-being. Together with the 'mind and the brain' he proposes 'a triangle of wellbeing' (see Figure 6.13): each aspect is mutually influencing and there is the harmony of integration between empathetic relationships, coherent mind and integrated brain. He proposes:

[The] brain is the mechanism of energy and information flow throughout the extended nervous system distributed throughout the entire body; relationships are the sharing of this flow; mind is the embodied and relational process that regulates the flow of energy and information.

(Siegel, 2010, p121)

'Mindsight' is the term he uses for the ability to see clearly the connectedness and which 'permits us to regulate – to monitor and modify – with more strength and flexibility' (Siegel, 2010, p120).

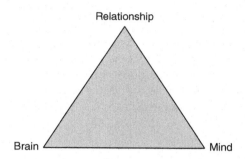

Figure 6.13 Siegel's triangle of well-being

Being resilient is about creating balance, and mindfulness as a practice has been identified as a significant approach in achieving such balance, particularly in terms of our mind states. The next section explores what mindfulness is.

What is mindfulness?

Mindfulness is the translation of the Pali word 'Sati', which translates as 'to remember'; although according to Goldstein (2013) its meaning goes far beyond our traditional understanding and application of 'memory'. Kabat-Zinn (2012, p1) describes mindfulness as 'Awareness, cultivated by paying attention in a sustained and particular way: on purpose, in the present moment, and non-judgmentally.'

Interest in mindfulness as a practice has exploded, with a plethora of research studies supporting the advantages of this approach. For example, Brown et al. (2007) identified the benefits to mental health, well-being, physical health, self-regulation and interpersonal behaviour, with many more valuable outcomes acknowledged below. According to Grossman (2013), mindfulness is a universal capacity we all have and are able to further cultivate through even short periods of training and, while based in Buddhist psychology, it does not require a religious or ideological perspective. The Mental Health Foundation (n.d.) describe it as a 'Mind-body based approach that helps people change the way they think and feel about their experiences, especially stressful experiences'.

Indeed, according to Keng et al. (2011, p1042), 'mindfulness has been theoretically and empirically associated with psychological well-being'. The components of mindfulness, specifically awareness and non-judgemental acceptance of an individual's present-moment experience, provide valuable protection and redress of a number of psychological manifestations, such as anxiety, rumination, worry, fear, anger, overwhelm, suppression and avoidance (Weinstein et al., 2009; Keng et al., 2011; Farb et al., 2012). Goldin (2011) would add the important role of emotion awareness and regulation. Hölzel et al. (2012) identified five facets of mindfulness (see Figure 6.14).

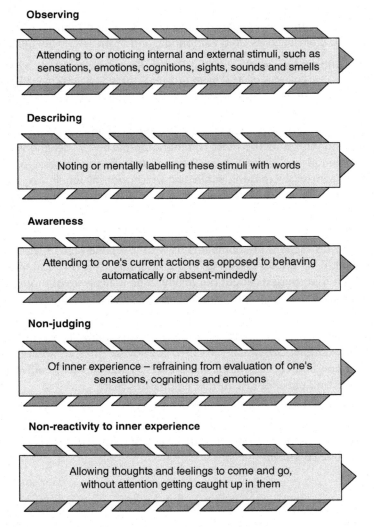

Observing

Attending to or noticing internal and external stimuli, such as sensations, emotions, cognitions, sights, sounds and smells

Describing

Noting or mentally labelling these stimuli with words

Awareness

Attending to one's current actions as opposed to behaving automatically or absent-mindedly

Non-judging

Of inner experience – refraining from evaluation of one's sensations, cognitions and emotions

Non-reactivity to inner experience

Allowing thoughts and feelings to come and go, without attention getting caught up in them

Figure 6.14 Five facets of mindfulness (Hölzel et al., 2012)

In 1979 Jon Kabat-Zinn (originally a molecular biologist) developed a programme for patients with chronic pain at Massachusetts University Hospital in America. The programme was named *mindfulness-based stress reduction* (MBSR). It constituted an eight-week course that trained patients to be mindful and relate better to both stress and pain. According to Grossman (2013), *mindfulness-based interventions* (MBIs) were derived from MBSR. These included both *informal* and *formal meditation* practices, with the latter involving focusing on the breath, sensations in the body, directing attention, compassion, loving kindness to self and others, and informal mindfulness about everyday life, for example as meaningful pauses, being fully in the moment in terms of experiencing body sensation.

From the successes of MBSR, British and Canadian psychotherapists developed a programme for individuals with psychological problems called mindfulness-based cognitive therapy (MBCT). This is a therapy that is currently recommended by the National Institute for Health and Care Excellence (NICE, 2011) to prevent individuals from relapsing into depression. Professor Mark Williams from Oxford University has been associated with this approach, together with Zindel Segal (Toronto University) and John Teasdale (formerly of the Cognition and Brain Sciences Unit, Cambridge, and of the University of Oxford).

From a survey undertaken by the Mental Health Foundation (2014, p22) with 2,330 adults, almost one in five people feel anxious nearly all of the time, or a lot of the time, with only one in twenty people saying they never feel anxious. An earlier survey by the Mental Health Foundation (2010) into stress revealed some significant implications in terms of its management, with individuals resorting to eating junk food, spending time alone or just living with it as the most common approaches to dealing with stress. The long-term detrimental implications are well recognised across all disease profiles. In addition, there is a reported increase in subjective perception of loneliness, which is a real mortality indicator (Singer, 2014). Indeed, Singer (2014) suggests that achievement and fear are out of balance and that stressed individuals have learnt to shut down, especially in front-line services, as the emotional contagion of caring for distressed others impacts.

Among the many distractions life bombards us with, Grossman (2013, p200) highlights a sobering thought: if we are so 'wavering' in our attention, so easily distracted, 'we might reflect upon what that suggests about our ability to be fully aware of more complex experience like attention to our work, our relationships, and our environment'.

MBIs such as mindfulness and mindfulness meditation implicitly are approaches that have a preventative beneficial impact not only in terms of mental resilience, but also in many more ways; for example, Grossman (2013, p200) advises that, in addition to 'learning powers of attention and concentration, mindfulness simultaneously cultivates powers of courage, kindness and patience'. He further emphasises that:

> *Mindfulness is a special kind of attention that can only occur when we turn towards whatever we are perceiving, without our emotions and intentions prejudiced or biased in the process – neither turning our attention away from the object of awareness, nor trying to hang on to or control it.*

> (Grossman, 2013, p200)

It generates an ability, with practice, to maintain a better presence in the moment, which includes whoever you are in contact with (Williams, 2012). Mindfulness also allows for more information to be elicited from the environment, including from others, and provides for a more accurate assessment of what is occurring in the moment without the prejudice of preconceived judgements, for example, *'typical – they always behave like this'*. Being fully present in the moment means reverting to awareness in the now; and returns a wandering mind from the future, or the past, where many of us can spend a great deal of time. Significantly, this not only allows individuals to deal with what is in the now, rather than putting it off or avoiding it, but ensures they are in a better headspace to respond. It provides a greater opportunity for others to really feel listened to, with a silence based on connection and being fully present.

Goldin (2011) also advises that mindfulness improves the way we talk to ourselves, which can often be surprisingly harsh. It helps, therefore, to tone down emotional responses, to help to label thought simply as just thought (Williams, 2012). In toning down emotional responses it also tones down the negative automatic, potentially inaccurate, biases and influences; all of which could potentially produce a negative contagion effect as non-verbal negative signs spill out into conversations.

Exercises in mindfulness

A mindfulness intervention would typically involve being aware of the breath, either by concentrating on the abdominal muscles moving in and out during inspiration and expiration, or the air moving in and out of the nostrils. This is about concentrating on the bodily sensations, and as the mind wanders off into default mode thinking, to bring it back in a non-judgemental way to the focus on the breath, which becomes the anchor point. This can be carried out simply for one cycle of inspiration and expiration, as a pause intervention, or in a more purposeful way, sitting down with feet flat on the floor, either eyes closed or half closed with focus down, and spine straight although relaxed; for, as Wallace (2006) reminds us, the emphasis is placed on relaxation. Concentrating on returning to the breath, as the anchor, provides a focus and is described as *attentional focusing* (Goldin, 2008).

The above exercise can be repeated, but instead of concentrating on the breath the attention can be shifted to open monitoring, noticing anything that crosses the mind, not holding on to the thought, simply observing. 'Typically participants are instructed to witness their thoughts without judgment or elaboration' (Atkins, 2014).

This exercise can be further adapted by simply listening, to let whatever is happening unfold – staying present, letting whatever sounds come and go without labelling them, for example that's a lawnmower, or an aeroplane. In this exercise the listening becomes the anchor, bringing the attention, when it wanders off into thought, back to listening. This exercise can be for any length of time from three minutes upwards.

It is not about putting further pressure on yourself to find a specific timeslot, it can be about capitalising on everyday activities to choose to be mindful of, for example, dressing – bringing your attention back to dressing as the anchor and being aware of the sensation of the fabric on the different parts of the body; brushing your teeth; washing up; folding the ironing; or mowing the lawn.

Attentional distraction would involve counting backwards in threes (Goldin, 2008). *Cognitive reappraisal* is helpful in addressing negative self-talk, self-criticism, rumination and worry (Goldin, 2008). Contrast the statement '*I am angry*' with '*I notice I am angry*' – this second perspective creates a sense of distance and with it a different impact. It creates more of an attitude of curiosity, acceptance and kindness to self. The above are basic examples of mindfulness, and further development would include focusing on different parts of the body and the accompanying sensations, directing attention on to a specific object.

Grossman (2013, p197) would suggest that mindfulness requires 'Exercising not only our powers of attention, but also our powers of openness and acceptance of what, at the moment, has, in fact, already occurred, and therefore we are unable to change.' He further proposes that 'we learn patience in the process . . . [together] with awareness of all aspects of our lives (Grossman, 2013, p197).

Mindfulness exercises have been found to have many benefits and a small number have been alluded to within this section. The particular role mindfulness plays in terms of compassion has some very interesting implications for Health and Social Care workers. This next section therefore explores this particular area in respect to its role in resilience.

The role of mindfulness in compassion and resilience

According to Atkins (2014), mindfulness demonstrably improves compassion and this positive impact is at least in part related to a changed relationship to the self and improved perspective taking. This ensures that being too empathetic in the caring environment does not cause burnout, or compassion fatigue, but allows instead an appropriate emotional separation from others and with it an ongoing resilience. For if an individual relates to another from a reference of self, they are likely to activate their own 'pain matrix and the amygdala' resulting in personal distress (Atkins, 2014).

This self–other merging is described by Atkins as 'detrimental to empathic concern'. Being able to self-regulate, creating a separate self–other perspective, promotes an appropriate empathetic response. This capacity to balance a felt sense of connection with ongoing differentiation and perspective taking of others (self-regulation) is created through mindfulness (Atkins, 2014). He suggests that even 'brief mindfulness . . . [training] can increase the degree to which participants consider others'.

Furthermore it enhances empathy because it helps individuals 'to take judgements of others less seriously and instead attend more closely to their moment-to-moment process' (Atkins, 2014). He summarises the important advantages of mindfulness training; it creates:

> a more flexible relationship to verbal content, enhances noticing of process, and creates a stable sense of self as an awareness that is beyond threat, and these effects all support more empathic responding rather than personal distress.

This has important implications for ensuring within the caring environments that individuals become and/or maintain their resilience, while remaining empathetic. Halifax (2013, p209) agrees and cites Duerr's research, which suggests that compassion can be a source of 'hardiness, resilience and wellbeing'. She also reminds us that it is 'an important feature of socialization essential to our individual and collective wellbeing' (Halifax, 2013, p209). Singer (2014) reminds us that compassion rather than achievement-based motivation is both intrinsically rewarding and increases resilience.

Neff and Germer (2013) add self-compassion as a central feature of being compassionate to others – self-kindness as opposed to self-judgement; they suggest that:

> Self-compassion gives us emotional strength and resilience, allowing us to recover more quickly from bruised egos so we can admit our shortcomings, forgive ourselves, and respond to ourselves and others with care and respect.

(Neff and Germer, 2013, p291)

They further suggest that self-compassion is pertinent when 'considering personal inadequacies, mistakes and failures, as well as when confronting painful life situations that are outside of our control' (Neff and Germer, 2013, p291). Self-compassion is expressed in the internal dialogue when things go wrong, instead of focusing simply on fixing things and beating ourselves up. Neff and Germer (2013, p295) cite the work of Filip Raes (2010) in relation to his study on rumination and worry and the significant role self-compassion can take in reducing the effects in terms of depression and anxiety. They suggest that 'a large body of research indicates that self-compassion enables people to thrive' (Neff and Germer, 2013, p295).

Furthermore, they report that self-compassion when compared to self-esteem affords more emotional stability because high self-esteem is based on comparisons and successful accomplishments and, therefore, relies on positive outcomes. In contrast, self-compassion can be present in both good and bad scenarios and therefore affords more protection in terms of resilience (Neff and Germer, 2013, p299).

In Neff's (2011) self-compassion model, discussed in Chapter 2, mindfulness is identified as playing a crucial role. Neff and Germer (2013) explain that mindfulness forms a central component in allowing for the awareness of suffering and, while it may seem obvious, many people do not acknowledge the degree, especially when this is related to their inner critics and they are preoccupied in problem solving. Mindfulness, instead, allows for an important pause and redresses the avoidance behaviour often attached to painful thoughts and emotions. Mindfulness also stops us getting swept along in the sometimes natural aversion reaction. Neff and Germer (2013, p295) state that 'When we observe our pain mindfully, however, we can acknowledge our suffering without exaggerating it, allowing us to take a wiser and more objective perspective on ourselves and our lives.'

Other benefits of mindfulness identified within the research are outlined in the next section.

The evidence base for mindfulness

Table 6.2 lists only a small number of research articles relating to the advantages of mindfulness training.

Table 6.2 Research evidence in relation to the effectiveness of mindfulness

Research article topic	Authors	Findings
Bibliotherapy to decrease stress and anxiety and increase resilience and mindfulness	Sharma et al. (2014)	This study demonstrated that a brief, self-directed programme to decrease stress and enhance resilience and mindfulness provided excellent short-term effectiveness for enhancing resilience, mindfulness and quality of life, and decreasing stress and anxiety.
Mindfulness-based training attenuates insula response to an aversion interoceptive challenge	Haase et al. (2014)	These results support the hypothesis that mindfulness training changes brain activation, such that individuals process more effectively an aversive interoceptive stimulus. Thus, mindfulness training may serve as a training technique to modulate the brain's response to negative interoceptive stimuli, which may help to improve resilience.
The mindful brain and emotion regulation in mood disorders	Farb et al. (2012)	In patients with mood disorders, limiting habitual cognitive evaluation and replacing it with present-moment awareness appears to reduce 'automatic negative self-evaluation', increases the ability to tolerate negative impacts and helps to produce self-compassion and empathy.

(Continued)

Table 6.2 (Continued)

Research article topic	Authors	Findings
Mindfulness practice leads to increases in regional brain grey matter density	Hölzel et al. (2012)	Changes in grey matter concentration in regions of the brain involved in learning and memory processing, emotion regulation, self-referential processing and perspective taking were found.
Regular, brief mindfulness mediation practice improves electrophysiological markers of attentional control	Moore et al. (2012)	Even short, regular meditation practice can hone our attentional systems.
Effects of mindfulness on psychological health: A review of empirical studies	Keng et al. (2011)	Describes a clear convergence of findings from correlated studies, which suggests that mindfulness is positively associated with psychological health. These effects ranged from increased subjective well-being, reduced psychological symptoms and emotional reactivity, to improved regulation of behaviour.
Neural correlates of dispositional mindfulness during affect labeling	Creswell et al. (2007)	In individuals who are more mindful the amygdala is deactivated with the amygdala actually turned off.
The mindful way through depression: Freeing yourself from chronic unhappiness	Williams et al. (2007)	This study found that the recurrence of depression could be decreased by 75 per cent with mindfulness training.

Summary

Within this chapter we have examined what resilience looks like, what is an appropriate professional judgement and the crucial role reflection plays in terms of resilience and good practice. Throughout the text resilience has featured as a significant component of self-leadership; this chapter has provided an opportunity to draw this information together in relation to the facets of self-leadership, and to extrapolate further some of the essential concepts in managing under pressure. For example, we have explored the key role of self-compassion and the implications of working too many hours; self-awareness and the cognitive biases; the ironic concept that exercising compassion actually increases resilience; the potential detrimental effect of our innate hypervigilance for negative threats; neuroplasticity, which gives us a chance to change bad thinking habits; and the vital role state of mind plays.

The neurobiology of attention has been discussed along with Goleman's (2013) suggestion that, as leaders, we need to place our attention on three important focuses, inner, other and outer, to create appropriate balance. Other considerations included the significance of the mind and body connection, and the important functions of sleep and physical exercise in building resilience. The role of the mind was examined to introduce mindfulness as a concept that is receiving considerable positive attention, as a plethora of research supports the many benefits of this approach, certainly in terms of sustained resilience. A special focus on the role of mindfulness and compassion was presented, with some of the supportive evidence base for mindfulness as a practice.

The list below perhaps best summarises what constitutes a resilient professional. Mindfulness is a key common denominator in terms of improving each of the identified facets of self-leadership and has been identified as an extremely useful practice for enhancing resilience in individuals under pressure. It has been demonstrated that it is an amenable and worthwhile approach that can easily be incorporated into busy schedules.

Resilience factors include:

- a high degree of *self- and social awareness*, with cognitive and emotional flexibility;

- *self-observation* – observing in the moment what is being played out and remaining curious;

- *self-regulation* – appreciating the important role unexpressed feelings can play and when these create blocks in self and others;

- *self-management* – being able to manage state of mind and to handle conflict within self and others;

- *self-compassion* – being able to exercise self-compassion, in order to be both resilient and compassionate to others;

- *relationship management* – combining self- and social awareness, empathy and self-management in order to appreciate and manage relationships with others;

- *effective communication* – in all aspects such as verbal, non-verbal and written communication, in order to increase clarity and involvement.

Appendix

A new framework for easy, effective and sustainable leadership development

Aaron Turner PhD

Introduction

This appendix presents a framework for understanding what drives the quality of a person's leadership moment to moment. I will propose that there is a single factor that drives leadership impact. Through understanding how this factor works, there is tremendous scope for improving the quality of leadership performance in a sustainable way with relatively little effort.

'State of mind' is the way we identify the underlying driver of performance. In every field there are unavoidable fluctuations in performance independent of environment, skill, knowledge, strategy and technique. Because every human being is in a state of mind in every moment, the quality of that state of mind is enabling or impeding their ability to be easily and naturally effective. In professions where outcomes are more immediate, this link between state of mind and performance is more recognised. Actors, athletes and traders all know that how they feel unavoidably affects their ability to be at their best.

This appendix also presents a framework for identifying state of mind as the driver of our effectiveness, for understanding how and why it has this determining effect, and for understanding how it works so we can clearly understand how our state of mind can be improved. In other words, this framework allows us to clearly understand what determines the quality of leadership so that it can be taken in hand. This offers a radically new option for leaders who are used to receiving a lot of information about leadership skills and behaviours with no clear path to improving their on-the-job capabilities.

State of mind identifies a fundamental underlying driver of human performance and operates in every field of human endeavour.

Because state of mind describes the intrinsic link between a person's clarity of mind and their emotions, an understanding of the concept enables leaders to more easily improve their overall effectiveness, reducing their stress and the emotional burden of leadership, and also experiencing increased energy, engagement and well-being at work and at home.

The discovery of a single underlying determinant of performance and experience allows leaders to raise their effectiveness in all areas of their work through addressing one single variable. This allows leaders a high-yield strategy for improving their effectiveness. Leaders and teams who start to see and understand state of mind tend to see across-the-board improvements in their work and the achievements of their organisations.

I have used leadership examples from a range of fields so the reader can get a feel for the way state of mind applies to leadership universally, regardless of industry and field of practice.

Leadership development for leaders: from observations to fundamental drivers

I have taken the following quotations from senior US military leaders and their civilian counterparts because they have typically been exposed to a wide range of leadership training and development. Their experiences are representative of a common experience of managers and leaders: there is a plethora of leadership theories and approaches but a relative absence of understanding of what determines effective leadership.

> *I have been to a lot of leadership training in my career and I have had enough of being exposed to a range of ideas and opinions about leadership and being told, 'the best one is what works for you'. This course was different, . . . it focused on the deeper more fundamental drivers that affect us as leaders.*

(Senior civilian executive, US Army)

Over time leaders often become fatigued and cynical about leadership theory and training. There are too many ideas that take up too much time without delivering enough results. Leaders often report that the promising ideas they encounter in training take effort and attention to apply and sustain: effort and attention that busy leaders cannot spare on an ongoing basis. So even the useful ideas they encounter are unusable. Consequently, many leaders lose faith and interest in leadership theory and training in the face of the unrelenting demands of their daily responsibilities. The following quotations, although expressed by military leaders, are common in all the fields we have worked in:

> *When I came here I was thinking, 'why me?' I have been to a lot of leadership courses . . . I thought it would be a waste of time.*

(Senior civilian executive, US Army)

> *I did not feel I had time to come to this program. I had a negative feeling about it coming in.*

(Senior HR Director, US Army)

A lack of a clear understanding of what drives effective leadership means that the field of leadership does not have clear, simple, usable answers for busy committed leaders. The discovery and understanding of an underlying determinant of leadership effectiveness allows us to escape from the seemingly endless discussion of observable behaviours and leadership qualities and provide a simple framework for leaders to improve their effectiveness in any area of their work.

Because state of mind is already determining people's abilities in everything they do, it applies in the same way to leadership in any industry. Increased understanding enables new possibilities and new, simple answers to old, previously difficult and persistent problems. Through new levels of leadership performance, new possibilities are discovered and previously stubborn problems are relatively easily resolved. As one leader recounts:

> *I initially discovered One Thought's concepts for enhanced performance through mind-state awareness at a senior leadership professional development seminar. Like many, I was initially sceptical that by simply learning to be aware of, and control, my state of mind, I could improve the quality of my thinking and free myself to consider truly transformational solutions to complex, strategic problems. Despite my scepticism, I committed to following Aaron's prescribed approach to mind-state management . . . My personal experience has been profound, leading to several new strategic lines of operation, consolidation and elimination of other lines of operation and the rapid advance of four strategic initiatives in my organization – which had been 'stuck', in the 'too hard', pile for years. As a result, I invited Dr Turner to provide training to my direct report senior leaders – and have seen a similar transformation in the quality of their thinking and problem solving. In my 25 years of leadership and management experience and countless training and professional development sessions, One Thought's seminar on state of mind management offers the fastest route to a high-performing leadership team.*

(US Army Colonel)

This same leader, a person who was intensely committed to his mission, later told me that when he attended the leadership programme described above he was 'burnt out' and ready to move on. In his description you can almost feel the enthusiasm and the practical outcomes that came from his new understanding. What is also interesting is that he observed the same pattern in his team. As they came to understand state of mind as an underlying driver of performance, their effectiveness increased (see Figure A.1).

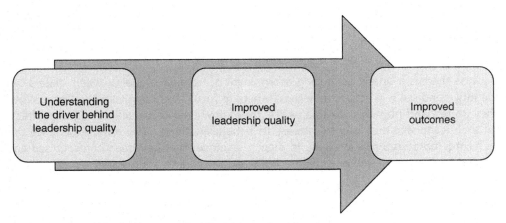

Figure A.1 State of mind as an underlying driver of performance

As they came to understand the role and nature of their state of mind in their leadership, the quality of their contribution improved. In the above example there was no change in the areas of skill, knowledge, processes or environment. What is not obvious, but none the less true, is that there was no technique or process to apply in order to achieve this improvement. Once the driver of performance is seen and understood, leaders make an automatic adjustment that has lasting results.

This is well illustrated by a small IT firm whose Managing Director and owner completed a four-day individual educational programme on state of mind. After the programme, with no significant change in employment numbers, sales, execution processes, products, technology or market conditions, the company saw a year-on-year increase in sales of 75 per cent and over two years doubled in size. It seems that what this MD learned had a direct and independent effect on his leadership and, through that, on the whole company. He said it was something he had not learned about before. This suggests there is something leaders are not learning about that directly, and significantly, affects the quality of what they are doing. As in the previous military example, this leader also reported a reduction in his experience of tension, stress and pressure without any decline in the demands of his job.

Leaders who have high demands on their time can have improved performance without additional time and effort by understanding what is determining their quality of work. Leaders in education are a good example. School leaders have both leadership and teaching responsibilities and report having little time for anything else.

The leadership team of a school academy went through a pilot educational programme to gain an understanding of state of mind. Their previous assessment from Ofsted graded them as 'good' on management and leadership. The assessment made after their leadership programme graded them as 'outstanding'. So there seems to have been a significant increase in the quality of their leadership. The change measured by Ofsted was echoed in anecdotal reports of an increase in comfort, trust and confidence in leadership from both year and subject teams.

Interestingly, the self-reported outcomes included a reduction of stress and of the feeling of time pressure. I mention this because it flies in the face of the idea that, in order to improve as a leader, you have to expend more time and effort to get and sustain improvement. Later in the appendix, I will explain how and why an almost automatic improvement in performance is common when leaders understand what is determining their quality of leadership. For now, I only want to highlight that this is possible and, in my observation, common.

Because there is a simple underlying determinant of leadership quality, when leaders can identify it and see it in action, they know where to focus their improvement efforts. When they understand how this variable works, they know how to reduce its negative effects on their leadership and how to increase its beneficial effects. They often experience this as having more resources available to them – resources that had been unrecognised and unused for years. As a senior leader in a hotel and restaurant group stated:

> *Gaining an understanding of the three principles and one's state of mind has provided me, and consequently my organisation, an endless supply of resource that had been underutilised for years. It has changed the way we do business, the way our relationships play out and become more resilient to circumstances that once seemed impossible to concur. Cascading this understanding to all levels of my organisation has not only created a better place to work but also visit and do business with – we can see the direct impact to our bottom line. This understanding is what makes all the difference when every other conventional method, tool and technique stops working.*

For leaders who had assumed such an improvement was not available without a lot of time and effort, this is both surprising and appreciated. Because the improvements come from an understanding and not the application of any techniques or practices, it is also a realistic development option for committed busy leaders:

> *When I came here I was thinking, 'why me?' I have been to a lot of leadership courses. It turned out to be more than I expected it would. It gave me a whole different perspective on state of mind that I didn't get from other courses I have been to. I thought it would be a waste of time but I am glad I was here.*

(Senior civilian executive, US Army)

What has self-leadership got to do with it?

Self-leadership points us beyond the behaviours, techniques and circumstances of leadership. This turning towards the person of the leader is important.

Leaders who have been through the same education and training programmes, perhaps even been mentored by the same person, possibly even using the same behavioural goals and standards, usually have very different kinds of outcomes. Since this is not explained by behaviours, skills, knowledge or environment, it needs to be understood in terms of the person of the leader (Quinn, 1996, 2004; Scharmer, 2008).

Attempts have been made to understand the 'x' factor of personal differences in leadership quality. I have heard them described as personality traits, or aspects of character. Although they describe what we observe, these understandings do not allow us to understand these differences in a way that makes them transferable.

Self-leadership is an important direction because it focuses our attention on understanding these differences in a way that allows us to generalise them to all leaders. Instead of assuming there is something special about the individual leader, we have the opportunity to look in the direction of a more general and shared potential and how all leaders might uncover this potential.

What is interesting about many outstanding leaders is that they can feel what makes them different, but they often do not understand it in a way that allows them to pass it on. One senior executive told me he did not struggle with the pressure and stress other leaders struggled with. He also found that clear, creative and responsive thinking came easily no matter how serious or pressurised the situation. He saw that his direct reports were not like this and they struggled with the stress and pressure of their jobs and also struggled to respond easily, effectively and strategically to their challenges. He could not understand this difference. He could see it was personal. He saw that he was different from his direct reports and that his input and guidance did not help them become more stable and strategic. So he concluded it was just an individual thing that was unexplainable and non-transferable. If he was right and his abilities were personal to him, they are not transferable. But if his abilities are an example of a more general human potential it could be uncovered in anyone. Understanding state of mind as a basis for self-leadership allows us to see and uncover a greater leadership ability in all leaders.

If self-leadership is the way we self-manage, this is where the answer lies. But what is this self-management? I want to suggest our self-management is the navigation of our state of mind. Here is the logic.

141

- Our state of mind is our mental clarity in any moment.

- State of mind determines how clearly and resourcefully we

and therefore how effectively we are able to operate and the influence we have on any person or situation.

- How we navigate our state of mind determines our level of clarity and that determines our level of ability and performance.

When I discussed the framework with the leader mentioned above, he said 'this explains why I am the way I am! Now I see how I can explain this to others so they can be this way too.' What he saw was that all leaders are managing the same variable. It is not a difference in individual capability that is the issue. The issue is how people manage the same capability in different ways. He also saw that anyone who understood how this self-management process worked could improve their leadership capability in a sustainable way. It was no longer personal, mysterious or elusive. That is the possibility of understanding the relationship of our state of mind to our performance.

State of mind and performance

I became aware of state of mind and its profound influence through the work being done at Pransky and Associates. George and Linda Pransky[1] were working with couples and helping them with their relationships. George asked me to do some research for a book he was writing. We decided I would sit in with him and observe the work he was doing. What I saw surprised, then fascinated me.

George and Linda's success rate with couples was unusually high. Just anecdotally, I worked with them for ten years and I cannot think of more than five cases that led to divorce. In fact, I can think of a couple of divorce mediations that ended in couples getting back together. Their standard for success was incredibly high. Most relationship counselling considers non-divorce and the successful resolution of problems a success. At Pransky and Associates success meant two happily married people who felt extremely confident about their ability to stay happy together no matter how long they had been together.

They achieved their unusual results by teaching people to deal with the influence of their state of mind on their relationship. This is worth illustrating because the same relationship exists in a leadership context.

They worked with couples whose relationships were struggling (to say the least). These couples would list the issues that were causing the problems in their relationships. Sometimes these were infidelities, disagreements, dissatisfactions, unhappiness or lack of commonality. They dealt with pretty much every relationship problem you can imagine, and more. Three things about the way they worked interested me.

1. They saw all these 'cases' as presenting the same problem and they addressed them that way. So instead of dealing with the presenting problem, they saw it as a symptom of a single generic relationship problem.

2. This generic 'relationship problem' was always seen as an individual problem relating to what I will be calling the person's state of mind and nothing else.

3. They had extremely consistent success in a field in which improvement tends to be hard won, insubstantial and often unsustainable. Not only that, their measure of success was higher than the rest of the field. I ended up interning and then working at the practice for ten years and I can honestly say, unsuccessful outcomes were the exception rather than the rule. As my appreciation for the role and nature of state of mind increased, this came to look perfectly normal and understandable to me too.

How did they do it?

The reason is simple. George and Linda focused and directly addressed what was causing all the observable problems: state of mind. A person's state of mind refers to their momentary level of clarity. This level of clarity is not purely intellectual, it encompasses a person's total internal state. This internal state includes the way a person feels, thinks and sees: emotion, cognition and perception.

I believe that the key to their uncommon success applies to leadership in the same way it applies to relationships. I have been applying the same logic and intervention to leadership development for ten years with similarly uncommon results. Most leaders and organisations are surprised by the range of outcomes and the impact of a better understanding of state of mind as illustrated in some of the preceding quotes.

Most people think of themselves as having a fairly consistent level of clarity. It is uncommon for people to appreciate that their level of clarity and mental capability varies as much as it actually does. This fluctuation is why you can try desperately to remember something without succeeding, while a second or two later you remember it instantly and effortlessly. I know this is an extremely trivial example, but it points to a highly underappreciated fact:

The clarity and capability of people's minds vary constantly.

You could think of it like a mobile phone signal. The difference is that we understand the variation in signal on our phone. When it is low we do not expect to have a good call quality. If we want a better signal we do not shake the phone, we move around to find a better signal. And we know exactly how to assess the quality of signal because we understand the feedback signal – the bars on the display screen. But what if we did not know what the bars meant and we did not know that signal strength varied? We would not know what was determining the quality of our calls. We might misdiagnose it, such as blame it on certain people we called, or our phone. The possibilities are endless.

I am suggesting that we have this problem with our use of our minds. We do not know that the signal quality varies – that the quality of our mind varies. At best, most people radically underestimate this. We have no idea how to assess our signal strength and very little idea how to improve it if we need to. The main issue is, how to assess or adjust something you are not even aware of. This is the problem with our state of mind. State of mind affects everything we do but, because we do not understand that, there is nothing we can do about it. Once you do understand state of mind you can avoid the negative effects of unclear states *and* more quickly and easily have an improvement of your state.

Signal strength

I would like to suggest that the primary indicator of people's clarity of mind or quality of state of mind is their emotions. More uncomfortable and unpleasant feelings (tension, discomfort or distress) indicate a drop in a person's clarity of mind. An increase in feelings without tension, such as ease, energy, well-being, indicate an increase in the quality of a person's state of mind.

This is why people's performance varies consistently with the way that they feel. In every area of activity, the worse people feel the harder they have to work to get results, and the better they feel the more easily they achieve better results. Therefore, our emotions are the most visible part of our state of mind.

This is also why relationship 'issues' are always consistent with a person's state of mind. In states of tension or distress the severity of issues increases. I know that you are thinking that it makes sense for people to be distressed about problems and things they do not like. But what I saw in the relationship work I observed over the years is that many of the issues couples think are causing all the distress have been a constant presence in their relationship. Let's start with something very trivial, such as one person being neat and the other messy. This is very common in relationships. What I observed is that this 'fact' remained a constant, but the level to which it becomes an important and distressing issue varies for couples depending on their emotional state. This indicates that:

> People's emotional state varies independently of the external issues and facts.

What I also observed was that:

> People's ability to see their issues with perspective, and have the creativity and clarity to deal with them productively and solve them, varies with their emotional state.

Some people's issues were trivial, like different levels of cleanliness. Other people's issues were more extreme, such as infidelity, bankruptcy or terminal illness. What they all had in common was that, when they were distressed, their problem loomed large so they felt destabilised emotionally. They could not think or see clearly enough to make any progress. When they were taught that their state of mind was independent of their circumstances, they learned how to have a clear mind and feel better without the situation changing. Once they felt better (their state of mind improved), they were not only emotionally resilient in the face of often quite serious challenges that previously destabilised them, but they also saw clearly and easily how to proceed productively or solve the issues.

The phenomenon of people being undisturbed by issues that previously distressed them *and* having perspective and answers they previously lacked was intriguing and got me hooked on the potential of understanding state of mind. Over the past 20 years I have yet to find a situation where people were struggling, in which an improvement in their state of mind, their clarity of mind and emotional stability, did not make a profound difference to the situation and its outcomes.

State of mind and the world of work

I know it is not anything new to suggest that emotions are important in relationships. But what I am suggesting is that emotions are a key indicator of something that is profoundly relevant no matter what we are doing (our state of mind). I have had clients tell me that their level of stress and distress determines how well they do in assembling flat-pack furniture. Our state of mind determines our level of clarity, capability and emotional resilience.

This is why leaders and teams start to struggle as their levels of stress increase. We have worked with a number of 'red teams'. These are chronically underperforming teams with important objectives. Sometimes red teams meet their challenges and 'go green' again. When we meet the red teams that go red and deteriorate, without fail, the teams are feeling very stressed and pressured. Understandable, you might say. But it is not as understandable as you might think, and if you could see how it does not actually make sense you would feel less stress yourself.

What I want you to see is that a high level of stress is completely consistent with compromised ability and hence impaired performance. Whether you are a leader, in a job interview, making a coffee or looking for your keys, stress and poor performance go together. This is because stress indicates a deteriorated state of mind. Everyone knows this to some degree. That is why no one wants to be nervous in an exam or driving test, on a date or when doing anything important. Once these red teams stop seeing their stress as a result of the pressure they are under and start to see how they could have less stress, a clearer state of mind, they start to feel better, and then they start to perform. Instead of panic, they are able to listen without reacting to each other. So they start to be able to work together. They are less worn out by their working hours and do not burn out by taking stress home. Soon, long-standing technical issues are being solved.

The team are surprised because they did not see two things.

1. Their state of mind made them incapable of clear strategic thought, team communication and emotional resilience.

2. Their state of mind could easily change without anything else changing.

With these two simple points of understanding I have seen red teams that were the bane of an organisation become the team showcase without learning any additional skills.

The framework of state of mind allows us to link:

*   the way people feel;

*   their clarity of mind and quality of thought.

This link is hugely underappreciated. Most professionals consider their feelings independent of their ability to see and think clearly and resourcefully. But in all of our experience, the kind of outcome improvements we see, such as increases in sales or profits, or the improved communication in the team example above or the school leadership team, always go hand in hand with a reduction of stress and increase in ease and emotional well-being. We also see a link between teams and individuals that are performing badly or in desperate need of help, and high levels of stress, pressure and other uncomfortable emotions. This is because our mental resources and emotional state are symptoms of the same variable: our state of mind. When our state of mind changes, our feelings and our capabilities change as a result. We can use this observation to identify another important, but underutilised fact:

> *People's feeling quality indicates the current clarity and capability of their mind.*

State of mind is a currently unrecognised performance variable but we consistently see that improvements in the state of mind of professionals lead to improvements in performance at work in every field of practice. We have seen the same pattern applied to sales effectiveness and client relationships, cross-department and company relationships, executive development and, of course, leadership. In fact we have seen improvements in state of mind across the board, and improvements wherever we have worked.

In his book *Building the Bridge as You Walk on It*, Quinn (2004) suggests that the qualities of an effective leader are not independent variables but the symptoms of the fundamental state of the leader. He calls this 'the essential state of leadership'. My observation is that a person's state of mind is what determines their quality of leadership capability, just as it determines their ability to do anything else. The qualities of effective leaders are often just the symptoms of a clearer mental state. So, focusing on the qualities themselves is a relative waste of time when compared to a focus on the state from which they come. We have found that improvements in state of mind come from nothing more than:

- seeing its existence and its relevance;
- understanding how it works.

In the following section we will give you an overview of how state of mind works.

How does state of mind work?

The way state of mind works is simple.[2] The challenge is seeing this simplicity in action. To the degree leaders can see this simplicity at work in the challenges they face every day, they will see an easier path to a clearer state of mind and find their effectiveness increasing without extra time or effort.

Our state of mind varies independently of circumstances. This indicates that our state of mind is a product of our mind, an internally created phenomenon that generates *the way* we experience our circumstances in every instance. This creation of feeling, perception and clarity of mind can be broken down into three elements. From these elements we can derive a very straightforward, yet profoundly enabling, understanding of the mind and our influence on it. In order to illustrate this, I will outline the three elements[3] and then explain the understanding of the mind that derives from it.

The three elements of state of mind

Mind

The idea is to suggest that the mind, before we do anything with it, has a nature. This is fundamentally important, because the nature of the mind would determine how it can best be used. For example, if the nature of the mind is an inert potential that must be used to be of value, then the best way of using it would be the most active way. This is a common assumption for many leaders and problem solvers. They will often say *'if I do not actively think of it I will not have any ideas or solutions'*.

If, however, the nature of the mind is an inherent intelligence constantly in action, then the mind does not require us to think so hard to benefit from its abilities. To me, this idea of mind fits better with the patterns of our experience. Most people I have worked with report that they have most of their best ideas when they are not thinking. They report them 'coming out of the blue'. Memory is often the same; the more you try the harder something is to remember. Leave it alone and it pops into mind. Rapport and connection are similar too. People recount that it is when they are least focused on trying to be connected and in rapport that it 'just happens'.

If we see emotions of ease, well-being and absence of tension and distress as indicating clearer states of mind, they also seem to 'just happen'. When I have asked people when they were at their best or happiest and to consider what they 'did' to get there, they report they cannot identify doing anything in particular; they just found themselves in a better place. This lack of doing often leads people to attribute the cause to something outside themselves, like good weather or ice cream or friends. The link of well-being to these stimuli is never a 100 per cent correlation. The 100 per cent correlation is with a mental freedom and better, more present states of mind.

The understanding of the nature of the mind as clarity, intelligence and well-being suggests that we do not need to 'do' anything to have clearer states of mind. This is why many successful leaders often say that what they are so good at 'comes naturally' and sometimes they find it hard to relate to the way others struggle with it. As one leader recounts:

> *Perhaps the most important thing I have discovered since my work with One Thought is that my business is not successful because of my ability to have constant anxious thought . . . I used to believe that I had to be constantly thinking . . . thinking of the next problem that might be coming around the corner, or thinking about what the next opportunity might be. If I wasn't doing this then I was neglecting my duty as business owner . . . I believed that I had to be anxious to be productive. This was a complete waste of time and must have had a hugely negative effect on those around me. Having this realization has been incredibly freeing.*

> (IT business owner and leader)

The element of mind also allows us to include the incredible potential of the mind as an inbuilt capability rather than as a property of the individual or his or her mental efforts. We have found that being open to the unknown potential of this resource is important. To me this is parallel to discussions of spirituality and leadership. This area of discussion is trying to point to a deeper capability and nature of human beings and the power and emotional stability that can be brought to the workplace. The element of mind allows us to include this aspect of experience and performance in a neutral way without having to link it to religion or spirituality as it often is.

If this understanding of the mind is at all correct, why are stress and distress so commonplace and emotional resilience, well-being and clarity more of an exception? This brings us to the second element in the equation.

Thought
You can think of thought as the medium through which we access and experience the nature of mind. The clearer our thought, the clearer our experience of the nature and

potential of mind. The more unclear our thought, the more unclear our experience of mind, so we do not experience the feelings of a clear mind, such as ease and well-being. Also, we do not experience as much of the power of mind. This explains why distress and capability are inversely related and why, when people are at peak performance, they talk of easily flowing yet fulfilling emotional experiences and effortless instinctive and responsive thought almost occurring on its own. This feature remains the same whether it is an athlete, musician, trader, public speaker or emergency response worker.

The inherent variable nature of thought is what determines the fluctuating signal strength I discussed earlier. This fluctuation is an unavoidable feature of state of mind because, through thought, you have the potential of mind forming moment to moment. Our thought in any moment creates our window on reality. The clarity of our thought in any moment determines the clarity of glass through which we are looking at it and the power of mind we are looking at it with.

The nature of thought is important. The idea that thought affects our perception and experiences is not new. The understanding of thought we are proposing is a fluctuating (ultimately self-righting) intermediary to the clarity and potential of the mind. We are pointing to the fact that, when people are upset or disturbed, if they do not focus on their suffering, they automatically and effortlessly calm down and feel better. The idea is that thought has no enduring existence of its own because thought has no substance. So it is a self-resolving function. The temporary insubstantial nature of thought is illustrated in the way people calm down without doing anything if they get upset, forget things they think of and have mood changes with no effort. The idea of thought as a temporary fluctuation is in opposition to the idea that distorting or negative thought has to be dealt with or removed in some way. From our perspective, addressing or dealing with the distortion of thought is just a way of focusing on a temporary fluctuation in a way that artificially prolongs the experience of it and the disturbance of clarity that it creates.

If our stress and distress are just a figment of thought: the moment-to-moment manifestation of our minds' creative ability, why do they affect us so badly? The answer to this question comes from the third and final element of state of mind.

Consciousness

I am not referring to any of the thought and literature on the concept or theory of consciousness. I am simply pointing to the conscious awareness of human beings. I am referring to every aspect of our awareness from vague sensations to specific cognitions, emotions and perceptions. Anything that a person is aware of is his or her consciousness. The element of consciousness allows us to appreciate the way people experience the moment-to-moment generation of thought as a full-fledged reality. If we think we are late, that thought manifests as a sensory reality for us. Our thought generally does not look or feel like a thought because we are conscious of it as our reality in that moment. Because of this it is easy to mistake distorted (painful) thought as something real and outside ourselves. This misunderstanding causes us to think about the felt 'problem' and fuel the thought that is creating the consciousness-based experience.

When you put the elements of mind, thought and consciousness together you get a potential for experience (mind) formulating content (thought) that we are aware of as a sensory experience (consciousness). This appearance of the temporary formulations of thought as a sensory reality for the individual explains why our experiences, although just momentary thought, feel so real to us and we take them to be real.

From the understanding above, managing one's state of mind becomes relatively simple and effortless. It could be distilled as follows.

- The way we feel is an indication of our clarity of mind and nothing else.

- We can consider our thoughts and perceptions in a clearer state of mind as reliable and those of unclear states unreliable. Therefore, acting on unclear perceptions and impulses is ill advised.

- Clarity of mind is a reliable default and a lack of clarity is the interruption of thought that by its nature is illusory (does not change the nature of mind) and temporary. Therefore, nothing has to be done to have an improvement in our state of mind.

Seeing the influence of our state of mind is the essence of self-leadership: a simple internal navigation to bring out the best in ourselves moment to moment. Because state of mind is a variable that applies to human capability in any field, it applies to leadership in any industry. From the military and private industry:

> State of mind has transformed the way I approach strategy thinking and critical decision-making. As a former senior executive for the United States Army and now a Chief Strategy Officer for a major IT company I have come to appreciate the relationship between the quality of my work and my state of mind. Dr Aaron Turner's work is an unpretentious common sense framework for results oriented thinking. Founded in a deep understanding of self and the inward dynamics that drive our creativity, state of mind navigation can replace gut feel and emotional overload with game changing strategic thinking!

To Health and Social Care:

> My own learning curve has continued to have a profoundly helpful impact in many areas including my career in the health service, in particular my experience of the work, my ability to operate more and more effectively within the workplace, and the joy I have found in doing so.

> After years of 'climbing the corporate ladder', achieving goal after goal, without feeling a sustainable sense of satisfaction, I have now realised that as I let go of the fundamental and innocent misunderstanding that my life situation is responsible for my experience, and seeing more and more that my experience of working life is only ever created from my own thinking in the moment, and that I can simply wait for a new and more empowering perspective to arise, I have experienced hugely increased clarity, resilience and wellbeing. The way I now experience work is in stark contrast to my previous experience of working life. More often than not I find ease and grace the default in navigating my working day with wisdom and efficiency. I no longer feel the need to act as if I have everything under control whilst living in perpetual concern about what is around the corner. Now I can simply be myself and know that what I need will come to me as I need it.

> I am now operating successfully, and to a very high standard, in a role that I assumed I might never be able to do; managing a range of multi-disciplinary hospital and

community services . . . the invisible and imagined boundaries I had innocently created in my reality have fallen away, leaving me with the freedom to take action.

(Senior NHS Manager)

Health and Social Care is a perfect example of how finding additional internal resources can make a dramatic difference in an environment that is increasingly pressured and demanding.

Why we manage our state of mind badly

As leaders come to understand state of mind and the elements behind it, it does become more straightforward and intuitive to manage/navigate. They begin to experience jumps in performance with less effort than they were previously expending:

I came in thinking 'why me?! I have so much to do'. Thanks to state of mind I was able to get my work done in less time with more clarity.

(US Army Program Executive)

I definitely have less stress. I have more going on, but I am getting it done quicker and getting it done better . . . [stress] used to be normal. But it does not look normal or necessary anymore. Now that I know what it is, it is easy to avoid.

(Hotel Director)

But if a clearer state of mind is more natural, why is it more the exception than the rule? Why do most leaders we introduce the idea to initially see it as effortful, difficult and unrealistic?

State of mind navigation is derailed by a couple of fundamental misunderstandings. As soon as the understanding outlined in the previous section is replaced by one of the misunderstandings below, a person's ability to have, or return to, a clear state of mind and effective leadership will be obscured. In this section I will outline two fundamental misunderstandings and how they derail our ability to have a better state of mind in the face of our challenges.

Misunderstanding 1
Our minds are (largely) reliable information processors

Most leaders we talk to assume their minds are reliable processors. They generally assume the mind takes in information and tells us what we are dealing with and comes up with largely credible suggestions for how we might deal with whatever it is. We assume our minds are like windows on the world.

This view of the mind is a central reason leaders live and work in unclear states of mind such as stress, pressure, resentment and overwhelm. This understanding of the mind leads us to relate to what we feel, see and think in a very undiscerning way. In other words, we trust, and use, what we feel, see and think in ways we would not if we recognised we are seeing a state of mind-dependent version of circumstances and information, not a neutral independent version of them. As I discussed earlier, our state of mind means that the version of reality we see and the clarity of thought we have about it changes as the quality of our state of mind changes. But if we attach to a particular version of circumstances it leads to us perpetuating it in our mind rather than experiencing the more fundamental and automatic return to clarity.

Misunderstanding 2
The circumstances of life directly affect the way we think and feel so you have to do something to have a clearer mind

As you will have seen in much leadership training, and the thinking behind it, the qualities of improved leadership have to be developed through certain techniques or practices. The basic assumption is that it is natural to be stressed and distressed by certain circumstances. Therefore, a somewhat disturbed mind is 'natural'. In order to counterbalance this natural tendency something has to be 'done'. The idea of 'stress management' is a good example. The assumption is that ongoing stress is unavoidable; therefore, the best we can do is manage it. In order to manage it there are certain things we need to do.

Much of the work in leadership development is similar. The desirable attributes of good leaders are identified and then approaches to achieving the identified quality are suggested. Even Quinn (2004), who suggests the qualities of effective leaders are all the symptom of the fundamental state of leadership, and hence cannot be achieved or created independently, spends the second half of his book suggesting approaches to achieving each quality separately.

As soon as someone believes they have to do something to improve their clarity of mind or feel better, they overlook the nature of the mind *as clarity* and the nature of *thought as inherently temporary* and they essentially override the default to a clearer mind by whatever thinking they are doing in order to clear their mind or feel better. But for this effort, they would easily and naturally default to a clearer state of mind.

Summary

State of mind influences the quality and effectiveness of everything we do. In the fields of sports, entertainment and financial trading its influence is visible and the ability to influence it is considered vital. In the areas of business and leadership, this influence has yet to be fully appreciated. Some analysts are starting to look in that direction. But there is limited acceptance of the existence of state of mind, let alone an appreciation of the profound influence it has on leadership and organisational performance.

In this appendix I have illustrated the consistent and predictable influence a leader's state of mind has on her or his quality of leadership in all industries and fields of practice. But we have gone a step further than identifying this fundamental driver of leadership quality. I have presented a framework for understanding what determines this underlying influence. This framework, based on the three principles originally outlined by Sydney Banks (1998, 2001), gives leaders the ability to avoid the negative impact of unclear states, improve their state of mind in any circumstance and therefore raise the quality of their leadership, while at the same time reducing their experience of stress, pressure and fatigue.

The primary issue for leaders is realising the existence and influence of state of mind. Regardless of all other factors, people are at their best in feelings of ease and confidence. People's abilities deteriorate as they start to experience growing levels of tension and distress. These feelings are the emotional aspect of our overall level of mental clarity and intelligence. With my executive development clients, I am generally asked to help in areas where executives are underperforming. These are always areas in which executives feel tense, pressured and uncomfortable. The problem areas of performance are also the ones the executives are trying hardest to address, usually with little significant improvement. If I am asked to help, I show executives how to have clearer minds (signified by more ease and confidence). As executives start to experience clearer minds in the same, previously troubling and challenging circumstances, their performance improves with no additional skills, just with a change of their mental clarity. Clarity of mind is a fundamental, but generally overlooked, aspect of leadership performance.

Just realising the existence of state of mind and the impact it has on us represents an increase in understanding and will lead to some performance improvement.

Once state of mind is identified as a driver of performance, understanding how it works brings further benefits and performance improvements. Our moment-to-moment clarity and potential of mind can be understood as the aggregate of three fundamental elements: mind, thought and consciousness. The words sound abstract but they are intended to point to aspects that drive and create our state of mind. Mind highlights the raw potential of the mind and the inbuilt impersonal intelligence of it. Mind is important because it points to the underlying, pre-existing power of the mind rather than the use of it by the individual. Thought points to the way we experience and access the potential of mind. We experience and access the power of mind thought by thought, moment to moment. So our clarity of thought in the moment determines our mental capability in that moment. If a person is nervous, not only are they a stunted awkward version of themselves, but their problem solving, creativity and memory recall suffers. This pairing of mental potential and feeling states shows us how we experience our moment-to-moment thought as a fully formed emotional-perceptual reality. If we get very nervous we tend to say 'that was a terrible situation', not 'I had a lot of unclear thought of the nervous variety and hence saw the situation in an intimidating light.'

To summarise, we are experiencing a tremendous mental potential through varying quality of thought experienced as an emotional-perceptual reality. The single variable that stands between us and a renewed clarity and potential of mind is our belief and preoccupation with the thought-created reality we currently occupy.

What these principles tell us about our state of mind is that it is essentially subject to an overarching intelligence that means it defaults to clarity and is only ever disturbed by fluctuations in thought. As we know, thoughts have no substance and, like leprechauns, if you take your eye off them, they have a habit of disappearing without a trace. That is why we have shopping lists. The thought of what to buy at the supermarket cannot be relied on to survive the walk to the shop, so we write it down.

Far from being complicated and elusive, as the discussions of leadership behaviours and qualities might suggest, a significant improvement in leadership quality can be achieved by understanding state of mind and navigating it more effectively. Because most leaders do not currently see or understand state of mind systematically, large improvements can be made with relatively little effort.

Without an awareness of state of mind and an understanding of how it works, leaders are left attempting to address demanding and complex challenges, while struggling with states of stress, pressure and the agitating, and sometimes overwhelming, barrage of thoughts that accompany these states. A realisation that this is just an unclear state and its barrage of unclear, unhelpful thought, frees leaders to have new clearer thought, and hence a more stable mind, without any change in circumstance.

Without this understanding of the nature and workings of state of mind leaders are left unknowingly, but actively, generating and using unclear states of mind as a matter of course. The symptom of this is the widespread accepted levels of stress, pressure and tension leaders associate with their workloads and responsibilities. With the understanding of a previously unseen performance variable comes a new potential for leadership performance. The framework outlined in this appendix presents a potential for reduced stress and increased ease, clarity and effectiveness as a new norm for leaders.

Most revolutionary is the realisation that a clearer, more effective state of mind is more of a natural default than an achievement. So, unlike most approaches to leadership development, addressing the clarity of mind of the leader is sustainable because it does not require the application of any ideas or techniques. Leaders can become more effective by realising and reducing the unproductive and inefficient ways they have been using the resource of their minds to date. Leadership impact can be increased by literally reducing the energy input just through an increase in understanding.

Challenges to improving leadership quality and potential lie in the acceptance of unproductive states of mind that are seen as 'normal' in our current understanding of leadership. Feelings of stress and pressure indicate unproductive states of mind, yet we accept and expect them based on the assumption that they are the experience of workload and environment. A key challenge to improving leadership in demanding jobs is the widely held misunderstanding that stress makes sense and hence is accepted. The acceptance of stress as inevitable translates to an unnecessary acceptance of impaired state of mind and hence impaired performance and results. Seeing the link between these feelings and a compromised state of mind allows leaders to move through these states to clearer, more capable ones.

Widespread improvements in leadership quality can be achieved by a relatively small amount of time spent understanding state of mind. But there is a much greater opportunity available. If the mind has an unknown potential, and our use of it depends on our ability to see past the limitations of our current thought-created reality, then the only limit to our discovery and use of a greater power of the mind is the degree to which we mistake our moment-to-moment, thought-created reality for a limit to our potential clarity. There is as yet no known limit to the power of the mind, so we have no known limit to the potential improvements in leadership quality through state of mind.

Notes

1. George and Linda Pransky are relatives. It was during my regular visits that I became aware of the work they were doing, its approach and the results they were getting.

2. The understanding of the mind that we are applying in our work is that originally outlined by Sydney Banks (1998, 2001). His perspective on the mind was based on a personal experience (see DVD or audio of *The Experience* from *The Long Beach Lectures*, Lone Pine Publishing), but was found to have huge potential in a number of fields (Pransky, 2001; Pransky, 2011b; Kramer, 2012; Neill, 2013).

3. I am using the term 'element' here as an elemental building block consistent with Sydney Banks's use of the term 'principle'.

References

AACN (American Association of Colleges of Nursing) (2002) Hallmarks of the professional nursing practice environment. *Journal of Professional Nursing*, 18: 295–304.

Adair, JE (1973) *Action Centred Leadership*. London: McGraw Hill.

Aguirre, DA, von Post, R and Alpern, M (2013) *Culture's Role in Enabling Organizational Change*. Available at www.strategyand.pwc.com/global/home/what-we-thin/reports-white-papers/article-display/cultures-role-organizational-change (accessed 14 April 2014).

Aiken, LH, Sloane, DM, Van den Heede, K, Griffiths, P, Busse, R, Diomidous, M, Kinnunen, J, Kozka, M, Lesaffre, E, McHugh, MD, Moreno-Casbas, MT, Rafferty, AM, Schwendimann, R, Scott, PA, Tishelman, C, von Achterberg, T and Sermeus, W (2014) Nurse staffing and education and hospital mortality in nine European countries: A retrospective observational study. *The Lancet*. Available at http://dx.doi.org/10.1016/SO140-6736(13) 62631-8 (accessed 26 February 2014).

Alimo-Metcalfe, B and Alban-Metcalfe, RJ (2001) The development of a new Transformational Leadership Questionnaire. *Journal of Occupational and Organizational Psychology*, 74(1): 1–27.

Alimo-Metcalfe, B and Alban-Metcalfe, J (2011) The 'need to get more for less': A new model of 'engaging leadership' and evidence of its effect on team productivity, and staff morale and wellbeing at work. *Management Articles of the Year*, June 2012, Chartered Management Institute (CMI): 6–12.

Allport, GW and Odbert, HS (1936) Trait-names: A psycho-lexical study. A study from the Harvard Psychological Laboratory. *Psychological Monographs*, 47, 1 (211). Published for the American Psychological Association by Psychological Review Company. Edited by Joseph Peterson, George Peabody College.

Amen, DG (2005) *Making a Good Brain Great*. New York: Three Rivers Press.

Amen, DG (2012) *Use Your Brain to Change Your Age*. New York: Crown Archetype.

Anderson, V (2007) *The Value of Learning: From Return on Investment to Return on Expectation: Research into Practice*. London: Chartered Institute of Personnel and Development.

Argyle, M, Salter, V, Nicholson, H, Williams, M and Burgess, P (1970) The communication of inferior and superior attitudes by verbal and non-verbal signals. *British Journal of Social and Clinical Psychology*, 9: 222–31.

Argyris, C (2010) *Organizational Traps: Leadership, Culture, Organizational Design*. Oxford: Oxford University Press.

Asebedo, S (2013) Well-being not a priority for workaholics, research says. Kansas State University, August 22. Available at www.k-state.edu/media/newsreleases/aug13/workaholics82213.html (accessed 15 April 2014).

Atkins, PWB (2014) Empathy, self–other differentiation, and mindfulness, in Pavlovich, K and Krahnke, K (eds) *Organizing Through Empathy*. New York and London: Routledge (Kindle version).

Attwood, M, Pedler, M, Pritchard, S and Wilkinson, D (2003) *Leading Change: A Guide to Whole Systems Working*. Bristol: Policy Press.

Avolio, BJ (2007) Promoting more integrative strategies for leadership theory-building. *American Psychologist*, 62(1): 25–33.

Avolio, BJ (2010) Pursuing authentic leadership development, in Nohria, N and Khurana, R (eds) *Handbook of Leadership Theory and Practice: A Harvard Business School Centennial Colloquium*. Boston, MA: Harvard Business Press.

Avolio, B and Gardner, W (2005) Authentic leadership: Getting to the root of positive forms of leadership. *The Leadership Quarterly*, 16(3): 315–38.

Avolio, BJ, Sosik, JJ, Jung, DI and Berson, Y (2003) Leadership models, methods, and applications, in Borman, WC, Ilgen, DR and Klimoski, RJ (eds) *Industrial and Organizational Psychology: Handbook of Psychology, vol. 12*. Hoboken, NJ: John Wiley and Sons.

Avolio, BJ, Gardner, W, Walumbwa, FO, Luthans, F and May, D (2004) Unlocking the mask: A look at the process by which authentic leaders impact follower attitudes and behaviours. *The Leadership Quarterly*, 15: 801–23.

Avolio, BJ, Walumbwa, FO and Weber, TJ (2009) Leadership: Current theories, research, and future directions. *Annual Review of Psychology*, 60: 421–49.

Banaji, MR and Greenwald, AG (2013) *Blind Spot: Hidden Biases of Good People*. New York: Delacorte Press (Kindle version).

Banks, S (1998) *The Missing Link*. Edmonton: Lone Pine Publishing.

Banks, S (2001) *The Enlightened Gardener*. Canada: International Human Relations Consultants.

Banks, S (2003) *Attitude: Using the Three Principles to Deal with Stress and Insecurity*. Edmonton: Lone Pine Media (audio CD).

Barnett, P, Malcolm, L, Wright, L and Hendry, C (2004) Professional leadership and organisational change: Progress towards developing a quality culture in New Zealand's health system. *The New Zealand Medical Journal*, 117(198): 1–11.

Barrett, JD (2010) Followers and situational factors, in Mumford, MD (ed.) *Leadership 101*. New York: Springer Publishing (Kindle version).

Bass, BM (1985) *Leadership and Performance Beyond Expectations*. New York: Free Press.

Bass, BM (1998) *Transformational Leadership: Industrial, Military and Educational Impact*. Mahwah, NJ: Lawrence Erlbaum Associates.

Bass, BM and Avolio, BJ (1997) *Full Range Leadership Development: Manual for the Multifactor Leadership Questionnaire*. Redwood City, CA: Mind Garden.

Bass, BM and Bass, R (2008) *The Bass Handbook of Leadership: Theory, Research and Managerial Applications* (4th edn). New York: Free Press.

Bass, BM and Riggio, RE (2006) *Transformational Leadership*. Mahwah, NJ: Lawrence Erlbaum Associates.

Bateson, G (1972) *Steps to Ecology of Mind*, foreword written by Catherine Bateson (2000). Chicago: University of Chicago Press.

Beck, AT and Beck, JS (2011) *Cognitive Behaviour Therapy: Basics and Beyond*. New York: The Guilford Press.

Beck, AT, Scott, J and Williams, JMG (2007) *Cognitive Therapy in Clinical Practice: An Illustrative Casebook*. London and New York: Routledge.

Beeler, CK (2010) Leader traits, skills, and behaviors, in Mumford, MD (ed.) *Leadership 101*. New York: Springer Publishing (Kindle version).

Begley, S (2009) *The Plastic Mind: New Science Reveals Our Extraordinary Potential to Transform Ourselves*. London: Constable and Robinson.

Bennett, N, Wise, C, Woods, PA and Harvey, JA (2003) *Distributed Leadership: A Review of Literature*. London: National College for School Leadership. Open Research Online.

Bennis, WG and Nanus, B (1985) *Leaders: The Strategies for Taking Charge*. New York: Harper and Row.

Benson, H (2005) Are you working too hard? A conversation with Herbert Benson. *Harvard Business Review*, November 2005.

Birey, F (2013) Mood disorders are glial disorders. Available at TEDxSBU, www.youtube.com/watch?v=Eo_OU344nZqc (accessed 20 January 2014).

Blakemore, SJ and Frith, U (2005) *The Learning Brain: Lessons for Education*. Oxford: Blackwell.

Bohm, D (1994) *Thought as a System*. New York: Routledge.

Bohm, D (1996) *On Dialogue*. London and New York: Routledge. Edited by Lee Nichol (Kindle version).

Bolden, R (2004) *What is Leadership: Leadership South West Research Report 1*. Exeter: University of Exeter, Centre for Leadership Studies.

Bolden, R and Gosling, J (2006) Leadership competencies: Time to change the tune. *Leadership*, 2: 147.

Bolden, R, Gosling, J, Marturano, A and Dennison, P (2003) *A Review of Leadership Theory and Competency Frameworks*. Exeter: University of Exeter, Centre for Leadership Studies.

Bolton, G (2010) *Reflective Practice Writing and Profession Development* (3rd edn). London: Sage.

Borg, J (2010) *Mind Power: Change Your Thinking, Change Your Life*. London: Pearson Education.

Borghi, AM and Cimatti, F (2010) Embodied cognition and beyond: Acting and sensing the body. *Neuropsychology*, 48(3): 763–73.

Bornemann, B and Singer, T (2013) What do we (not) mean by training, in Singer, T and Bolz, M (eds) *Compassion: Bridging Practice and Science*. Munich: MaxPlanck Society (e-book).

Bosman, M (2012) *How Your Brain Fights for Social Survival in the Workplace*. Available at www.strategicleadershipinstitute.ne/news/neuroleadership (accessed 20 May 2012).

Bowden, AO (1926) Study of the personality of student leaders in colleges in the United States. *Journal of Abnormal and Social Psychology*, 21: 149–60.

Boyatzis, R (2012) *What is Great Leadership: Inspiring Leadership Through Emotional Intelligence*. Cleveland, OH: Case Western Reserve University, USA (video).

Boyd, E and Fales, A (1983) Reflective learning: Key to learning from experience. *Journal of Humanistic Psychology*, 23(2): 99–117.

Bradford, DI and Cohen, AR (1998) *Power Up: Transforming Organizations Through Shared Leadership*. New York: John Wiley and Sons.

Braye, RH (2002) Servant-leadership: Leading in today's military, in Spears, LC and Lawrence, M (eds) *Focus on Leadership: Servant-Leadership for the 21st Century*. New York: John Wiley and Sons.

Brookes, S and Grint, K (2010) *The New Public Leadership Challenge*. Basingstoke: Palgrave Macmillan (Kindle version).

Brooks, M (1989) *Instant Rapport*. New York: Warner Books.

Brown, B (2012) *Daring Greatly: How the Courage to Be Vulnerable Transforms the Way We Live, Love, Parent, and Lead*. New York: Portfolio Penguin.

Brown, K (1996) Planning and evaluation in training: some thoughts on 'how to evaluate'. Paper presented at the National Association of Training Officers in Personal Social Services Annual Conference.

Brown, K, Ryan, RM and Creswell, JD (2007) Mindfulness: Theoretical foundations and evidence for its salutary effects. *Psychological Inquiry*, 18(4): 211–37.

Brown, K, McCloskey, C, Galpin, D, Keen, S and Immins, T (2008) Evaluating the impact of post-qualifying social work education. *Social Work Education*, 27(8): 853–67.

Brown, P (2011) Interview with Professor Paul Brown. *The Bulletin of the Association for Coaching*, 6 (Autumn): 3–7.

Brown, P and Brown, V (2012) *Neuropsychology for Coaches: Understanding the Basics*. London: McGraw Hill, Open University Press.

Brown, P and Hales, B (2011) Neuroscience: New science for new leadership. *Developing Leaders: Executive Education in Practice*, 5: 36–42.

Buchanan, DA, Addicott, R, Fitzgerald, L, Ferlie, E and Baeza, JI (2007) Nobody in charge: Distributed change agency in healthcare. *Human Relations*, 60(7): 1065–90.

Burns, JM (1978) *Leadership*. New York: Harper and Row.

Burns, JM (2003) *Transforming Leadership: A New Pursuit of Happiness*. New York: Grove Press.

Byrne, CL (2010) How leaders think, in Mumford, MD (ed.) *Leadership 101*. New York: Springer Publishing (Kindle version).

Cameron, OG (2002) *Visceral Sensory Neuroscience: Interoception*. New York: Oxford University Press.

Care Quality Commission (CQC) (2012) *The State of Healthcare and Adult Social Care in England: An Overview of Key Themes in Care 2011/2012*. London: CQC.

Carlyle, T (1888) *On Heroes, Hero-Worship and the Heroic in History*. New York: Frederick A. Stokes and Brother.

Carpenter, J (2005) *Evaluation Outcome in Social Work Education*. Dundee: Scottish Institute for Excellence in Social Work Education (SIESWE) and the Social Care Institute for Excellence (SCIE). Available at www.scie.org. uk/publications/misc/evalreport.pdf (accessed 26 March 2012).

Carpenter, J (2011) Evaluating social work education: A review of outcomes, measures and research designs and practicalities. *Social Work Education*, 30(2): 122–40.

Carroll, M and Gilbert, MC (2011) *On Being a Supervisee Creating Learning Partnerships* (2nd edn). Vukani Publishing (online).

Cashman, K (2008) *Leadership From the Inside Out: Becoming a Leader for Life* (2nd edn). San Francisco, CA: Berrerr-Koehler.

Cashman, K (2012) *The Pause Principle: Step Back to Lead Forward*. San Francisco, CA: Berrerr-Koehler Publishers Inc.

Caughron, JJ (2010) Perspectives on leadership research, in Mumford, MD (ed.) *Leadership 101*. New York: Springer Publishing (Kindle version).

Caver, CS and Scheier, MF (2011) Self-regulation of action and affect, in Vohs, KD and Baumeister, RF (eds) *Handbook of Self-Regulation: Research, Theory and Application* (2nd edn). New York: Guilford Press.

Chadwick, P (2013) Leaders fit for the future. *Developing Leaders: Executive Education in Practice*, 13.

Chochinov, HM (2007) Dignity and the essence of medicine: The A, B, C and D of dignity conserving care. *British Medical Journal*, 334: 184–7.

Chödrön, P (2001) *The Places that Scare You: A Guide to Fearlessness*. London: Element, HarperCollins.

Choi, J (2006) A motivational theory of charismatic leadership: Envisioning, empathy, and empowerment. *Journal of Leadership and Organisational Studies*, 13(1): 24–43.

Chomsky, N (2000) *The Architecture of Language*. Oxford: India Paperbacks.

CIPD (Chartered Institute of Personnel and Development) (2010) *Real-world Coaching Evaluation: A Guide for Practitioners*. London: CIPD.

CIPD (2011) *Developing Resilience*. London: Produced by Affinity Health at Work for the CIPD.

CIPD (2012) *Evaluating Learning and Talent Development*. Available at www.cipd.co.uk/hr-resources/factsheets/evaluating-learning-talent-development.aspx (accessed 6 April 2014).

CIPD (2013) *Employee Outlook: Focus on Employee Well-being*. London: CIPD.

CIPD (2014) *Cultivating Trustworthy Leaders*. Research report. London: CIPD.

Clift, RT, Houston, WR and Pugach, M (1991) *Encouraging Reflective Practice in Education: An Analysis of Issues and Programs*. New York: Teachers' College Press.

Coles, C (2002) Developing professional judgment. *Journal of Continuing Education Health Professions*, 22(1): 3–10.

Collins, DB and Holton, EF (2004) The effectiveness of managerial leadership development: A meta-analysis of studies from 1982 to 2001. *Human Resource Development Quarterly*, 15(2).

Collins, J (2001) *Good to Great: Why Some Companies Make the Leap … and Others Don't*. London: Random House Business Books.

Connelly, MS, Gilbert, JA, Zaccaro, SJ, Threlfall, KV, Marks, MA and Mumford, MD (2000) Exploring the relationship of leader skills and knowledge to leader performance. *The Leadership Quarterly*, 11: 65–86.

Creswell, JD, Way, BM, Eisenberger, NI and Lieberman, MD (2007) Neural correlates of dispositional mindfulness during affect labelling. *Psychosomatic Medicine*, 69: 560–5.

Crosby, BC and Bryson, JM (2005) *Leadership for the Common Good: Tackling Public Problems in a Shared-power World*. San Francisco, CA: Jossey-Bass.

Cruess, SR, Cruess, RL and Steinert, Y (2008) Role modelling: Making the most of a powerful teaching strategy. *British Medical Journal*, 336: 718.

Csikszentmihalyi, M (2002) *Flow: The Classic Work on How to Achieve Happiness*. London: Rider.

Cuddy, A (2012) *Your Body Language Shapes Who You Are*. Available at www.ted.com/tals/amy_cuddy_your_body_language_shapes_who_you_are (accessed 20 September 2013).

Currie, G and Lockett, A (2011) Distributing leadership in Health and Social Care: Concertive, conjoint or collective? *International Journal of Management Reviews*, 13: 286–300.

Damasio, AR (1994) *Descartes' Error: Emotion, Reason, and the Human Brain*. New York Putnam.

Damasio, AR (1999) *The Feeling of What Happens: Body, Emotion and the Making of Consciousness*. London: Vintage Books.

Damasio, A (2006) *Descartes' Error: Emotion, Reason and the Human Brain*. London: Vintage Books.

Darzi, L (2008) *High Quality Care for All: NHS Next Stage Review, Final Report*. London: Department of Health.

Davis, J, Balda, MJ and Rock, D (2014) Keep an eye on the time. *Leadership Development*. Available at www.astd.org/Publications/Magazines/TD/TD-Archive/2014/01/Keep-An-Eye-on-the-Time (accessed 14 April 2014).

Deci, EL and Flaste, R (1995) *Why We Do What We Do: Understanding Self-Motivation*. London: Penguin Books.

Dehaene, S (2011) Signatures of consciousness, in Brockman, J (ed.) *The Mind: Leading Scientists Explore the Brain, Memory, Personality, and Happiness*. New York: HarperCollins.

De Mello, A (1990) *Awareness*. Nashville, TN: Zondervan.

Dennett, DC (2013) The normal well-tempered mind, in John Brockman (ed.) *Thinking: The New Science of Decision-Making, Problem-Solving, and Prediction*. New York: HarperCollins.

Department of Health (1998) *Modernising Social Services: Promoting Independence, Improving Protection, Raising Standards*. London: DH.

Department of Health (2009) *Inspiring Leaders: Leadership for Quality*. London: DH.

Department of Health (2012) *Compassion in Practice: Nursing, Midwifery and Care Staff: Our Vision and Strategy*. London: DH.

Department of Health (2013) Delivering high quality, effective, compassionate care: Developing the right people with the right skills and the right values. A mandate from the Government to Health Education England, April 2013 to March 2015. London: DH.

DeSteno, D (2012) *Compassion Science*. Available at www.poptech.org/popcasts/david_desteno_compassion_science (accessed 30 November, 2013).

Dispenza, J (2007) *Evolve Your Brain: The Science of Changing Your Mind*. Deerfield Beach, FL: Health Communications.

Dispenza, J (2012) *Breaking the Habit of Being Yourself: How to Lose Your Mind and Create a New One*. London: Hay House.

Doidge, N (2007) *The Brain That Changes Itself*. London: Penguin.

Dolan, R (2011) *Neuroscience of Emotion*. The Royal Society, blogs.royalsociety.org/science-live/2011/07/09neuroscience-of-emotion (accessed 12 December 2013).

Draper, J and Clark, E (2007) *Evaluating the Impact of Continuing Professional Education on Healthcare Practice: The Rhetoric and the Reality*. Milton Keynes: The Open University.

Dumdum, UR, Lowe, KB and Avolio, BJ (2003) A meta-analysis of transformational and transactional leadership correlates of effectiveness and satisfaction: An update and extension, in Avolio, BJ and Yammarino, FJ (eds) *Transformational Leadership: The Road Ahead*. Oxford: Elsevier Press.

Edwards, N (2014) *Community Services: How They Can Transform Care*. London: The King's Fund.

Eicher-Catt, D (2005) The myth of servant-leadership. *Women and Language: A Feminist Perspective*, 28(1): 17–25.

Ekman, P (2003) *Emotions Revealed: Understanding Faces and Feelings*. London: Phoenix.

Ernst, A, Alkass, K, Bernard, S, Salehpour, M, Perl, S, Tisdale, J, Possnert, G, Druid, H and Frisen, J (2014) Neurogenesis in the striatum of the adult human brain. *Cell*, 156(5): 1072–83.

Eurich, T (2013) *Bankable Leadership: Happy People, Bottom Line Results and the Power to Deliver Both*. Austin, TX: Greenleaf Book Group Press.

Evans, M (2011) *90:10 – The Single Most Important Thing You Can Do For Your Stress.* Available at www.youtube.com (accessed 20th April 2012).

Farb, NAS, Anderson, AK, Mayberg, H, Bean, J, McKeon, D and Segal, ZV (2010) Minding one's emotions: Mindfulness training alters the neural expression of sadness. *Emotion: American Psychological Association,* 10(1): 25–33.

Farb, NAS, Anderson, AK and Segal, ZV (2012) The mindful brain and emotion regulation in mood disorders. *Canadian Journal of Psychiatry,* 57(2): 70–7.

Fenner, P (2007) *Radiant Mind: Awakening Unconditioned Awareness.* Boulder, CO: Sounds True.

Fiedler, FE (1967) *A Theory of Leadership Effectiveness.* New York: McGraw-Hill.

Fiedler, FE and Garcia, JE (1987) *New Approaches to Effective Leadership: Cognitive Resources and Organizational Performance.* New York: Wiley.

Figley, C (1995) *Compassion Fatigue: Coping with Secondary Traumatic Stress Disorder in Those Who Treat the Traumatized.* New York: Brunner-Routledge.

Finlay, L (2008) Reflecting on 'reflective practice'. Practice-based Professional Learning Centre, paper 52, The Open University. Available at www.open.ac.uk/opencetl/file/ecms/web-content/Finlay-(2008)-Reflecting-on-reflective-practice-PBPL-paper-52.pdf (accessed 20 May 2012).

Fleenor, JW (2007) Trait approach to leadership, in Rogelberg, SG (ed.) *Encyclopaedia of Industrial and Organizational Psychology, vol. 1.* London: Sage.

Fleishmann, EA (1953) The description of supervisory behaviour. *Journal of Applied Psychology,* 37: 1–6.

Fleming, P (2006) Reflection: A neglected art in health promotion. *Health Education Research,* 22(5): 658–64.

Foster, R (2013) *Why Do We Sleep?* Available at www.ted.com/talks/russell_foster_why_do_we_sleep (accessed 10 May 2014).

Frankl, VE (2004) *Man's Search For Meaning: The Classic Tribute to Hope from the Holocaust.* Croydon: Random House.

Fredrickson, BL (2001) The role of positive emotions in positive psychology: The broaden-and-build theory of positive emotions. *American Psychology,* 56(3): 218–26.

Friedrich, TL (2010) The history of leadership research, in Mumford, MD (ed.) *Leadership 101.* New York: Springer Publishing (Kindle version).

Frith, C (2007) *Making Up The Mind: How the Brain Creates Our Mental World.* Oxford: Blackwell Publishing.

Gale, TJ, Shields DC, Ishizawa, Y and Eskandar, EN (2014) Reward and reinforcement activity in the nucleus accumbens during learning. *Frontier Behavioral Neuroscience,* 3 April, doi: 10.3389/fnbeh.2014.00114. Available at http://journal.frontiersin.org/Journal/10.3389/fnbeh.2014.00114/full (accessed 12 May 2014).

Gallup (2013) *State of the American Workplace. Employee Engagement Insights for U.S. Business Leaders.* Washington, DC: Gallup.

Gardner, J (1990) *On Leadership.* New York: The Free Press.

Gardner, W, Avolio, B, Luthans, F, Walumbwa, F and May, D (2005) *'Can you see the real me'* – A self-based model of authentic leader and follower development. *Leadership Quarterly,* 16(3): 343–72.

Garland, EL, Froeliger, B and Howard, MO (2013) State of mindfulness during meditation predicts enhanced cognitive reappraisal. *Front Psychiatry,* 4: 173. Available at www.ncbi.nlm.nih.gov/pmc/articles/PMC3887509/ (accessed 10 February 2014).

Garratt, B (2010) *The Fish Rots From the Head: Developing Effective Board Directors* (3rd edn). London: Profile Books.

Gazzaniga, MS (2012) *Who's in Charge: Free Will and the Science of the Brain*. London: Robinson (Kindle version).

George, B (2003) *Authentic Leadership: Rediscovering the Secrets to Creating Lasting Value*. San Francisco, CA: Jossey-Bass.

George, B, Sims, P, McLean, A and Mayer, D (2007) Discovering your authentic leadership. *Harvard Business Review*, 85(2): 129–38.

Gerhardt, S (2004) *Why Love Matters: How Affection Shapes a Baby's Brain*. London: Routledge.

Gibb, CA (1947) The principles and traits of leadership. *Journal of Abnormal and Social Psychology*, 42: 267–84.

Gill, R (2011) *Theory and Practice of Leadership* (2nd edn). London: Sage.

Girardeau, G, Benchenane, K, Wiener, SI, Buzsáki, G and Zugaro, MB (2009) Selective suppression of hippocampal ripples impairs spatial memory. *Nature Neuroscience*, 12: 1222–3. Available at www.nature.com/neuro/journal/v12/n10/abs/nn.2384.html (accessed 12 March 2012).

Gladwell, M (2005) *Blink: The Power of Thinking Without Thinking*. London: Penguin Books.

Gleeson, J and Berman, SP (2012) *Inside Job: 8 Secrets to Loving Your Work and Thriving*. San Francisco, CA: Career Wisdom Institute (Kindle version).

Glynn, MA and DeJordy, R (2010) Leadership through an organization behavior lens: A look at the last half-century of research, in Nohria, N and Khurana, R (eds) *Handbook of Leadership Theory and Practice: A Harvard Business School Centennial Colloquium*. Boston, MA: Harvard Business Press.

Goldin, P (2008) *The Neuroscience of Meditation*, 6 November. Available at www.youtube.com/watch?v=Q52HFos18wY (accessed 28 August 2012).

Goldin, P (2011) *Mindfulness Meditation Part 1*, Stanford University. Available at www.youtube.com/watch?v=SbWlzxzzgk (accessed 28 April 2012).

Goldstein, J (2013) *7 Treasures of Awakening: The Benefits of Mindfulness*. Sounds True Inc. (Kindle e-book).

Goleman, D (2000) Leadership that gets results. *Harvard Business Review*, March–April.

Goleman, D (2011) *The Brain and Emotional Intelligence: New Insights*. Northampton, MA: More Than Sound (Kindle version).

Goleman, D (2013) *Focus: The Hidden Driver of Excellence*. London: Bloomsbury (Kindle version).

Goleman, D, Boyatzis, R and McKee, A (2013) *Primal Leadership: Unleashing the Power of Emotional Intelligence*. Boston, MA: Harvard Business Review Press.

Google (2013) *Leadership Books*. Available at www.google.co.uk/search?q=leadership+books&oq=leadership+books&aqs=chrome..69i57j0l3.3566j0&sourceid=chrome&ie=UTF-8 (accessed 8 March 2014).

Gordon, R (2008) Dispersed leadership, power and change: An empirical study using a critical management framework – Australia and New Zealand Academy of Management 22nd ANZAM Conference 2008: Managing in the Pacific Century. Auckland, New Zealand, December 2008. Bond University Faculty of Business ePublications.

Gosling, J, Jones, S and Sutherland, I (2012) *Key Concepts of Leadership*. London: Sage.

Graeff, CL (1997) Evolution of situational leadership theory: A critical review. *Leadership Quarterly*, 8(2): 153–70.

Graen, GB and Uhl-Bien, M (1995) Relationship based approach to leadership: Development of leader exchange theory of leadership over 25 years – applying a multilevel domain perspective. *Leadership Quarterly*, 60: 219–47.

Greenleaf, RK (1970) *The Servant as Leader.* Indianapolis, IN: Robert K. Greenleaf Center.

Greenleaf, RK (1977) *Servant Leadership: A Journey into the Nature of Legitimate Power and Greatness.* Mahwah, NJ: Paulist Press.

Greenwood, J (1993) Reflective practice: A critique of the work of Argyris and Schön. *Journal of Advanced Nursing*, 19: 1183–7.

Grint, K (2010) *Leadership: A Very Short Introduction.* Oxford: Oxford University Press

Gronn, P (2002) Distributed leadership, in Leithwood, KA and Hallinger, P (eds) *Second International Handbook of Educational Leadership and Administration.* Dordrecht: Kluwer.

Gronn, P and Hamilton, A (2004) A bit more life in the leadership: co-principalship as distributed leadership practice. *Leadership and Policy in Schools*, 3(1): 3–35.

Grossman, P (2013) Kindness and compassion as integral to mindfulness, in Singer, T and Bolz, M (eds) *Compassion Bridging Practice and Science.* Munich: MaxPlanck Society (e-book).

Gyurak, A, Goodkind, MS, Madan, A, Kramer, JH, Miller, BL and Levenson, RW (2009) Do tests of executive functioning predict ability to down regulate emotions spontaneously and when instructed to suppress? *Cognitive, Affective and Behavioural Neuroscience*, 9(2): 144–52.

Haase, L, Thom, NJ, Shukla, A, Davenport, PW, Simmons, AN, Paulus, MP and Johnson, DC (2014) Mindfulness-based training attenuates insula response to an aversion interoceptive challenge. *Social Cognitive and Affective Neuroscience*, 8 April.

Hackman, JR (2010) What is this thing called leadership?, in Nohria, N and Khurana, R (eds) *Handbook of Leadership Theory and Practice: A Harvard Business School Centennial Colloquium.* Boston, MA: Harvard Business Press.

Hackman, MZ and Johnson, CE (2009) *Leadership: A Communication Perspective* (5th edn). Long Grove, IL: Waveland Press.

Hafford-Letchfield, T (2007) *Practising Quality Assurance in Social Care.* Exeter: Learning Matters.

Hafford-Letchfield, T and Bourn, D (2011) 'How am I doing?': Advancing management skills through the use of a multi-source feedback tool to enhance work based learning on a post qualifying post graduate leadership and management programme. *Social Work Education: The International Journal*, 30(5): 497–511.

Hafford-Letchfield, T and Lawler, J (2010) Guest editorial: Reshaping leadership and management: The emperor's new clothes? *Social Work and Social Sciences Review*, 14(1): 5–8.

Halifax, J (2010) Compassion and the true meaning of empathy. Available at www.ted.com/talks/joan_halifax (accessed 4 May 2014).

Halifax, J (2013) Understanding and cultivating compassion in clinical settings. The A.B.I.D.E Compassion Model, in Singer, T and Bolz, M (eds) *Compassion Bridging Practice and Science.* Munich: MaxPlanck Society (e-book).

Halpin, AW and Winer, BJ (1957) A factorial study of the leader behaviour descriptions, in Stogdill, RM and Coons, AE (eds) *Leader Behaviour: Its Description and Measurement.* Columbus, OH: Ohio State University, Bureau of Business Research.

Ham, C and Walsh, N (2013) *Lessons from Experience: Making Integrated Care Happen at Scale and Pace.* London: The King's Fund.

Ham, C, Dixon, A and Brooke, B (2013) *Transforming the Delivery of Health and Social Care: The Case for Fundamental Change.* London: The King's Fund.

Hamilton, J (2008) *Multitasking Teens May be Muddling Their Brains.* Available at www.npr.org/templates/story/story.php?storyId=95524385 (accessed 10 November 2013).

Hartley, J and Allison, M (2000) The role of leadership in the modernization of public services. *Public Money and Management*, 20: 35–40.

Hayes, P (2006) *NLP Coaching.* London: Open University Press, McGraw Hill.

Heffernan, M (2011) *Wilful Blindness: Why We Ignore the Obvious At Our Peril.* London: Simon and Schuster.

Hernandez, M, Eberly, MB, Avolio, BJ and Johnson, MD (2011) The loci and mechanisms of leadership: Exploring a more comprehensive view of leadership theory. *Leadership Quarterly*, 22(6): 1165–85.

Hersey, P and Blanchard, KH (1969) Life cycle theory of leadership. *Training and Development Journal*, 23(2): 26–34.

Hersey, P and Blanchard, KH (1993) *Management of Organizational Behaviour: Utilizing Human Resources* (6th edn). Englewood Cliffs, NJ: Prentice Hall.

Hersey, P, Blanchard, KH and Johnson, DE (2013) *Management of Organisational Behaviour: Leading Human Resources* (10th edn). London: Pearson.

Hitti, FL and Siegelbaum, SA (2014) The hippocampal CA2 region is essential for social memory. *Nature.* Available at http://dx.doi.org/10.1038/nature13028 (accessed 15 March 2014).

Hobbs, V (2007) Faking it or hating it: Can reflective practice be forced? *Reflective Practice*, 8(3): 405–17.

Hofman, W, Friese, M, Schmeichel, BJ and Baddeley, AD (2011) Working memory and self-regulation, in Vohs, KD and Baumeister, RF (eds) *Handbook of Self-Regulation Research, Theory and Applications* (2nd edn). New York: The Guilford Press.

Holroyd, J (2012) *Improving Personal and Organisational Performance in Social Work.* London: Sage.

Holroyd, J and Brown, K (2011) *Leadership and Management Development for Social Work and Social Care: Creating Leadership Pathways of Progression.* Bournemouth: Bournemouth University Centre for Post-Qualifying Social Work and Learn to Care.

Hölzel, BK, Carmody, J, Vangel, M, Congleton, C, Yerramsetti, SM, Gard, T and Lazar, SW (2012) Mindfulness practice leads to increases in regional brain gray matter density. *Psychiatry Research*, 191(1): 36–43. Available at www.ncbi.nlm.nih.gov/pmc/articles?PMC3004979 (accessed 10 May 2014).

House, RJ (1971) A path-goal theory of leader effectiveness. *Administrative Science Quarterly*, 16: 321–39.

House, RJ and Mitchell, TR (1974) Path-goal theory of leadership. *Journal of Contemporary Business*, 3: 81–97.

Howell, JP and Costley, DL (2006) *Understanding Behaviours for Effective Leadership* (2nd edn). Upper Saddle River, NJ: Prentice Hall.

Hunt, JG, Boal, KB and Dodge, GE (1999) The effects of visionary and crisis-responsive charisma on followers: An experimental examination of two kinds of charismatic leadership. *The Leadership Quarterly*, 10: 423–48.

Huppert, FA and Baylis, N (2004) Well-being: towards an integration of psychology, neurobiology and social science. *Philosophical Transactions of The Royal Society London*, 359: 1447–51.

Iacoboni, M (2009) *Mirroring People: The Science of Empathy and How We Connect With Others*. New York: Picador.

IBM (2008) *IBM Global Study: Majority of Organizational Change Projects Fail: Changing Mindsets and Culture Continue to be Major Obstacles*. Available at www-03.ibm.com/press/us/en/pressrelease/25492.wss (accessed 12 November 2013).

Ilardi, S (2013) *Depression is a Disease of Civilization – Stephen Ilardi at TEDxEmory*. Available at www.youtube.com/watch?v=I9fl-YPWFzM (accessed 14 April 2014).

Isaacs, W (2008) *Dialogue: The Art of Thinking Together*. New York: Currency Publishing (Kindle version).

Jack, AI, Dawson, A, Begany, K, Leckie, R, Barry, K, Ciccia, K and Snyder, A (2012) fMRI reveals reciprocal inhibition between social and physical cognitive domains. *Neuro-Image*, 66: 385–401.

James, W (1880) Great men, great thought and the environment. *Atlantic Monthly*, 0046(276): 441–59, from Cornell University Library.

Jay, JK and Johnson, KL (2002) Capturing complexity: A typology of reflective practice for teacher education. *Teaching and Teacher Education*, 18: 73–85.

Johns, C (2009) *Becoming a Reflective Practitioner* (3rd edn). Oxford: Wiley-Blackwell.

Johnson, CE (2005) *Meeting the Ethical Challenges of Leadership: Casting Light or Shadow* (2nd edn). Thousand Oaks, CA: Sage.

Joseph, A (2009) *Cognitive Behavioural Therapy*. Chichester: Capstone Publishing.

Judge, TA, Bono, JE, Ilies, R and Gerhardt, MW (2002) Personality and leadership: A qualitative and quantitative review. *Journal of American Psychology*, 87(4): 765–80.

Jung, DI (2001) Transactional and transformational leadership and their effects on creativity in groups. *Creativity Research Journal*, 13(2): 185–95.

Kabat-Zinn, J (2012) *Mindfulness for Beginners: Reclaiming the Present Moment and Your Life*. Boulder, CO: Sounds True.

Kahneman, D (2011) *Thinking Fast and Slow*. London: Allen Lane.

Katz, D, Maccoby, N, Gurin, G and Floor, L (1951) *Productivity, Supervision, and Morale in an Office Situation*. Ann Arbor, MI: Institute for Social Research.

Keng, SL, Smoski, MJ and Robins, CJ (2011) Effects of mindfulness on psychological health: A review of empirical studies. *Clinical Psychology Review*, 31: 1041–56.

Kenner, N and Poldrack, R (2009) Portrait of a multitasking mind: What happens when you try to do three things at once? *Scientific American*, 15 December 2009.

Kets de Vries, MFR and Korotov, K (2012) Transformational leadership development programs: Creating long-term sustainable change, in Snook, S, Nohria, N and Khurana, R (eds) *The Handbook for Teaching Leadership: Knowing, Doing and Being*. London: Sage.

Keverne, EB (2004) Understanding well-being in the evolutionary context of brain development. *Philosophical Transactions of the Royal Society London*, B 359: 1349–58.

Keysers, C (2011) *The Empathic Brain: How the Discovery of Mirror Neurones Changes our Understanding of Human Nature*. London: Social Brain Press (Kindle version).

Kidder, RM (2005) *Moral Courage*. New York: HarperCollins.

The King's Fund (2011) *The Future of Leadership and Management in the NHS: No More Heroes. Report from The King's Fund Commission on Leadership and Management in the NHS*. London: The King's Fund.

Kirkpatrick, DL (1959) Techniques for evaluating training programs. *Journal of the American Society of Training and Development*, 33(11): 93–9.

Kirkpatrick, JD and Kirkpatrick, WK (2010) ROE's rising star: Why return on expectations is getting so much attention, in *The Best of Measuring and Evaluating Learning*, Training and Development sponsored by DDI, pp63–7.

Kirkpatrick, SA and Locke, EA (1991) Leadership: Do traits matter? *The Executive*, 5(2): 48–60. Published by the Academy of Management.

Kisfalvi, V (2014) How personal history influences leaders' emotions and capacity for empathy, in Pavlovich, K and Krahnke, K (eds) *Organizing Through Empathy*, New York and London: Routledge (Kindle version).

Klenke, K (2005) The internal theatre of the authentic leader: Integrating cognitive, affective, conative and spiritual facets of authentic leadership, in Gardner, W, Avolio, B and Walumba, F (eds) *Authentic Leadership Theory and Practice: Origins, Effects and Development, vol. 3*, Monographs in Leadership and Management. New York: Elsevier.

Kline, N (2009) *More Time to Think: A Way of Being in the World*. Pool in Wharfedale: Fisher King Publishing.

Knight, S (2009) *NLP at Work: The Essence of Excellence* (3rd edn). London: Nicholas Brealey Publishing.

Kolb, DA (1984) *Experiential Learning: Experience as the Source of Learning and Development*. Englewood Cliffs, NJ: Prentice Hall.

Koole, SL, vanDillen, LF and Sheppes, G (2011) The self-regulation of emotion, in Vohs, KD and Baumeister, RF (eds) *Handbook of Self-Regulation: Research, Theory and Application* (2nd edn). New York: Guilford Press.

Kouzes, JM and Posner, BZ (2002) *The Leadership Challenge* (3rd edn). San Francisco, CA: Jossey-Bass.

Kramer, G (2012) *Stillpower: Excellence with Ease in Sports and Life*. Hillsboro, OR: Beyond Words Publishing.

Lansley, A (2011) Modernisation Speech, The King's Fund, Leadership Conference, 18 May, Department of Health, London.

Lawler, J (2007) Leadership in Social Work: A case of caveat emptor? *British Journal of Social Work*, 37: 123–41.

Leadership Academy (2011) *The Clinical Leadership Competency Framework and The Leadership Framework*, published on behalf of the NHS Leadership Academy by NHS Institute for Innovation and Improvement, Coventry House, University of Warwick Campus, Coventry.

Lencioni, P (2005) *Overcoming the Five Dysfunctions of a Team: A Field Guide For Leaders, Managers and Facilitators*. San Francisco, CA: Jossey-Bass.

Lieberman, MD (2013) *Social: Why Our Brains Are Wired to Connect*. Oxford: Oxford University Press (Kindle version).

Lieberman, MD and Eisenberger, N (2008) The pains and pleasures of social life: A social cognitive neuroscience approach. *NeuroLeadership Journal*. Available at www.neuroleadership.org (accessed 12 January 2012).

Likert, R (1967) *The Human Organization: Its Management and Value*. New York: McGraw-Hill.

Lorsch, J (2010) A contingency theory of leadership, in Nohria, N and Khurana, R (eds) *Handbook of Leadership Theory and Practice: A Harvard Business School Centennial Colloquium*. Boston, MA: Harvard Business Press.

Luthans, F and Avolio, BJ (2003) Authentic leadership: A positive development approach, in Cameron, KS, Dutton, JE and Quinn, RE (eds) *Positive Organizational Scholarship*. San Francisco, CA: Berrett-Koehler.

Lyubomirsky, S, King, L and Diener, E (2005) The benefits of frequent positive affect: Does happiness lead to success? *APA Psychological Bulletin*, 131(6): 803–55.

Macaulay, S (2010) *Are You a Good Role Model?* Available at www.som.cranfield.ac.uk/som/p14216/Think-Cranfield/2010/February-2010/Are-you-a-good-role-model (accessed 20 March 2013).

Mandela, N (2011) *Nelson Mandela By Himself. The Authorised Book of Quotations.* London: Macmillan in association with PQ Blackwell (Kindle version).

Manz, CC (1998) *The Leadership Wisdom of Jesus: Practical Lessons for Today.* San Francisco, CA: Berrett-Koehler Publishers.

Martin, GP, Currie, G and Finn, R (2009) Leadership, service reform, and public-service networks: The case of cancer-genetics pilots in the English NHS. *Journal of Public Administration Research and Theory*, 19(4): 769–94.

Matthews, G, Deary, IJ and Whitemen, MC (2003) *Personality Traits* (3rd edn). Cambridge: Cambridge University Press.

Matthewson, P (2007) Professional leadership in mental health social work: An examination of a professional leadership role in the mental health division of a New Zealand district health board. *Social Work Review*, 19(3): 38–47.

McAdam, R, Mason, B and McCrory, J (2007) Exploring the dichotomies within the tacit knowledge literature: Towards a process of tacit knowing in organizations. *Journal of Knowledge Management*, 11(2): 43–59.

McAllan, W and MacRae, R (2010) Learning to lead: Evaluation of a leadership development programme in a local authority social work service. *Social Work and Social Sciences Review*, 14(2): 55–72.

McBain, R, Ghobadian, A, Switzer, J, Wilton, P, Woodman, P and Pearson, G (2012) *The Business Benefits of Management and Leadership Development.* London: Chartered Management Institute.

McCall, MW (2010) The experience conundrum, in Nohria, N and Khurana, R (eds) *Handbook of Leadership Theory and Practice: A Harvard Business School Centennial Colloquium.* Boston, MA: Harvard Business Press.

McCartney, M (2014) Attention pays: Mindfulness as a key to leadership. *Developing Leadership*, 14: 10–13.

McCrimmon, M (2010) Why servant leadership is a bad idea. *Management Issues*, 16 August. Available at www.management-issues.com/2010/8/16opinion/why-servant-leadership-is-a-bad-idea.asp? (accessed 10 November 2012).

McEwen, L, Strachan, G and Lynch, K (2010) 'Shock and awe' or 'reflection and change': Stakeholder perceptions of transformative learning in higher education. *Learning and Teaching in Higher Education*, 5 (2010–11): 34–55.

McGonigal, K (2013) How to make stress your friend. Available at www.ted.com/talks/kelly_mcgonigal_how_to_make_stress_your_friend (accessed 20 January 2014).

McGregor, D (1960) *The Human Side of Enterprise.* McGraw-Hill, 1960; annotated edn, McGraw-Hill Companies Inc. (1st January 2006). Edited by Joel Cutcher-Gershenfeld.

McKay, S (2014) Brain-immune communication: Meet the expert Dr Mark Hutchinson. Available at http://yourbrainhealth.com.au/brain-immune-communication-meet-expert-dr-mark-hutchinson/ (accessed 14 April 2014).

Medina, J (2008) *Brain Rules: 12 Principles for Surviving and Thriving at Work, Home and School.* Seattle, WA: Pear Press.

Mental Health Foundation (n.d.) *Mindfulness.* Available at www.mentalhealth.org.uk/help-information/mental-health-a-z/M/mindfulness/ (accessed 15 May 2014).

Mental Health Foundation (2010) British approach to dealing with stress runs risk of serious mental health problems. Available at http://www.mentalhealth.org.uk/our-news/news-archive/2010/2010-11-03/?view=Standard (accessed 27 December 2014).

Mental Health Foundation (2014) *Living with Anxiety: Understanding the Role and Impact of Anxiety in our Lives.* London: Mental Health Foundation.

Merleau-Ponty, M (2012) *Phenomenology of Perception,* trans. Donald A Landes. London and New York: Routledge.

Merzenich, M (2013) *Soft-wired: How the New Science of Brain Plasticity Can Change Your Life.* San Francisco, CA: Parnassus Publishing (Kindle version).

Merzenich, M (2014) Ginger Campbell, MD interview with Dr Michael Merzenich: Brain plasticity: Soft-wired: How the new science of brain plasticity can change your life, 21 January. Available at http://brainsciencepodcast.com/bsp/2014/bsp-105-merzenich#sthash.v1HKdiG6.dpuf (accessed 5 May 2014).

Meyer, D, Bonhoeffe, T and Scheuss, V (2014) Balance and stability of synaptic structures during synaptic plasticity. *Neuron,* 82(2): 430, doi: http://dx.doi.org/*10.1016/j.neuron*.2014.04.005 (accessed 17 April 2014).

Mitchell, C (2001) Partnership for continuing professional development: The impact of the Post Qualifying Award for Social Workers (PQSW) on social work practice. *Social Work Education,* 20(4): 434–45.

Moore, A, Gruber, T, Derose, J and Malinowski, P (2012) Regular, brief mindfulness meditation practice improves electrophysiological markers of attentional control. *Frontiers in Human Neuroscience,* 6: 18.

Moylan, D (1994) The dangers of contagion: Projective identification processes in institutions, in Obholzer, A and Zagier Roberts, V (eds) *The Unconscious at Work: Individual and Organizational Stress in the Human Services.* London: Routledge.

Mumford, MD (ed.) (2006) *Pathways to Outstanding Leadership: A Comparative Analysis of Charismatic, Ideological, and Pragmatic Leaders.* Mahwah, NJ: Lawrence Erlbaum Associates.

Mumford, MD (2010) *Leadership 101.* New York: Springer Publishing (Kindle version).

Mumford, MD and Licuanan, B (2004) Leading for innovation: Conclusions, issues and directions. *The Leadership Quarterly,* 15: 217–21.

Mumford, MD and Van Doorn, J (2001) The leadership of pragmatism: Reconsidering Franklin in the age of charisma. *The Leadership Quarterly,* 12: 279–309.

Mumford, MD, Connelly, MS and Gaddis, B (2003) How creative leaders think: Experimental findings and cases. *The Leadership Quarterly,* 14: 411–32.

Mumford, MD, Scott, GM and Hunter, S (2006) Charismatic, ideological, and pragmatic leaders: How do they lead, why do they lead, and who do they lead?, in Mumford, MD (ed.) *Pathways to Outstanding Leadership.* Mahwah, NJ: Lawrence Erlbaum Associates.

Mumford, MD, Hunter, ST, Eubanks, DL, Bedell, KT and Murphy, ST (2007a) Developing leaders for creative efforts: A domain-based approach to leadership development. *Human Resource Management Review,* 17: 402–17.

Mumford, MD, Friedrich, TL, Caughron, JJ and Byrne, CL (2007b) Leader cognition in real-world settings: How do leaders think about crises? *The Leadership Quarterly,* 18: 515–43.

Munro, E (2011) *The Munro Review of Child Protection, Final Report: A Child-centred System.* London: Department for Education.

Nagar, A (2005) *Re-critiquing John Keats*. New Delhi: Sarup and Sons.

National Skills Academy for Social Care (2013) *The Leadership Qualities Framework for Adult Social Care: Leadership Starts with Me*. London: National Skills Academy for Social Care.

Naylor, C, Imison, C, Addicott, R, Buck, D, Goodwin, N, Harrison, T, Ross, S, Sonola, L, Tian, Y and Curry, N (2013) *Transforming Our Health Care System: Ten Priorities for Commissioners*. London: The King's Fund.

Neck, CP and Manz, CC (2010) *Mastering Self-Leadership: Empowering Yourself for Personal Excellence* (5th edn). Upper Saddle River, NJ: Prentice Hall.

Neff, K (2011) *Self-Compassion: Stop Beating Yourself Up and Leave Insecurity Behind*. New York: HarperCollins.

Neff, K and Germer, C (2013) Being kind to yourself: The science of self-compassion, in Singer, T and Bolz, M (eds) *Compassion: Bridging Practice and Science*. Munich: MaxPlanck Society (e-book).

Neill, M (2009) *SuperCoach: 10 Secrets to Transform Anyone's Life*. London: Hay House.

Neill, M (2013) *The Inside Out Revolution*. London: Hay House.

Newberg, A and Waldman, MR (2012) *Words Can Change Your Brain*. New York: Penguin Group USA.

NHS Confederation (2014) *The 2015 Challenge Declaration*. London: NHS Confederation.

NICE (2011) *NICE Guidelines for Common Mental Health Disorders: Identification and Pathways to Care* (CG123). London: National Institute for Health and Care Excellence.

Nicholls, JR (1985) A new approach to situational leadership. *Leadership and Organisation Development Journal*, 6(4): 2–7.

Nohria, N and Khurana, R (2010) *Handbook of Leadership Theory and Practice*. Boston, MA: Harvard Business Press.

Northouse, PG (2013) *Leadership: Theory and Practice* (6th edn). London: Sage (Kindle version).

O'Connor, PMG and Quinn, L (2004) Organizational capacity for leadership, in McCauley, CD and Van Velsor, E (eds) *The Center for Creative Leadership Handbook of Leadership Development* (2nd edn). San Francisco, CA: Jossey-Bass.

O'Driscoll, T, Sugrue, B and Vona, MK (2005) The c-level and the value of learning: Organisational change. *Training and Development*, 59(10): 70–3, 76–8.

O'Hanlon, M and Doddy, J (2013) Managing resilience in difficult times. CIPD Ireland Centenary Conference, 30 April 2013. Available at www.cipd.co.uk/binariesCIPDResiliencePresentationFinal.pdf (accessed 10 May 2014).

O'Sullivan, T (2005) Some theoretical propositions of the nature of practice wisdom. *Journal of Social Work*, 5(2): 221–42.

Oxford Dictionaries (2011) *Concise Oxford English Dictionary*. Oxford: Oxford University Press.

Oxford Dictionaries (2013) Foundation definition. Available at www.oxforddictionaires.com/definition/english/foundation?q=foundations (accessed 11 November 2013).

Pangle, TL (1980) *The Laws of Plato: Translated with Notes and Interpretive Essays*. London: University of Chicago Press.

Patel, L (2010) Overcoming barriers and valuing evaluation, in *The Best of Measuring and Evaluating Learning*, Training and Development sponsored by DDI, p61.

Pavlovich, K and Krahnke, K (2014) *Organizing Through Empathy*. London: Routledge (Kindle version).

Pearce, CL and Conger, JA (2003) *Shared Leadership: Reframing the Hows and Whys of Leadership*. London: Sage.

Phillips, A (2006) *Side Effects*. London: Penguin Books.

Phillips, PP (1994) *Measuring Return on Investment, vol. 1*. Alexandria, VA: American Society for Training and Development.

Pink, D (2010) *The Surprising Truth About What Motivates Us*. Available at www.youtube.com.RSAAnimate-Drive the Surprising Truth about What Motivates Us (accessed 30 May 2012).

Pinker, S (2011) Organs of computation, in Brockman, J (ed.) *The Mind: Leading Scientists Explore the Brain, Memory, Personality, and Happiness*. New York: HarperCollins Publishers.

Politis, JD (2005) Dispersed leadership predictor of the work environment for creativity and productivity. *European Journal of Innovation Management*, 8(2): 182–204.

Post, J, Ruby, K and Shaw, E (2002) The radical group in context: 1. An integrated framework for the analysis of group risk for terrorism. *Studies in Conflict and Terrorism*, 25: 73–100.

Pransky, GS (2001) *The Relationship Handbook: A Simple Guide to Satisfying Relationships*. La Conner, WA: Pransky and Associates (Kindle version).

Pransky, J (2003) *Prevention From the Inside-Out*. Moretown, VT: North East Health Realization Institute.

Pransky, J (2011a) *Somebody Should Have Told Us! (Simple Truths for Living Well): The Mind-Spirit Connection* (3rd edn). Terrace, British Columbia: CCB Publishing.

Pransky, J (2011b) *Modello: A Story of Hope for the Inner City and Beyond*. Terrace, British Columbia: CCB Publishing.

Quinn, RE (1996) *Deep Change: Discovering the Leader Within*. San Francisco, CA: Jossey-Bass.

Quinn, RE (2004) *Building the Bridge as You Walk on It: A Guide for Leading Change*. New York: John Wiley and Sons.

Ramachandran, VS (2009) The neurons that shaped civilization. Available at www.ted.com/talks_ramachandran_the_neurons_that_shaped_civilization (accessed 21 March 2014).

Ramachandran, VS (2011) *The Tell-tale Brain: Unlocking the Mystery of Human Nature*. London: Windmill Books (Kindle version).

Ratliff, KA and Nosek, BA (2011) Negativity and outgroup biases in attitude formation and transfer. *Personality and Social Psychology Bulletin*, 37: 1692–703.

Richardson, MP, Strange, BA and Dolan, RJ (2004) Encoding of emotional memories depends on amygdala and hippocampus and their interactions. *Nature Neuroscience*, 7: 278–85.

Riggio, J (2012) *The State of Perfection: Your Hidden Code to Unleashing Personal Mastery*. IM Press (Kindle version).

Ringleb, AH and Rock, D (2012) Teaching leadership with the brain in mind, in Snook, S, Nohria, N and Khurana, R (eds) *The Handbook for Teaching Leadership: Knowing, Doing and Being*. London: Sage Publications.

Rizzolatti, G, Fogassi, L and Fallese, V (2002) Motor and cognitive functions of the ventral premotor cortex. *Current Opinion in Neurobiology*, 12: 149–54.

Roberts, BW and DelVecchio, D (2000) The rank-order consistency of personality traits from childhood to old age: A quantitative review of longitudinal studies. *Psychological Bulletin*, 126(1): 3–25.

Robinson, S (2012) *Why We Have to Go Back to a 40-Hour Work Week to Keep Our Sanity*. AlterNet. Available at www.alternet.org/story/154518/why_we_have_to_go_back_to_a_40-hour_work_week_to_keep_our_sanity?pagining=off&current_page=1#bookmark (accessed 20 April 2012).

Rock, D (2007) *Quiet Leadership: Six Steps to Transforming Performance at Work: Help People to Think Better – Don't Tell Them What to Do*. HarperCollins e-books.

Rock, D (2008) SCARF: A brain-based model for collaborating with and influencing others. *NeuroLeadership Journal*, 1. Available at www.davidrock.net/files/NLJ_SCARFUS.pdf (accessed 13 March 2013).

Rock, D (2009) *Your Brain at Work: Strategies for Overcoming Distraction, Regaining Focus and Working Smarter All Day Long*. New York: Harper Business, HarperCollins.

Rock, D (2010) SCARF model: Influencing others with David Rock. Available at www.youtube.com/watch?v=isiSOeMVJQk (accessed 12 February 2013).

Rock, D (2013) Learning about the brain changes everything. TEDxTalks. Available at www.youtube.com/watch?v=uDyxxayNig (accessed 20 January 2014).

Rock, D and Cox, C (2012) SCARF in 2012: Updating the social neuroscience of collaborating with others. *NeuroLeadership Journal*, Neuroleadership Institute. Available at www.Neuroleadership.org (accessed 20 October 2013).

Rock, D, Siegel, DJ, Poelmans, SAY and Payne, J (2012) *The Healthy Mind Platter*. Neuroleadership Institute. Available at www.NeuroLeadership.org (accessed 20 November 2012).

Rock, D, Jones, B and Davis, J (2013) One simple idea that can transform performance management. Research Corner, *People Strategy*, 36(2): 16–19.

Roebuck, C (2011) *Developing Effective Leadership in the NHS to Maximise the Quality of Patient Care: The Need for Urgent Action*. London: The King's Fund.

Royal College of Nursing (RCN) (2008) The RCN's definition of dignity. Available at www.rcn.org.uk/_data/assets/pdf_file/0003/191730/003298.pdf (accessed 20 April 2014).

Royal College of Physicians (RCP) (2012) *Care Closer to Home: Narrative Report*. London: Royal College of Physicians.

Russell, RF (2001) The role of values in servant leadership. *Leadership and Organization Development Journal*, 22(2): 76–83.

Russell, RF and Stone, AG (2002) A review of servant leadership attributes: Developing a practical model. *Leadership & Organization Development Journal*, 23: 145–57.

Sabo, B (2011) Reflecting on the concept of compassion fatigue. *The Online Journal of Issues in Nursing: A Scholarly Journal of the American Nurses Association*, 31 January 2011.

Santos, L (2010) A monkey economy as irrational as ours. Available at www.ted.com/talks/laurie_santos (accessed 12 June 2012).

Satpute, AB, Mumford, JA, Naliboff, BD and Poldrack, RA (2012) Human anterior and posterior hippocampus respond distinctly to state and trait anxiety. *Emotion*, 1(February): 58–68. Available at www.ncbi.nlm.nih.gov/pubmed/22309734 (accessed 12 January 2013).

Scharmer, CO (2008) Uncovering the blind spot of leadership. *Executive Forum*, 47(Winter): 52–9.

Scharmer, CO (2009) *Theory U Leading from the Future as it Emerges: The Social Technology of Presencing.* San Francisco, CA: Berrett-Koehler Publishers.

Schön, DA (1991) *The Reflective Practitioner: How Professionals Think in Action.* Farnham: Ashgate Publishing.

Scott, S (2002) *Fierce Conversations: Achieving Success in Work and in Life, One Conversation at a Time.* London: Piatkus.

Senge, PM (2006) *The Fifth Discipline: The Art & Practice of The Learning Organisation.* London: Random House Business Books.

Seppala, EM (2012) The brain's ability to look within: A secret to well-being: Tapping into our ability to turn attention inward empowers and heals. *Psychology Today.* Available at www.psychologytoday.com/blog/feeling-it/201212/the-brains-ability-look-within-secret-well-being (accessed 31 December 2012).

Serani, D (2014) The emotional blindness of alexithymia. *Scientific American.* Available at http://blogs.scientificamerican.com/mind-guest-blog/2014/04/03the-emotional-blindness-of-alexithymia/ (accessed 11 April 2014).

Shakespeare, W (1987) Hamlet, Act 2, Scene 2, in *The Complete Oxford Shakespeare, III: Tragedies.* London: Book Club Associates by arrangement with Oxford University Press.

Sharma, V, Sood, A, Prasad, K, Loehrer, L, Schroeder, D and Bauer, B (2014) Bibliotherapy to decrease stress and anxiety and increase resilience and mindfulness: A pilot trial. *Explore: Journal of Science and Healing,* 10(4): 248–52.

Shaw, S, Rosen, R and Rumbold, B (2011) *What Is Integrated Care? An Overview of Integrated Care in the NHS.* London: Nuffield Trust.

Shipman, AS (2010) Future directions, in Mumford, MD (ed.) *Leadership 101.* New York: Springer Publishing (Kindle version).

Siegel, DJ (2010) *The Mindful Therapist: A Clinician's Guide to Mindsight and Neural Integration.* New York: WW Norton.

Singer, T (2014) How to train your mind and your heart. *Social Neuroscience.* Available at www.youtube.com/watch?v=HQKoWehp8no (accessed 10 May 2014).

Skills for Care (n.d.) *Dignity: Dignity Must Be at the Centre of Everything We Do.* Available at http://SkillsforCare.org.uk/Skills/Dignity/Dignity.aspx (accessed 20 April 2014).

Skinner, BF (1974) *About Behaviourism.* New York: Vintage Books.

Skodol, AE (2010) The resilient personality, in Reich, JW, Zautra, A and Hall, JS (eds) *Handbook of Adult Resilience.* New York: Guilford Press.

Smart, J (2013) *Clarity: Clear Mind, Better Performance, Bigger Results.* Chichester: Capstone Publishing.

Smith, BN, Montagno, RV and Kuzmenko, TN (2004) Transformational and servant leadership: Content and contextual comparisons. *Journal of Leadership and Organizational Studies,* 10(4): 80–91.

Smith, JA and Foti, RJ (1998) A pattern approach to the study of leader emergence. *Leadership Quarterly,* 9(2): 147–60.

Smith, MK (2003) Michael Polanyi and tacit knowledge, in *The Encyclopedia of Informal Education.* Available at http://infed.org/mobi/michael-polanyi-and-tacit-knowledge (accessed 10 May 2014).

Snook, S, Nohria, N and Khurana, R (2012) *The Handbook for Teaching Leadership: Knowing, Doing and Being.* New York: Sage.

Social Care Institute for Excellence (n.d.) *Choice and Control are Key Defining Aspects of Dignity.* Available at www.scie.org.uk/publications/guides/guide15/factors/ (accessed 20 April 2014).

Solomon, ND (2010) *Impact: What Every Woman Needs to Know to Go From Invisible to Invincible.* Hoboken, NJ: John Wiley and Sons.

Southwick, SM and Charney, DS (2012) *Resilience: The Science of Mastering Life's Greatest Challenges.* New York: Cambridge University Press.

Sparrow, RT (2005) Authentic leadership and the narrative self. *The Leadership Quarterly,* 16: 419–39.

Spears, L (1995) Servant leadership and the Greenleaf legacy, in Spears, L (ed.) *Reflections on Leadership: How Robert K. Greenleaf's Theory of Servant Leadership Influenced Today's Top Management Thinkers.* New York: John Wiley and Sons.

Spillane, JP (2006) *Distributed Leadership.* San Francisco, CA: Jossey-Bass.

Starkey, K and Hall, C (2012) The spirit of leadership: New directions in leadership education, in Snook, S, Nohria, N and Khurana, R (eds) *The Handbook for Teaching Leadership: Knowing, Doing and Being.* London: Sage.

Stephenson, S (2009) *Get Off Your 'But': How to End Self-sabotage and Stand up for Yourself.* San Francisco, CA: Jossey-Bass.

Stogdill, RM (1948) Personal factors associated with leadership: A survey of the literature. *Journal of Psychology,* 25: 35–71.

Stogdill, RM (1974) *Handbook of Leadership.* New York: The Free Press.

Stogdill, RM and Bass, BM (1990) *Handbook of Leadership: A Survey of Theory and Research* (3rd edn). New York: The Free Press.

Stokes, J (1994) The unconscious at work in groups and teams: Contributions from the work of Wilfred Bion, in Obholzer, A and Zagier Roberts, V (eds) *The Unconscious at Work: Individual and Organizational Stress.* London: The Human Services, Routledge.

Stone, AG and Patterson, K (2005) *The History of Leadership Focus.* Virginia Beach, VA: School of Leadership Studies, Regent University. Available at www.regent.edu/acad/global/publications/sl_proceedings/2005/stone_history.pdf (accessed 8 November 2012).

Stone, AG, Russell, RF and Patterson, K (2004) Transformational versus servant leadership: A difference in leader focus. *Leadership and Organisation Development Journal,* 25(4): 349–61.

Stone, D, Patton, B and Heen, S (1999) *Difficult Conversations.* London: Penguin Books.

Stone, L (1998) Continuous partial attention. Available at www.wordspy.com/words/continuouspartialattention.asp (accessed 18 March 2012).

Storey, J and Holti, R (2013) *Possibilities and Pitfalls for Clinical Leadership in Improving Service Quality, Innovation and Productivity, Final Report.* London: NIHR Service Delivery and Organisational Programme.

Strange, JM and Mumford, MD (2002) The origins of vision: Charismatic versus ideological leadership. *The Leadership Quarterly,* 13: 343–77.

Summers, RF and Barber, JP (2010) *Psychodynamic Therapy: A Guide to Evidence Based Practice.* New York: The Guilford Press.

Surowiecki, J (2005) *The Wisdom of Crowds: Why the Many Are Smarter Than the Few.* London: Abacus.

Tang, Y and Posner, MI (2009) Attention training and attention state training. *Trends in Cognitive Sciences,* 13: 222–7.

Tannenbaum, R and Schmidt, W (1958) How to choose a leadership pattern: Should a leader be democratic or autocratic – or something in between? *Harvard Business Review*, 37: 95–102.

Terry, RW (1993) *Authentic Leadership: Courage in Action.* San Francisco, CA: Berrett-Koehler.

Thorpe, R, Lawler, J and Gold, J (2007) *Systematic Review.* Leeds: University of Leeds, Northern Leadership Academy.

Thorpe, R, Gold, J and Lawler, J (2011) Locating distributed leadership. *International Journal of Management Reviews,* 13: 239–50.

Tichy, N and Devanna, MA (1986) *Transformational Leadership.* New York: Wiley.

Torres, R (2013) What it takes to be a great leader. Available at www.ted.com/talks/roselinde_torres_what_it_takes_to_be_a_great_leader (accessed 30 January 2014).

Tosey, P and Mathison, J (2009) *Neuro-linguistic Programming: A Critical Appreciation for Managers and Developers.* Basingstoke: Palgrave Macmillan.

Tourish, D (2013) *The Dark Side of Transformational Leadership: A Critical Perspective.* London: Routledge.

Van Wart, M (2003) Public-sector leadership theory: An assessment. *Public Administration Review,* 63(2): 214–28.

Vessey, WB (2010) Outstanding leadership, in Mumford, MD (ed.) *Leadership 101.* New York: Springer Publishing (Kindle version).

Vroom, VH and Jago, AG (2007) The role of the situation in leadership. *American Psychologist,* 62(1): 17–24.

Vroom, VH and Yvetton, PW (1973) *Leadership and Decision-making.* Pittsburg, PA: University of Pittsburg Press.

Wagner, DD and Heatherton, TF (2011) Giving in to temptation: The emerging cognitive neuroscience of self-regulatory failure, in Vohs, KD and Baumeister, RF (eds) *Handbook of Self-Regulation: Research, Theory and Application* (2nd edn). New York: Guilford Press.

Wagner, M (2013) Bringing outside innovations into health care. *Harvard Business Review Blog Network.* Available at www.blogs.hbr.org (accessed 28 October 2013).

Wake, L (2010) *NLP Principles in Practice.* St Albans: Ecademy Press.

Walker, MP (2007) The human emotional brain without sleep: A pre-frontal amygdala disconnect. *Current Biology,* 17(20): 877–8.

Wallace, BA (2006) *The Attention Revolution: Unlocking the Power of the Focused Mind.* Somerville, MA: Wisdom Publications.

Walumbwa, FO, Avolio, BJ, Gardner, WL, Wernsing, TS and Peterson, SJ (2008) Authentic leadership: Development and validation of a theory-based measure. *Journal of Management,* 34(1): 89–126.

Ward, J (2010) *The Student's Guide to Cognitive Neuroscience* (2nd edn). Hove and New York: Psychology Press.

Weber, M (1947) *The Theory of Social and Economic Organization.* Translated by A. M. Henderson & Talcott Parsons. New York: The Free Press.

Weinstein, N, Brown, KW and Ryan, RM (2009) A multi-method examination of the effects of mindfulness on stress attribution, coping, and emotional well-being. *Journal of Research in Personality,* 43: 374–85.

Western, S (2013) *Leadership: A Critical Text.* London: Sage.

Whetstone, T (2002) Personalism and moral leadership: The servant leader with a transforming vision. *Business Ethics: A European Review*, 11(4): 385–92.

Whiting, J, Jones, E, Rock, D and Bendit, W (2012) *Lead Change With the Brain in Mind.* Neuroleadership Institute. Available at www.davidrock.net/resources/ (accessed 12 November 2013).

WHO (World Health Organization) (2014) WHO mental health: Strengthening our response. World Health Organization, Fact sheet No 220. Available at www.who.int/mediacentre/factsheets/fs220/en/ (accessed 5 May 2014).

Whybrow, A and Wildflower, L (2011) Humanistic and transpersonal psychology, in Wildflower, L and Brennan, D (eds) *The Handbook of Knowledge-based Coaching: From Theory to Practice.* San Francisco, CA: Jossey-Bass.

Williams, M (2012) Mindfulness Professor Mark Williams Lecture, 3 April. Available at www.Youtube.com/watch?v=wAy_3Ssyqqg (accessed 25 April 2013).

Williams, M and Penman, D (2011) *Mindfulness: A Practical Guide to Finding Peace in a Frantic World.* London: Piatkus.

Williams, M, Teasdale, JD, Segal, ZV and Kabat-Zinn, J (2007) *The Mindful Way Through Depression: Freeing Yourself from Chronic Unhappiness.* New York: The Guilford Press.

Williamson, M (1992) *A Return to Love: Reflections on the Principles of 'A Course in Miracles'.* London: HarperCollins.

Wofford, JC and Liska, LZ (1993) Path-goal theories of leadership: A meta-analysis. *Journal of Management*, 19(4) (August): 857–76.

Yukl, G (1998) *Leadership in Organizations* (4th edn). Upper Saddle River, NJ: Prentice Hall.

Yukl, G (2006) *Leadership in Organizations* (6th edn). Upper Saddle River, NJ: Prentice Hall.

Zaccaro, SJ (2007) Trait-based perspectives of leadership. *American Psychologist*, 62: 6–16.

Zaccaro, SJ and Horn, ZNJ (2003) Leadership theory and practice: Fostering an effective symbiosis. *The Leadership Quarterly*, 14: 769–806.

Zaccaro, SJ, Kemp, C and Bader, P (2004) Leader traits and attributes, in Antonakis, J, Cianciolo, AT and Sternberg, RJ (eds) *The Nature of Leadership* (pp101–24). Thousand Oaks, CA: Sage.

Zak, PJ, Kurzban, R and Matzner, WT (2005) Oxytocin is associated with human trustworthiness. *Hormones and Behavior*, 48: 522–7.

Zautra, AJ, Hall, JS and Murray, KE (2010) Resilience: A new definition of health for people and communities, in Reich, JW, Zautra, A and Hall, JS (eds) *Handbook of Adult Resilience.* New York: The Guilford Press.

Zheltoukhova, K (2014) *Leadership – Easier Said Than Done: Research Report.* London: Chartered Institute of Personnel Development.

Index

achievement 130
action-centred leadership model 9
Adair, JE 9
adverse reactions, and limbic system arousal 91
affect heuristic 87
Aguirre et al. 97
alexithymia 82
Alimo-Metcalfe, B and Alban-Metcalfe, RJ 14, 19, 55, 58
amygdala 27, 45, 82, 84, 98, 107, 121
analytical cognitive network 97
analytical reasoning 103
anchoring effect 87
anger 46, 65, 66, 119, 120
anxiety 91, 121, 127, 130, 132–3
approach state 98
Argyle et al. 31
Argyris, C 115
assumptions 114
Atkins, PWB 30, 120, 132
attention: deployment of 123–5; neurobiology of 134
attentional distraction/ attentional focusing 131
authentic leadership theory 3, 18–19
autism 80
autonomy 53, 99, 101, 116
avoidance 121
Avolio, BJ 8, 19
Avolio et al. 15, 19
awareness: and compassion 29; and consciousness 67, 126; of others 101; and self-observation 25

Banaji, MR and Greenwald, AG 90
Banks, S 45, 70, 151, 153n.2
Barrett, JD 10, 11
Bass, BM 13, 14
Bass, BM and Avolio, BJ 15
Bass, BM and Bass, R 4, 6, 10, 11, 13, 16
Bateson, G 114
Beeler, CK 4, 7
Beeman, M 83
behaviour, changes in 61
behaviourist theories 2, 6–8
behaviours: leadership 7; Model I and Model II 115–16
beliefs: and decision making 114; limiting 122–3; religious/spiritual 107; and state of mind 64; as thoughts made real 70, 85
belonging, sense of 100
Bennis, WG and Nanus, B 1
Benson, H 95
bias(es): to believe 87; confirmation 87, 88; in-group/out-group 100; instinctive 115; optimistic 87; potential 88; and professional judgement 114; and self-awareness 118–19; thinking 103; and tiredness 118; types of 87; unconscious 94; understanding 114

Bion, W 4, 53
Birey, F 89
blame 46, 74
Bohm, D 47, 68
Bolden et al. 5, 11
Bolden, R and Gosling, J 8
Bornemann, B and Singer, T 37
Bosman, M 99
Bower et al. 84
Boyatzis, R 95, 124
Boyd, E and Fales, A 113
Bradford, DI and Cohen, AR 51, 58
brain 88–90; brownout in 91; and change 97–102; and consciousness 126; neuroplasticity of 92, 93, 107, 121–2
brain-derived neurotrophic factor (BDNF) 93
brain fitness 107–8
Braye, RH 23
breakout principle 95
Brookes, S and Grint, K 1, 40, 50, 53, 57, 58
Brooks, M 81
Brown, B 30, 92
Brown et al. 128
brownout 91
Broyard, A 48
Buchanan et al. 56
Building the Bridge as You Walk on It 146
burnout 38, 102
Burns, JM 13
business school educational model, private sector 37

Cameron, P 32, 84
capability 145, 148
care: closer to home 39; integrated models of 40, 58; quality of 36
caring 49, 130
Carlyle, T 3
Carpenter, J 60
Carroll, M and Gilbert, MC 110
Cashman, K 36
Caughron, JJ 14
Caver, CS and Scheier, MF 26
certainty 99, 101, 116
change management 97–8, 101
change(s): in behaviour 61; and the brain 97–102; cognitive 84; motivation to 114; need for fundamental 39–40; and self-observation 25; workplace 116–17
charisma 16
charismatic leadership 13, 16–17, 18, 50
Chartered Institute of Personnel and Development (CIPD) 33, 60, 99
Chödrön, P 85

clarity of mind 144, 145, 151, 152, 153
clinical engagement 53
clinical leadership 52, 55
clinical networks 58
clinicians, distributing leadership to 58
cognitive biases, and self-awareness 118–19 *see also* bias(es)
cognitive change 84 *see also* change(s)
cognitive flexibility 107
cognitive reappraisal 131
cognitive reasoning, and empathetic thinking 97
cognitive resources leadership theory 20
cognitive theories 3, 20–1
Coles, C 108
collective leadership 53, 56–9
collectively smart 49
Collins, DB and Holton, EF 60
Collins, J 16
command and control style 55
common humanity 29
communication: compassionate 94–5; effective 30, 31, 38, 135; improving 103; non-verbal 31–2; and professional judgement 110; and rapport building 81; silent 32; and stress 92, 94, 103; team 32
compassion 49 *see also* self-compassion; and awareness 29; and fear 120; and hardiness/resilience/well-being 132; lack of/fatigue 37–8; and leadership 119–20; and mindfulness 132–3; and state of mind 47
compassionate communication 94–5
Compassion in Practice 37
confirmation bias 87, 88
conflict avoidance 115
conflict, resolving 97, 115
connecting with others 81, 102, 127
connection 49, 147
conscious awareness 67, 126
consciousness 65, 67–8, 126, 148–50, 152
conscious systems, of brain 88
consideration behaviour 7
consistency 19
contagion effect 37; of emotions 27, 96, 120, 130; teams 118
contingency theories 2, 8–10
continuous improvement 60
continuous partial attention (CPA) 91, 94
cortisol 25, 92
Creswell, JD 84
Crosby, BC and Bryson, JM 50
Csikszentmihalyi, M 122
Cuddy, A 125
culture: of engagement 55; learning 59; 'me first' 122; organisational 38; and organizational change 97; working 49–50
curiosity 119, 131
Currie, G and Lockett, A 15, 56, 58
cyclical thinking feedback loop 127

Damasio, AR 82, 96, 113
Davis et al. 94

Deci, EL and Flaste, R 114
decision making: and emotions 83, 113; and empathetic/analytical reasoning 103; of groups 115; and negative thinking 116; and panic 106; and stress 102; and values/beliefs/assumptions 114
defensive traps 115–16
Dehaene, S 126
Delivering High Quality, Effective, Compassionate Care 37
De Mello, A 25, 28
dependency, and paternalism 53
depression 92, 130, 132–3
DeSteno, D 119
devolved models of leadership 55–9, 62, 102, 116
difficult situations, addressing 115
dignity 48–9
Dispenza, J 70, 85, 92, 93
dispersed leadership 57, 58, 102
dissonant effects, of leaders 96
distress 45, 145, 148 *see also* stress
distributed leadership 56–7, 58
diversity 119
doing and seeing 80
Dolan, R 82
dopamine 98
dual process model, thinking 86–8

Eco-leadership 56
Edwards, N 33
effectiveness, and state of mind 137
effortful activity 86
Ekman, P 32
elitism, professional/managerial 55
emotional blindness 82
emotional contagion *see* contagion effect
emotional flexibility 107
emotional intelligence 95–7, 103
emotional resilience 145 *see also* resilience
emotional responses 25
emotional self-control 26
emotional states, and insight 83
emotional strength, and self-compassion 132
emotional well-being 106 *see also* well-being
emotions: and communication 31; contagion effect of 27, 96, 120, 130; controlling 27; and decision making 83, 113; defined 26; expressing/suppressing 83, 85; and feelings 82; in groups 125; and judgement 83; labelling 84; managing 116; originating from the mind 65–6; and reasoning 83, 113; regulation of 26, 27, 84, 93, 107; and relationships 145; and resilience 26; role of 81–5; and self-awareness 113; and state of mind 66, 144; and thoughts 66, 85; universal 82
empathetic reasoning 103 *see also* reasoning
empathetic thinking 97 *see also* thinking
empathy: developing 29; of leaders 97; in leadership 96; in men 100; and mirror neurones 80; neurones 81; as organising principle 120; and self-regulation 132; and social awareness 30; sustainable 120
employee engagement 38

engagement: clinical 53; culture of genuine 55; employee 38; lack of 38–9; and self-leadership 39
environmental factors, and resilience 108
environmental mindfulness 124
Erikson, E 109
Ernst et al. 89
ethics, of leaders 19
evaluation: of impact 62; impact of leadership development 44, 59–61; Kirkpatrick's model 60
exchange relationships 15
experience(s): created by the mind 66; human 69–77; as a product of the mind 71–4, 77; as a resource 20
experiential know-how 54, 55
experiential learning 111–12
expert intuition 87–8
external factors, and feelings/thinking 69–71, 77
extreme listening 49

fairness 100, 102, 115, 116
familiar, pervasiveness of 90
Farb et al. 29, 84
Farb, NAS 72
fear: and achievement 130; and anger 120; and anxiety 121, 127; and compassion 120; facing it 106–7; and mindfulness 107; of redundancy 117
feedback, and status 101
feeling, and thinking 85
feelings: and emotions 82; and external factors 69–71, 77; of helplessness/hopelessness 37; subjective 81
Fiedler, FE 8, 9
Fiedler, FE and Garcia, JE 20
fight or flight response 25, 53, 92, 106; new 120–1
Finlay, L 111
Fish Rots from the Head, The 90
fitness, physical 107
flow, concept of 122
follow-ship 13
Foster, R 126
Frankl, VE 108
Fredrickson, BL 116
Friedrich, TL 9
Frith, C 32, 113
frontal lobes 89, 92

Gardner, J 56
Garratt, B 90
Gazzaniga, MS 121, 126
George, B 18
Gill, R 11, 14, 16, 19
Gladwell, M 32
Gleeson, J and Berman, SP 122–3
glial cells 89
Glynn, MA and DeJordy, R 9
Goldin, P 130
Goldstein, J 128
Goleman, D 105, 119, 123, 124
Goleman et al. 26, 27, 28, 30, 31, 95, 96
Gordon, R 56
Gosling et al. 13
Graeff, CL 11

Graen, GB and Uhl-Bien, M 15
great man theory 2, 3–4
Greenleaf, RK 11
Greenwood, J 109
Gross, J. 83
Grossman, P 129, 130, 131
groups: decision making of 115; emotions in 125; overthinking 76; resilience of 125
group think 90, 94, 103
growth mindset 102, 103

habitual worry 46
Hackman, JR 9
Hackman, MZ and Johnson, CE 53
Halifax, J 37
halo effect 87
Ham, C and Walsh, N 40
Ham et al. 39
happiness 75, 102, 122
hardiness 132
hardwiring 85, 121
Hartley, J and Allison, M 57
Health and Social Care sectors: and artistry/science 109; current landscape 33; managerial changes 54; need for fundamental change 39–40; need to implement self-leadership 40
healthcare: compassion in 37; leadership development in 36–7
health, innate 51, 123
Hebb, D. 85
Hebb's law 85, 102
Heffernan, M 90
helplessness 37
heroic concept of leadership 3–4
hero leader model 23, 51
Hersey et al. 28, 32, 61
Hersey, P and Blanchard, KH 10
hippocampus 89, 91, 92
Hofman et al. 94
Hölzel et al. 129
hopelessness 37
hot buttons, and limbic system arousal 83
House, RJ 9
How Your Brain Fights for Social Survival in the Workplace 99
human connection 49, 81 see also connecting with others; connection
human experience 69–77 see also experience(s)
human functioning, and stress 66
hypervigilance 121

ideological leadership 17–18
Ilardi, S 92, 125
immune system 92, 93
impact: evaluation 44, 59–61, 62; of leadership 137, 153
individuals: as leaders 16–19; as victims of something 74–5, 77
in flow 47
in-group/out-groups 15, 16, 90, 100
initiating structure behaviour 7

innate health 51, 123
inner knowing 36
inside-out approach: leadership development 40, 51; self-awareness 28; self-leadership 10, 36, 37, 41, 55
insight, and emotional states 83
integrated models of care 40, 58
intelligence 20–1, 76, 152
internal mental rehearsal 121
internal resilience 45, 51
interoceptive awareness 84
interpreter module 126
intuition 87–8
Isaacs, W 114

Jack et al. 97
Johns, C 111
Johnson, CE 4, 52
Judge et al. 5
judgement: and emotions 83; professional 53, 108–11, 114–16

Kabat-Zinn, J 105, 128, 129
Kahneman, D 70, 83, 86, 87, 88, 103, 113
Keng et al. 128
Keverne, EB 89
Keysers, C 96
Kidder, RM 107
King's Fund 40
Kirkpatrick, SA and Locke, EA 4
Kirkpatrick, DL 60
Kline, N 45
Knight, S 81
know-how, experiential 54, 55
knowledge retrieval, and stress 114
Kolb, DA 112
Koole et al. 26
Kouzes, JM and Posner, BZ 5, 24, 31, 50

labelling emotions 84
laissez-faire leadership 14
Langer, E. 124
language circuits, and stress 92, 103
Lansley, A 54
leader–member exchange (LMX) 3, 15–16
leader plus 57
leaders: balanced 123–4; charismatic 16, 50; dissonant effects of 96; in education 140; emotional function of 97; empathy of 120; female 4; hero leader 23, 51; individuals as 16–19; morality/ethics of 19; performance of 38–9; problem-solving skills of 20; qualities of effective 146; resilience of 103; resonant effects of 96, 103; servant leaders 12; state of mind 45, 151–2; successful 124; three focuses of 134
leadership: behaviours 7; blind spots 90–1, 94; capacity for 50; charismatic 13, 16–17, 18, 50; clinical 52, 55; collective 53, 56–9; and compassion 119–20; coupling/partnership 57; defined 1, 24; devolved models of 55–9, 62, 102, 116; dispersed 57, 58, 102; distributed 56–7, 58; Eco-leadership 56; empathy in 96; foundations of 119; heroic concept

of 3–4, 23, 51; ideological 17–18; impact 137, 153; importance of 50; and individual relationships 50; lack of professional 52–5; laissez-faire 14; as learned behaviour 6; and management 1–2, 21; patriarchal 13; practice 56; pragmatic 17, 18; preoccupation of general 36–7; primal 95–7; professional 37, 52–5; public 53; quality of 140, 141, 151, 153; and relationships 24, 31, 50; reviews pointing to ineffective 34–5; self and others 29–32; and self-awareness 28; shared 57–8; in social services sector 36; and state of mind 46, 138–41, 146, 152; styles of 6, 8, 11; theories of see leadership theories; traditional 21
leadership development: evaluating the impact of 44, 59–61; focus of 44; fundamental drivers 138–41; in healthcare 36–7; inside-out approach 40, 51; outcomes of 40; outside-in approach 37, 40, 41, 51; in public sector 36
Leadership Qualities Framework for Adult Social Care 27, 28
Leadership Starts with Me 37
leadership theories: cognitive theories 3, 20–1; focusing on followers 11–16; focusing on the individual as leader 3–8, 16–19; focusing on the situation or context 8–11; historical overview 2–3
learning: culture 59; evaluation of 60; from experience 111–12; impact of 59; lifelong 110; and reflection-in-action/on-action 109; transformative 61
level of clarity 143, 145
Lieberman, MD 81, 84, 97, 120, 125
lifelong learning 110
limbic system 82, 83, 84, 91, 102
line management 51, 53
listening, extreme 49
logic, and intuition 88
loneliness 130
Lorsch, J 9
loss aversion 86, 87
Luthans, F and Avolio, BJ 19

management: as everyone's responsibility 51; and leadership 1–2, 21; line 51, 53; under pressure 134
managerial elitism 55
Manz, CC 13, 24
Marmot, M. 99
Martin et al. 57
Matthews et al. 5
Matthewson, P 53
McAdam et al. 109
McCartney, M 91
McEwen et al. 61
McGonigal, K 48, 81, 93
meaning 108
Medina, J 92, 93
meditation 107, 129
memory 91, 94, 147
men, empathy/motivation in 100
mental health 93, 105
Mental Health Foundation 130

mental internal practice 121
Merzenich, M 90, 121, 122
Meyer, D 91
mind 67, 77; automatic responses of 113; clarity of 144,
    145, 151, 152, 153; intelligence in the 76, 152;
    misunderstandings of 69; nature of 146–7; role of
    126; and stress 65, 66, 127; and thought 68, 69; as
    unreliable 150
mind and body connection 125, 134
mindful, being 126–7
mindfulness: benefits of 133–4; and compassion/
    resilience 132–3; defined 105; environmental 124;
    exercises in 131–2; facets of 129; and fear 107; and
    resilience 84, 132–3, 135; and self-awareness 118;
    and self-compassion 29; and self-leadership 84; and
    sustainable empathy 120; what is it? 128–34
mindfulness-based cognitive therapy (MBCT) 130
mindfulness-based interventions (MBIs) 129
mindfulness-based stress reduction (MBSR) 129
mindful presence 124
mindsight 128
mind-state management 139
mirror neurones 80–1, 102, 125
Model I and Model II behaviours 115–16
Modernising Social Services 48
monetary pressures, public sector 39
mood 82
mood disorders 89
moral compass 107
Moral Courage 107
morality, of leaders 19
motivation 54, 98, 100, 114
Moylan, D 37
multi-professional environments 115
multitasking 91, 94, 103, 118
Mumford et al. 20
Mumford, MD 11, 15, 17, 57
Myers-Briggs Type Indicator (MBTI) 6

Narcissism Epidemic: Living in the Age of Entitlement,
    The 122
National Institute for Health and Care Excellence (NICE) 130
National Skills Academy for Social Care 37
Neck, C 24
Neck, C and Manz, CC 24, 25
Neff, K 29, 38, 95, 133
Neff, K and Germer, C 132, 133
negative thinking 27, 102, 116, 121
Neill, M 47, 68
Nesse, R 121
neurones 81, 89 see also mirror neurones
neuroplasticity, of the brain 92, 93, 107, 121–2
Newberg, A and Waldman, MR 92, 95
New Public Management (NPM) 1–2
NHS Clinical Leadership Framework 27, 28
NHS Confederation 55
NHS, professional leadership 52
Nicholls, JR 11
non-verbal communication 31–2
Northouse, PG 1, 5, 11, 19, 52

Obama, Barack 49
O'Hanlon, M and Doddy, J 117
On Heroes, Hero Worship and the Heroic in History 3
optimism, realistic 106
optimistic bias 87
organisational culture, and staff performance 38
organisations, stress in 117
organizational change 97
organizational resilience 108
Organizing Through Empathy 97
O'Sullivan, T 114
Our Health, Our Care, Our Say: A New Direction for
    Community Services 39
outcomes, of leadership development 40
out-group threat 115
outside-in approach: leadership development 37, 40, 41, 51;
    self-awareness 28
outstanding leadership approaches 18
overanalysis 121
overthinking 76
oxytocin 81, 107

pairing assumption 54
panic 106 see also stress
paradoxical active–passive dynamic 95
participation, principle of 114
Pascual-Leone, A 90
paternalism, and dependency 53
path–goal leadership theory 9
patriarchal leadership 13
Pavlovich, K and Krahnke, K 96, 97
performance: of leaders 38–9; of staff 38; and state
    of mind 137, 139, 142–4, 146, 152; and stress/
    distress 46, 145; of teams 57
performance regimes 58
personality traits 82, 108
Phillips, A 30, 60, 114
physical exercise 126
physical fitness 107
Pinker, S 126
plasticity 90
Polanyi, M 109
political nature, of public services 33
power: relationships 58; and shared leadership 58;
    sharing of 56
practice wisdom 114–15
practitioners, resilient 115
Pransky, G and L 142
Pransky, GS 31
Pransky, J 36, 45, 47, 49
prefrontal cortex 91, 92, 98, 102, 106
premature cognitive commitment 114
presence of mind, and self-leadership 32
pressure 45, 116–17
primary task, focussing on 55
principle of participation 114
private sector, business school educational model 37
problem solving, intelligence and 20
productive deduction 115
professional autonomy 53

professional elitism 55
professional experiential leadership 54–5
professional hierarchy 58
professional judgement 53, 108–11, 114–16
professional leadership 37, 52–5
professional practice 110
professional will 54
prospect theory 87
psychodynamic theories 3
psychometric testing 5
public leadership 53
public sector 33, 36, 39
public services, political nature of 33
purpose 108

quality: of care and services 36; of leadership 140, 141, 146, 151, 153; and state of mind 144
Quinn, RE 146, 151

Raes, F 132
Ramachandran, VS 80
rapport 30–1, 81, 102, 147
Ratliff, KA and Nosek, BA 115
reappraisal 84, 131
reasoning: and emotions 83, 113; empathetic 103
re-balancing 45
redundancy, fear of 117
reflection 109, 111–14
reflection-in-action/on-action 109
regulation, of emotions 26, 27, 84, 93, 107 see also self-regulation
rejection, social 103
relatedness 99–100, 101–2, 115, 116
relational leadership theories 3, 15–16
relationship-focused behaviour 7
relationships: based on self-leadership 35; and emotions 145; exchange relationships 15; interpersonal 31; and leadership 24, 31, 50; management of 31, 135; power 58; and state of mind 142–3, 144; and well-being 127; working 31
relaxation 131
religious beliefs 107
remembering self 87
resilience: and compassion 132; creating 102; emotional 145; and emotions 26; and environmental factors 108; of groups 125; and human connection 81; internal 45, 51; of leaders 103; and mindfulness 84, 132–3, 135; natural 77; organizational 108; and professional judgement 114–16; and relatedness 115; and role modelling 107; and self-awareness 115; and self-compassion 132; and self-leadership 116, 134; and state of mind 47, 122–3; and stress 48, 49, 81, 105; a summary 116–17; of teams 108, 120; what does it look like? 106–8
resistance to change 98
resonant effects, of leaders 96, 103
respect 49
response-ability 31
restructuring 33
reviews, pointing to ineffective leadership 34–5

reward, and the brain 90
rewiring the brain 93
Ringleb, AH and Rock, D 26
Robinson, S 118
Rock, D 16, 83, 91, 94, 97, 98, 102
Roebuck, C 38
role modelling 8, 107
Royal College of Nursing 48
Royal College of Physicians 39
Russell, RF 12
Russell, RF and Stone, AG 12

safety, sense of 124–5
Santos, L 86
satisfaction 65
Satpute et al. 91
SCARF model 16, 97, 98–102, 103
Scharmer, CO 48
Schein, E 109
Schön, DA 108
Sedgeman, J 51
Segal, Z 130
self-awareness 28–9; and cognitive biases 118–19; and consistency 19; and emotional intelligence 96; and emotions 113; and leadership 28; and lifelong learning 110; and professional leadership 55; and resilience 115; and SCARF model 101; and self-leadership 85, 93, 94; and self-mastery 30; and self-regulation 119; testing 119
self-compassion 29; and compassion 49; and depression 132–3; and emotional intelligence 95; and emotional strength/resilience 132; and helping others 94; and mindfulness 135; model 133; and resilience 47; and self-leadership 38; and working too many hours 118
self-control 26, 84, 86
self-criticism 25
self-esteem 133
self-importance 85
self-kindness 29, 132
self-leadership: for all 50–5; as an approach 21; case for 32–40; as a concept 23–4; the context 33–9; defined 23, 24; foundations of 43–50, 61–2; principles of 44
self-management 27–8, 30, 88, 93, 135
self-mastery 30
self-observation 25–6, 55, 81, 88, 94, 116, 135
self-other merging 132
self-regulation 26–7; and biases 88; and consistency 19; and empathy 132; and mindfulness 84; and resilience 116; and self-awareness 119; and self-leadership 81; and thinking 93; and working memory 94
Senge, PM 27, 29
sensory experiences 67
Seppala, EM 72
Serani, D 82
servant leadership theory 2, 11–13
services, quality of 36
shared leadership 57–8

Shipman, AS 17, 57
Siegel, DJ 45, 127–8
silent communication 32
Singer, T 130, 132
situational leadership theory 10, 11
situational theories 2, 10–11
skills, developing new 121–2
Skinner, BF 6
sleep 93, 107, 118, 125–6
social awareness 30–1, 96, 120, 135
social care: compassion in 37; professional
    leadership 52
Social Care Institute for Excellence 48
social intelligence 4
socialization, and well-being 132
social pain 97
social rejection 103
social services sector, leadership in 36
social support 107
Solomon, ND 48
Southwick, SM and Charney, DS 92, 105, 106–8, 122
Sparrow, RT 19
spending, reducing and management structures 59
Spillane, JP 51
spiritual beliefs 107
staff, performance of 38
standard of living 122
standards of care 37
state of mind 45–7; and effectiveness 137; and emotions
    66, 144; how does it work? 146–51; invisibility
    of 65–9; key principles 64–5, 67–9; leaders 45,
    151–2; and leadership 46, 138–41, 146, 152;
    managing 149, 150–1; misunderstandings of
    150–1; and performance 137, 139, 142–4, 146,
    152; preconceived ideas of what determines 63–4;
    quality of 144; and relationships 142–3, 144; and
    resilience 47, 122–3; and self-leadership 32, 44, 51,
    61–2, 149; and stress 45, 153; three elements of
    146–50; and world of work 145–6
status 99, 101, 116
Stephenson, S 70
stereotypes 90, 94
Stogdill, RM 4, 9
Stogdill, RM and Bass, BM 6
Stokes, J 4
Stone et al. 113
Stone, L 91
Storey, J and Holti, R 40, 53
stress: and ability to think clearly 27, 70; acceptance
    of 153; attributing blame for 74; and the brain
    92–3; causes of 122; and communication 92, 94,
    103; and connecting with others 81, 102; and
    decision making 102; detrimental effects of 130;
    and the hippocampus 91; and human functioning
    66; and intuitive wisdom 114; and knowledge
    retrieval 114; and language circuits 92, 103;
    management 102, 151; and the mind 65, 66, 127;
    in organisations 117; and performance 46, 145; in
    public sector 33; reduction in 140; and resilience
    48, 49, 81, 105; and self-leadership 93–5; and

sleep 118, 125–6; and state of mind 45, 153; and
    supporting others 102; tolerance 20; work 117
styles of leadership 6, 8, 11
subjective feelings 81
suffering 74
sunk-cost fallacy 87
supporting others, and stress reduction 102
suppression, of emotions 83
Surowiecki, J 49
sustainable empathy 120
System 1/System 2 thinking 86, 88

Tang, Y and Posner, MI 27
Tannenbaum, R and Schmidt, W 8
task orientation 7
team communication 32
teams: contagion effect 118; and empathy 97;
    performance of 57; resilience of 108, 120; state of
    mind of 145
Teasdale, J 130
technological surfing 91
temperament 82
Terry, RW 18
theory X and Y 6–7
thinking: bias 103; empathetic and cognitive reasoning
    97; and external factors 69–71, 77; faulty forms of
    113; and feeling 85; group think 90, 94, 103; limited
    122–3; negative 27, 102, 116, 121; new ways of
    93; overthinking 76; and self-regulation 93; System
    1 and 2 86, 88; traps 122; two systems 86–8, 103
Thinking Fast and Slow 86
Thorpe et al. 54, 56
thought 68–9, 76–7; capacity of 64–5; and
    consciousness 65; and emotions 66, 85; and
    experience 71; is not reality 71–3, 77; kinds of
    72; nature of 151; and nature of the mind 147–8;
    negative 27, 102, 116, 121; and state of mind
    152; suppression of 123; variable nature of 148
threat and avoid response 98
threat response 99, 100, 101, 121
threats 90, 98, 115
Tichy, N and Devanna, MA 13
tiredness 93–4, 114, 118 *see also* sleep
tolerance 84
Tourish, D 15
trait contingency model 8–9
trait theory 2, 4–6
transformational change 97
Transformational Leadership Questionnaire (TLQ) 14
transformational leadership theory 2–3, 13–15
transformation, and impact of learning/development 59
transformation programmes 38
transformative learning 61
*Transforming Community Services, Ambition, Action,
    Achievement: Transforming Services for Acute Care
    Closer to Home* 39
two systems thinking 86–8, 103

uncertainty 99
unconscious alert system 92

unconscious awareness 126
unconscious bias 94
unconscious processing, of brain 88, 89
unfairness 100
universal emotions 82

values: and decision making 114; of health clinicians/
    social workers 28
Van Wart, M 11
Vessey, WB 16, 17
victims of something, individuals as 74–5, 77

Wallace, BA 131
Walumbwa et al. 19
Wegner, D 123
well-being 47–8; and attention 123; and compassion 132;
    emotional 106; and mindfulness 128; psychological
    107;and socialization 132; triangle of 127–8; in
    Western society 122; and working hours 118
Western, S 56, 57
Western society, well-being/happiness in 122
Whetstone, T 12
Whiting et al. 99
whole-system working 40
Whybrow, A and Wildflower, L 25

Wilful Blindness 90
Williams, M 123, 126, 127, 130
Williams, M and Penman, D 48
wisdom: harvesting 124–5; intuitive 54, 114; practice
    114–15
Wolff, S 124
women, leaders 4
workaholics 118
work, and state of mind 145–6
workforce, resilience in 116
working culture 49–50
working memory 94 *see also* memory
working relationships 31 *see also* relationships
working too many hours 118
workloads 33
workplace change 116–17
World Health Organization (WHO) 105
worry, habitual 46

Yukl, G 7

Zaccaro, SJ 5
Zaccaro, SJ and Horn, ZNJ 6
Zak et al. 81
Zheltoukhova, K 51, 58